The Myth and Ritual School

Theorists of Myth
Robert A. Segal, Series Editor

Jung and the Jungians on Myth
An Introduction
by Steven F. Walker

René Girard and Myth
An Introduction
by Richard J. Golsan

Political Myth
A Theoretical Introduction
by Christopher G. Flood

The Poetics of Myth
by Eleazar M. Meletinsky
translated by Guy Lanoue and Alexander Sadetsky

Northrop Frye on Myth
An Introduction
by Ford Russell

Cassirer and Langer on Myth
An Introduction
by William Schultz

Myth and Religion in Mircea Eliade
by Douglas Allen

The Myth and Ritual School

J. G. Frazer and the Cambridge Ritualists

Robert Ackerman

Routledge
New York and London

Published in 2002 by
Routledge
29 West 35th Street
New York, NY 10001
www.routledge-ny.com

Published in Great Britain by
Routledge
11 New Fetter Lane
London EC4P 4EE
www.routledge.co.uk

Routledge is an imprint of the Taylor & Francis Group

10 9 8 7 6 5 4 3 2 1

Library of Congress Cataloging-in-Publication data forthcoming.
Ackerman, Robert, 1935–
  The myth and ritual school : J. G. Frazer and the Cambridge ritualists /
Robert Ackerman
  p.   cm. — (Theorists of myth)
  Includes bibliographical references and index.
  ISBN 0-415-93963-1
    1. Myth and ritual school—England—Cambridge—History. 2. Classical
philology—Study and teaching—England—Cambridge—History. 3. Literature
and anthropology—England—Cambridge—History. 4. Frazer, James George,
Sir, 1854-1941—Influence. 5. Cambridge (England)—Intellectual life. 6.
Mythology, Classical—Historiography. 7. Harrison, Jane Ellen, 1850-1928. 8.
Ritual—Historiography. I. Title. II. Theorists of myth (Routledge (Firm))

BL304.2.A35 2002
801'.95'0904—dc21   2002021329

Contents

Series Editor's Foreword

For most theorists of myth, there is no special connection between myth and ritual. Any connection that exists is either irregular or happenstance. For those theorists labeled "myth-ritualists," myth is necessarily linked to ritual. Myth-ritualists assume not that all rituals are inherently linked to myths but that all myths are inherently linked to rituals.

What the link is varies from myth-ritualist to myth-ritualist. For Biblicist William Robertson Smith, the pioneering myth-ritualist, myth is inferior to ritual. It arises as an explanation of a ritual only after the ritual, which antedates myth, is no longer considered magically potent and so is no longer understood. For James Frazer, the classicist and anthropologist, myth is the equal of ritual and arises alongside it to serve as its script: myth explains what ritual enacts. Myth operates while ritual retains its magical power. The classicist Jane Harrison and the Biblicist S. H. Hooke follow Frazer's version of myth-ritualism but in addition bestow magical efficacy on myth itself, not just on ritual.

The Semiticist Theodor Gaster and the anthropologist Adolf Jensen offer versions of myth-ritualism that make myth superior to ritual. Claude Lévi-Strauss, the structural anthropologist, argues that whenever myth and ritual work together, they work as dialectical opposites. Not only myths and rituals but also texts and practices of other kinds have been traced back to one version or another of myth-ritualism. Other leading myth-ritualists include anthropologist A. M. Hocart, Lord Raglan, and Clyde Kluckhohn; historians of religion E. O. James and Margaret Murray; classicists Gilbert Murray, F. M. Cornford, A. B. Cook, George Thomson, and Rhys Carpenter; Biblicists Ivan Engnell, Aubrey Johnson, and Sigmund Mowinckel; and literary critics Jessie Weston, E. M. Butler, Francis Fergusson,

John Speirs, C. L. Barber, William Troy, most fervently Stanley Edgar Hyman, while at times Herbert Weisinger.

Robert Ackerman's *The Myth and Ritual School* is the first book-length analysis of the most famous and influential school of myth-ritualists; the Cambridge Ritualists, a group of classicists all but one of whom were affiliated with Cambridge. The central member of the group was Jane Harrison. The others were Gilbert Murray, alone affiliated with Oxford; F. M. Cornford; and, more marginally, A. B. Cook.

Beginning with a comprehensive overview of theorizing about myth in the eighteenth and nineteenth centuries, Ackerman proceeds to trace the varying influences on the Cambridge group. He then analyzes the chief works of each member. By profession an intellectual historian rather than either a classicist or an anthropologist, Ackerman reconstructs the cultural milieu of the Ritualists. In analyzing their views, he scrutinizes their unpublished as well as published writings.

The prime influence on the group was James Frazer, on whom the prime influence in turn was William Robertson Smith. Smith was the first to see the era of primitive, though not modern, religion as practice rather than belief—as ritual rather than either creed or myth. Myth for Smith arises to account above all for the ritual of the annual killing of the totem, or god.

From Smith, Frazer took both the association of myth with ritual and the ritual of killing the god. He altered the exact connection between the myth and the ritual, made the god the god of vegetation, and made the function of the ritual agricultural: causing the crops to grow. Frazer also introduced the role of the king, the incarnation of the god of vegetation. Where Smith restricts himself to Semitic cultures, Frazer boldly generalizes to primitive and ancient ones worldwide. Strictly speaking, myth-ritualism for Frazer arises neither in his stage of magic nor even in his stage of religion but only in a subsequent, less clearly demarcated stage of magic and religion combined—the stage to which nearly all of *The Golden Bough* is devoted.

As Ackerman documents, Frazer was in fact an inconsistent myth-ritualist. He was simultaneously both a Tylorian intellectualist and euhemerist as well as a myth-ritualist and is even singled out by Hooke as the nemesis of myth-ritualists! Frazer turns out to have been a myth-ritualist above all at the outset of his career, when he was most under the influence of the uncompromising ritualist Smith.

Nevertheless, it is Frazer *qua* myth-ritualist who most influenced the Cambridge Ritualists. From him, they took his myth-ritualist scenario, though not his set of stages. More broadly, they took an anthropological and comparativist rather than a philological and particularistic approach to Greek myth, ritual, and religion. The Ritualists argue that ancient Greeks were far closer to primitives than had been assumed—indeed, were much more like primitives than like moderns.

At the same time the Ritualists were interested not just in the primitive origin of Greek myth, ritual, and religion but also in the myth-ritualist origin of some other, seemingly secular, Greek phenomena: tragedy, comedy, epic, philosophy, art, and even sport. It is on the myth-ritualist origin of Greek tragedy and comedy that Ackerman focuses on. In his final chapter he summarizes the application of the myth-ritualist approach to non-Greek literature of all kinds. As often as not, that application has skirted the Ritualists themselves and has gone back directly to Frazer, though often altering his own formulation of the scheme. Still, it is the Cambridge Ritualists who pioneered the analysis of literature as myth. In literary lingo, they were the first "myth critics." Contemporary literary critics like Northrop Frye are their successors.

Ackerman is concerned to show that Frazer was by no means the sole influence on the Cambridge group. Other influences range from cultural luminaries like Durkheim, Nietzsche, Bergson, Freud, and Jung to local academicians like the classicists William Ridgeway and A. W. Verrall. Moreover, even as a myth-ritualist Frazer views myth, ritual, and religion differently from the Ritualists. Where he deems all three fundamentally intellectual in nature, the Ritualists deem them primarily sociological and psychological affairs. The Ritualists prove far closer to William Robertson Smith, even though they were influenced by him only indirectly through Durkheim and others.

Ackerman charts at once the impact of the Cambridge Ritualists on literary scholars and the vitriolic dismissal of them by fellow classicists. That dismissal doubtless accounts for what till recently has been dormant scholarly interest in the group. There have been sporadic articles on the group, but until now no book. The reawakening of interest has been partly spurred by Ackerman's own acclaimed intellectual biography of Frazer: *J. G. Frazer: His Life and Work* (Cambridge University Press, 1987). Another spur has been Sandra Peacock's *Jane Ellen Harrison: The Mask and the Self* (Yale University Press, 1989). Both books are the first full biographies of their subjects. In 1989 a conference on the Cambridge Ritualists was held at the University of Illinois, the proceedings of which, edited by organizer William M. Calder III, were published as *The Cambridge Ritualists: A Reconsideration*, Illinois Classical Studies, Supplement No. 2 (1990). Shelley Arlen, of the University of Florida Library, has compiled a bibliography of the group: *The Cambridge Ritualists: An Annotated Bibliography* (Scarecrow Press, 1990). Ackerman's present book on the Cambridge Ritualists is a masterly and indispensable addition that goes far toward completing the picture of the group.

Preface

This is an essay in the history of mythography in general and of modern literary criticism in particular. It offers a critical narrative account of the origins of "myth-and-ritual criticism" (hereafter, for brevity's sake, "myth criticism"): a school or tendency influential from the 1920s through the 1960s that sought to discover mythic and/or ritual patterns underlying literary works. This approach to literature is an application and adaptation of the work of a group of British classical scholars—J. G. Frazer and the "Cambridge Ritualists"—Jane Ellen Harrison, Gilbert Murray, F. M. Cornford, and A. B. Cook—around the turn of the century. The problem they worked on was the origins of Greek drama. On the basis of the comparative anthropological study of "primitive" religion they concluded that drama evolved from certain magical fertility rituals performed in the worship of a deity who died and was reborn. Dionysus was the Greek exemplar of this class of gods, called by Jane Harrison "eniautos-daimons," or "year-spirits."

In view of the seismic shift in the objects and methods of both mythography (structuralism) and literary criticism (deconstruction) over the last twenty years, it is perhaps not surprising that no thorough study of this subject exists today. The only book-length work in English on the history of modern mythography, Richard Chase's rather skimpy *Quest for Myth* (1948), is marred by tendentiousness and is in any case inimical to the Ritualists.[1] Aside from Chase there exist several essays and chapters in books, all more or less helpful, but none of them more than a sketch. Some, like that of Haskell M. Block, are concerned with the effects of the myth-and-ritual approach on contemporary criticism in the 1950s, and therefore are not especially concerned with origins.[2] Others are polemics for or against the myth critics: examples are the panegyrics of Stanley Edgar Hyman and the denigrations of Philip Rahv.[3]

There are, in addition, writers generally sympathetic to the Ritualists but unwilling to go the whole of the extravagantly long way with them.[4] In my judgment the most astute assessments of myth criticism have been made from this position, but unfortunately the occupants of this middle ground are in a minority.[5] Writing about myth and mythically inspired criticism offers as depressingly good an example of old-style *odium scholasticum* as one might wish. Moreover, not only were the Ritualists an embattled minority within the ranks of literary critics, but because their theoretical foundations lay within the purview of anthropologists and classicists, criticism from those quarters, most of it harsh indeed, has not been lacking.[6] The reasons for this will be discussed below.

With fire and brimstone being thus freely called down, it seems necessary to declare myself. I find that although I am not convinced by the arguments of the Ritualists, I am at least willing to listen. That, I imagine, makes me one of their partisans, at least in the eyes of the many root-and-branch extirpators of the group and all its works. Nevertheless, this essay is intended to be a reasonably objective investigation into an interesting and important chapter in the history of twentieth-century literary criticism. The exposition will be analytic, but I shall attempt to avoid the polemic note by focusing on the origins of the movement. Indeed, the historical approach seems especially appropriate to this subject because the first generation of myth critics themselves were all deeply concerned with origins.

1

At the close of his discussion of Frazer in *The Tangled Bank*, Stanley Edgar Hyman writes:

> In the work of Murray and the Cambridge Ritualists—Harrison, Francis Cornford, and A. B. Cook—the influence of Frazer permanently transformed and revitalized the field of classics, and however much it may have appeared to return to its old deaf-adder ways in recent years (and Frazer was the first

to swing back from his own insights), it will never be the same again. The application of these ideas from classical to medieval and modern literature by a brilliant series of literary critics—William Troy, Francis Fergusson, Herbert Weisinger, John Speirs, C. L. Barber, and others—has given Frazer an importance in literary criticism at least equal to that of Marx and Freud.[7]

But to imply that the only begetter of myth criticism was Sir James Frazer is to indulge in drastic simplification. In fact the origins of myth criticism, as it was developed by the Ritualists, were very complicated. No one would wish to deny Frazer's real importance; he was, however, necessary but not sufficient. In fact the Cambridge group levied on Durkheim, Bergson, and Freud nearly as much as on Frazer. They used the materials he had amassed on the dying god and the "tragic rhythm" of death and resurrection that was implied in *The Golden Bough*, but they jettisoned Frazer's rather simple-minded rationalism and replaced it with a vitalism that he found objectionable. Not only did he "swing back from his own insights," as Hyman puts it, but in 1921 he was so far out of sympathy with ritualism and its practitioners that he took pains to attack them.

Therefore, the opening chapters of this essay survey the intellectual complex that produced Frazer and the Ritualists. Only when one understands the background can one judge the extent to which they were indeed innovators. These chapters are not intended as a full-dress history of the theories about myth—that would be to write Chase's book again. In order to keep the preliminaries to a reasonable size, the criterion has been throughout: What does the reader need to know to understand "Anglo-Saxon" thought and writing about myth at the turn of the century? Put that way, the question has a threefold answer. The most significant influences on myth studies were Enlightenment rationalism, romantic historicism and philology, and comparative evolutionary anthropology: appropriately, they are the subjects of Chapters One, Two, and Three. Unlike the rest of this essay, these early chapters rely heavily on secondary material. The reasons are that (1) much of Herder and the philologists must be quarried out of extensive *Sämtliche Werke*, and (2) good recent studies of much of this material exist, although not written with the interest of the historian of myth in mind: I refer especially to the books by Manuel, Burrow, and Stocking.

With regard to myth and ritual the "rise of anthropology" means especially the work of Andrew Lang, E. B. Tylor, and William Robertson Smith. With them as background, we arrive at J. G. Frazer and *The Golden Bough*. Frazer was a late-eighteenth-century mind in a late-nineteenth-century setting: Enlightenment anticlerical rationalism overlaid with late Victorian evolutionary progressivism. I offer a map of the labyrinth of *The Golden Bough*, with special attention to the twistings and turnings of its maker's mind so far as the origins and meaning of myth are concerned. I argue that he moved from a generally ritualist position (that myth is the spoken or written description or accompaniment to ritual) to a generally euhemerist position (that myth recapitulates, albeit in distorted form, real events that occurred to real heroes).

Of the Ritualists Gilbert Murray was (and is) clearly the best known, particularly to nonclassicists; nevertheless, I maintain that Jane Harrison was the center of the group. I explore the connections between her life and her scholarly work in order to explain in what sense she stood at its heart (in more than one sense). Harrison and her relations with the other members of the group are discussed in the context of the scholarship of the time.

Finally, in Chapter Seven, we arrive at the works that constitute the theoretical foundations for myth-and-ritual criticism: Harrison's *Themis* (1912) and *Ancient Art and Ritual* (1913), Cornford's *The Origin of Attic Comedy* (1914), and Murray's "Excursus on the Ritual Forms Preserved in Greek Tragedy" (in *Themis*) and "Hamlet and Orestes" (1914). The arguments of these works are analyzed in considerable detail. This is followed, in the last chapter, by a discussion of the Ritualists' (generally adverse) critical reception, along with a discussion of those critics of the 1920s who attempted to generalize the basic approach of the Ritualists and extend it to nonclassical, nondramatic literature: Jessie Weston, Roger Tiddy, and others. The essay closes with an overall critical evaluation of myth criticism and a sketch of later trends within this critical tendency.

2

It is my pleasant obligation here to express my deep appreciation to all those persons and institutions that have helped me at various stages in the preparation of this essay.

Patience Burne, former Librarian of Newnham College, Cambridge, was gracious enough to put the Jessie Stewart papers at my disposal. To her my thanks, as to the helpful staff of the Anderson Room in the Cambridge University Library, where I consulted them. My thanks as well to the late Dr. Philip Gaskell, Fellow and Librarian of Trinity College, Cambridge, and his staff, for permitting me access to the voluminous Frazer papers, and the librarians of the Bodleian Library, Oxford, for leave to use the Murray correspondence.

The following were helpful in answering queries and making suggestions: Sir C. M. Bowra, Warden of Wadham College, Oxford; Mr. J. Diggle, Acting Librarian and Director of Studies in Classics, Queens' College, Cambridge; Professor Stanley Edgar Hyman, of the State University of New York at Buffalo; and Professor Theodor H. Gaster, of Barnard College.

My friend and sometime colleague Sidney Feshbach, then of the City University of New York, first broached the idea for this study many years ago and has often helped me since then by his generous willingness to talk about the subject.

Of my colleagues at The University of the Arts, I wish especially to thank Laura Markham, the immensely competent secretary who processed the words into the computer, and Michael Bonitatibus, who offered invaluable expert help with technical aspects of its production.

Versions of two chapters have been published elsewhere, and I wish here to acknowledge permission of the editors of the journals in question. A revised Chapter Four appeared as "Frazer on Myth and Ritual" in the *Journal of the History of Ideas* 36 (1975) 115-34; a revised Chapter Five appeared as "Jane Ellen Harrison: The Early Work" in *Greek, Roman and Byzantine Studies* 13 (1972) 209-30.

Lastly I wish to thank my friend Professor Robert Segal, of Lancaster University, in the United Kingdom, whose idea it first was to publish this work.

One

The Eighteenth Century—Rationalism and Reaction

The interest in myth among the *philosophes* and the Scottish philosophical historians of the eighteenth century derived from their attitude toward the past. Frank Manuel has said that one of the leading characteristics of the *philosophes* was their "state of profound wonder about origins."[1] Their original Lockean premise was that men came into the world *tabula rasa*, and that all ideas were therefore learned. What they determined to do was to work backwards, charting the history of human institutions and stripping away the layers of superstition and ignorance until they discovered how and when it was that the initial right ordering of things was disturbed and "error"—that favorite notion of the savants—crept in. Once this was known, remedial action might be taken by men of reason. In this way the entire ancient world became a subject of ardent inquiry, because it obviously held the answers to these questions.

The *philosophes* were not primarily trying to effect immediate social change (indeed they had no hope of doing so in France) but in fact to do something more audacious and profound. They were attempting to reconstruct man's entire view of himself and of his world. Theirs was no disinterested inquiry into the past, such as was claimed by the "scientific historians" of the nineteenth century, but an attack on the established order of society. In the name of reason they wished to illuminate what had lain dark for centuries. Manuel has acutely observed that in fact they were replacing one set of myths ("myth" both as a story concerning origins and as an unquestioned social assumption) with another.[2] Their investigations into the nature of human nature and into those of the rest of creation—civil society, language, and religion—may be seen as authentic attempts at constructing a new secular mythology.

Perhaps the most baffling question to these emancipated minds was the genesis of religion. How, when, and why did it start? The first great step toward answering these questions was to ask them. For whereas religious controversy was certainly no novelty in Europe, these men were not sectarian partisans but students of religion as a phenomenon, as a creation of the human spirit. As Hume put it in the title of his well-known essay, they wished to examine "The Natural History of Religion." However, even to pose such questions so boldly and in such a spirit in a religiously divided Europe was dangerous. Their transparent ruse, therefore, was to claim that they were really studying ancient paganism, and one of the best ways to do so was through a close analysis of pagan mythology. In order, however, to understand the contribution of this new group of writers on mythology it is worth reviewing briefly the most important of the older, more traditional attitudes concerning its meaning and origins: allegorism and euhemerism.

Even in the ancient world, conjectures had abounded as to the origins and proper method of interpreting the myths, as well as how the gods and their worship had originated. Among the pagans, sensitive spirits, appalled by the depravity and violence of many of the traditional stories, decided that their apparent, repellent meaning could not be the true one. Instead they decided that the myths were philosophical allegories formulated by the ancient sages. These men had deemed the story to be the best vehicle, considering the dim intelligences of their audiences, for transmitting their wisdom. According to the allegorists, then, the many repulsive narratives were merely episodes in the unending struggle between good and evil that was the true meaning of mythology. This approach was adopted as well by Jews and Christians when it suited their purposes, as it often did, and it remained popular through the Christian centuries. It was the most widespread method through the seventeenth century, although the systems to be named below also had their adherents.

The other noteworthy Greek viewpoint was euhemerism, after Euhemerus, a Greek romancer.[3] He claims, in a story, to have discovered a remote island where he read an account of how the gods were born as men, ruled as great heroes, and were apotheosized by a grateful populace. Although euhemerism is plainly a doctrine that can be turned against all religions, it was used by the early Christians to confute pagan apologists, and thus received Christian sanction; it has had many proponents over the centuries.

These and other doctrines jostled one another through the centuries, each with its advocates and critics. As noted above, the allegorical method of interpretation had the better of it through the seventeenth century. But this all changed at the end of that century and the beginning of the next. As Manuel puts it, "One of the striking expressions of the new [post-Renaissance] scientific and material civilization of western Europe was an overwhelming tendency to become matter-of-fact, to eschew wonder, to reduce the fantastic to a commonsense narrative. There was a general movement to de-allegorize. . . ."[4] The most important of these new mythographers was the erudite, acerbic, skeptical Pierre Bayle (1647–1706).[5] Bayle insisted that these recitals of degraded and degrading events (and he emphasized their sordidly sexual aspect) were felt by their pagan audiences to be merely racy stories and nothing more. Bayle and those who followed him insisted that the myths were to be interpreted euhemeristically in the sense that they were accounts of events that had really occurred.

Bayle seems to have been the first to make the parallel between Greek religion, as shown in the myths, and modern "savagery," which was then being described to Europeans in an ever-increasing number of accounts and relations by travelers and missionaries. Although he made this comparison in a polemic spirit—he was an untiring partisan of the Moderns in their warfare with the Ancients—it was to become widely accepted and stand as a cornerstone in later anthropological thinking about myth. He amassed mountains of data that show the folly of men in all times; and implicitly the reader of his *Dictionary* (1700) is asked to contemplate his own times in the lurid light of the chaotic past. Although it was still dangerous to attack Christianity openly, Bayle made it plain that he thought

Christianity to be but a modern variant of the primitive brutality and absurdity that he so painstakingly documented.

1

Another line of inquiry began with the impulse of some of the *philosophes*, given to system-building and universal history, to mesh the accounts of ancient history given in the Bible with the history of pagan antiquity contained in the chronicles and myths from that era. The Mosaic chronology, which was assumed by all *faute de mieux*, presented a problem. It was believed that the pure monotheism that had existed before the Flood was perpetuated among the Semites, but that this pure doctrine had been permitted, God alone knew why, to become corrupted among the Hamites and Japhetites. The question was whether any system was to be discerned among the chaos of the thousands of pagan gods and their stories. Given the systematizing bent of the investigators, it is no surprise that they succeeded in reducing this multiplicity to a relative handful of deities from some leading nation—Egypt, Babylon, Phoenicia—which they then argued was the center from which all other institutions of paganism derived. These writers thus required some method to demonstrate how cultural diffusion was accomplished, and their usual approach was etymological. By seizing upon chance resemblances between words of geographically distant countries,[6] these savants attempted to show, by piling conjecture on conjecture, that their own candidate for primacy in the ancient world had indeed been the originator of the world's religion. It was in this atmosphere that the great orientalist Sir William Jones in 1786 asserted that the religion of the gentiles was descended not from any Mediterranean nation at all but from India, thus giving rise to the "Aryan" theory.

Throughout the eighteenth century etymology was employed in a steady stream of works which purported to chart the spread of paganism in the ancient world. Etymology was the most "scientific" method then available, but the true principles governing the relationships between languages were then not known and would not be known for another fifty years. However, it is useful to see the works of the comparative philologists, and following them the philologically based comparative mythologists, as the continuators of a long line of linguistic speculation on this subject. Methodologically too, for all the conjecture connected with these etymological speculations, such work required its practitioner to inspect texts closely in order to establish trustworthy versions of the narratives, and this training in analysis was to be useful as a foundation in the textual work of the comparative philologists.

Although the majority of the writers on myth through the middle of the eighteenth century were euhemerists of one sort of another, several of the most influential writers were not. The most important of these on the Continent were Fontenelle and Vico; in England, Hume. These three all represented the more liberated wing of those pursuing this question all over Europe. Fontenelle and Vico achieved a certain local fame during their lifetimes, but the importance of their work on the subject was not really appreciated until the next century, when they were rediscovered and enthusiastically praised.

The earliest of these writers was Bernard Fontenelle (1657–1757), the younger and more original contemporary of Bayle. Unlike most of the mythographers of his time, who embalmed their conclusions in elephantine folios, Fontenelle wrote only two brief, elegant essays on the subject—one on the orgins of myth (*fables*) and the other on the mechanics of oracles. In these he sketched a view of primitive mankind that was to be influential throughout the eighteenth century. His great contribution was to assume that myth originated not as the vehicle for some sage's wisdom, nor as some enormous imposition by wily priests in antiquity, but as the direct and inevitable consequence of man's psychological nature. Myth therefore provided a remarkable insight into the thought processes of primitive humanity. Fontenelle's primitive was a dreamer and a storyteller. His initial lack of concern with factual accuracy, along with the inevitable changes wrought by generations of oral transmission, have caused the tales to change out of mind and assume the shapes they now possess.

Fontenelle asserted what had often been said—that the ancients created their gods in their own image. But he added something new when he announced that this act of projection of man's psychic nature had not been done once and for all but continuously and

progressively. Therefore he was able to explain what had been puzzling up to that time—how it was that the crude Homeric Greeks
had gods cut to their own swaggering, heroic measure whereas the
later, more civilized pagans had more philosophical deities.

Fontenelle was also the first (in this too he was followed by Vico
and Hume) to adopt the hypothesis of parallel development to
explain the similarities between the myths of geographically distant
nations. In this he opposed those earlier writers, already mentioned,
who had asserted on etymological grounds that myths had originated in some one country and then spread to all the others.
Fontenelle and his successors rejected this form of diffusionism
because they hypothesized a universal human nature; if myth was a
natural and inescapable product of the human psyche, then no
mechanism for cultural transmission was either possible or necessary. Like so much else in the study of myth, this very dispute (in a
more sophisticated form) between the evolutionists and the diffu-
sionists was to break out again in the late nineteenth and early twentieth centuries (and indeed is still a point of controversy today).

Finally, Fontenelle is noteworthy for his picture of the primitive
mythopoet. An inveterate fantasist, with no special interest in or care
for facts or accuracy, he is also, as the nineteenth-century anthropologist E. B. Tylor was to call him in a famous phrase, a "savage
philosopher." That is, myths originate as primitive science, in that
they are the answers to questions about the universe that primitive
man raises. This view has been very long-lived, reappearing in the
work of Frazer and Tylor and other like-mindedly rationalistic and
positivistic thinkers; it is represented today by the Popperian historian of anthropology I. C. Jarvie.

2

Max Fisch has put it succinctly:

> Modern historiography, so far as it differs from ancient and
> medieval in principle and not merely in technical proficiency,
> range and quantity of output, rests on the discovery of man as
> a particularly historical being, subject to a development tran-

scending the life of any individual, nation or race. . . . So far as this discovery and the adumbration of those auxiliary disciplines [anthropology, genetic and social psychology, sociology, comparative mythology, comparative law, and philosophy of history] can be ascribed to a single man or book, the man is Vico and the book is the *New Science.*[7]

Giambattista Vico (1668–1744) is the first enunciator of the new historicism that will characterize the outlook of the next century.

To appreciate how radical his position was, it is only necessary to recall the ideas of history widely shared by the philosophers of the Enlightenment. They began by assuming a universal, unchanging human nature. This granted, the existence of reason implied that there was and could be but one permanent, unwavering standard for judging human behavior. History, which was a record only of ceaseless change, was thus essentially meaningless. It embodied no norm and was therefore useless for demonstrating the workings of reason. Its only possible worth was that it provided a series of exemplary individuals who might be adopted as models for personal conduct. Furthermore, the enemies of the Enlightenment always appealed to tradition and to the past to justify the present, and this further discredited history in the eyes of the *philosophes.*

To an eighteenth-century gentleman, *philosophe* or no, Vico's history was incomprehensible on its face because its leading actors were not princes and dynasties and its leading events were not battles and treaties:[8] instead, Vico traced the rise, fall, and conflict of institutions, classes, and languages. Vico attempted to isolate and express the deepest spirit of the various nations and ages of the past by analyzing the dynamic, even chaotic, panorama presented by history. He asserted that men's everyday acts, though perhaps meaningless on the small scale, nevertheless did compose a unity when viewed overall: that unity was the pattern of Providence. Far from being meaningless, history offered mankind "a rational civil theology of divine providence."[9] But the study of history, the divine plan for man, also showed men living their lives in the spirit of their age. And since Vico's master principle, methodologically, is that all sciences must begin where their subject matters begin, the study of the science of

history must involve an investigation into how civil societies originated and maintained themselves.

Vico said that history was cyclical and that each cycle was composed of three parts—the ages of the gods, of heroes, and of men—
each with its special characteristics. According to this scheme Vico
himself was living in the advanced third phase of the second cycle;
despite this, he spent most of his book (which implies that he was
most interested) on the earliest phases, in primitive history. He
reconstructed the rise of civil society, of religion, and of language,
and through this he touched on mythology.[10]

Vico began his researches into antiquity with the rationalist pre-
conceptions that he was later to demolish. He started by accepting
the common assumption that the ancients had developed vast
amounts of arcane wisdom, which imbued their whole civilization.
Vico, a professor of Latin, attempted (in the spirit of the seven-
teenth-century etymologists) to read back into various Latin legal
phrases his own metaphysics and philosophy, characteristic of his
own times. His problem arose when he tried to assess the many traditions that narrated how various ancient lawgivers had founded
their respective states and presented them with fully formed consti-
tutions. He refused to believe this was possible because he was convinced that such Cartesian clarity simply did not describe real experience. Like the romantics later, Vico believed that any completely
defined idea was sterile and dead. And since these myths were anything but dead to his mind, some other explanation was needed. He
could not accept them as Platonic "noble lies," for this was equally
rationalistic and, what is more, vitiated the myths as historical evidence from a period in which there was practically nothing else
(before archaeology). He then made his great conceptual leap.
Jettisoning his rationalist assumptions, he conjectured that the earliest men were *not* rationalist lawgivers, primitive versions of Hugo
Grotius or René Descartes, but in fact poets who spoke in what he
called "poetic characters": that is, unable to abstract, they were
forced by the peculiar limitations of their languages to speak in a
kind of concentrated, heightened metaphor.

His contribution to the study of myth stems directly from this theory of primitive language. Myths were nothing but this *Ursprache* mis-

understood by later times. Mythology, "the universal language of gentile nations in the early period of their existence,"[11] was to him a kind of cultural allegory, composed by the spirit of the naturally mythopoeic age, that enlarged particular men or events or institutions to representative stature. Thus there never was such a man as Romulus, literally; instead he was the type of the fathers of the families that founded Rome. And likewise the other ancient Roman (Numa Pompilius) and Greek (Cadmus, Minos) leading figures were symbolic representations of general popular sentiment. Later, however, in historical times, the true meaning of these myths was lost, and historians, believing (like Vico's contemporaries) that these mythopoeic primitive ancestors were like themselves, took these stories for historical facts. The task, then, of the mythographer was to analyze these tales and attempt thereby to return to the mentality (if not the literal facts) of the eras that produced them.

Vico made other observations that prefigured future developments. His idea of myth being the representation in imaginative form of popular sentiment will be repeated by Herder and other German romantics. His notion of a purely metaphorical primitive language in which myths were produced naturally and misunderstood by later ages will be revived by Max Müller and the comparative mythologists. Lastly he analyzed the Homeric epics (fifty years before Wolf, on whom more below) and announced that the *Iliad* and the *Odyssey* were not the work of one man but the distilled essence of the spirit of the Greek people in a barbarous time.

Vico was also the author of the fateful idea that all societies must pass through three stages. It was picked up later in the century by Turgot, who added the all-important elements of progress and perfectibility to the schema. That is, he asserted that each succeeding stage was necessarily better socially, morally, and technologically than its predecessor. From Turgot it was adopted by Comte, for his three stages of social development, which Frazer then anthropologized when he asserted that all societies proceed inexorably from a stage of Magic (understood as a worldview), to a stage of Religion, and culminate in the stage of Science.

Unfortunately, Vico was not widely read in his own time. He was writing in Naples, on the southern fringe of the European "civilized" world, in Italian, then no longer a major language, and in an extremely difficult style; it is therefore no wonder that his advanced ideas received less than justice when they appeared. But Herder read him, as did Goethe, and he was triumphantly "discovered" by Michelet, who reinterpreted him to a sympathetic audience a century after he died. Had his circumstances been different, had he received the hearing that his genius merited, there can be little doubt that the historiography of the eighteenth century would have been considerably different.

3

David Hume's (1711–76) contribution to the hotly debated question of the origins of religion was made in his provocatively titled "Natural History of Religion" of 1757. In it Hume for the first time approached religion as an artifact, a completely human institution; like all human institutions it is amenable to study and analysis. Hume is in the same naturalist line as Bayle and Fontenelle.

Hume denied what had been asserted by the deists in the past— that religion was the result of primitive men rationally contemplating the harmony of the universe. And of course he refused to admit that religion was the result of any innate idea of God. His denial arose from his theories concerning primitive mentality. For Hume, primitive people were, like most ordinary people everywhere and at all times, creatures endowed with reason but unable or unwilling to use it. The cause of this situation was simply that primitives were engaged in a struggle for survival and had neither the time, the inclination, nor the excess energy to spend on abstraction. Instead of ratiocinating, then, they were completely creatures of passion. They reacted first to the vast natural upheavals that occurred from time to time in the environment—floods, earthquakes, lightning, and the like—and the gods they created were embodiments of these natural powers. Thus the origin of religion lay in terror of a multitude of natural forces that had to be placated.

It is therefore not surprising that Hume asserted that polytheism everywhere antedated monotheism. Monotheism was the result of centuries of slow endeavor; men had to be persuaded that the evi-

dence of their eyes was not to be believed and that multiple immediate causes were only indications of a single greater cause that lay
behind them. The monotheism that finally did develop in the great
historical religions was not the result of a true insight into the cosmic order on the part of the men of antiquity; on the contrary, it was
simply an act of generalization (favoring one god over all the others) that did not differ in its origins or motives from the fear that
inspired primal polytheism. This was shown by the fact that the mass
of the people, even in "advanced" Europe, had attained monotheism only nominally but in fact needed and worshiped the symbols of
God such as saints and miracle workers (and feared the equally concrete torments of hell).

Hume concludes his essay with a discussion of popular religious
activities as they have been recorded by chroniclers from all times
and places. To him all rites and ceremonies have but one function—
to appease the powers that be. Thus religion is not a system of beliefs
but a set of relationships between the believer and his god. As
Richard Chase notes:

> The importance of Hume's observations is that he sees that
> idol worship and religious ritual are in one sense invocations
> of power, that power flows back and forth, so to speak, between
> men and gods, and that primitive religion endeavors to elicit
> power or sanction from the gods toward the accomplishment
> of specific tasks, or the avoidance of specific calamities. Men
> believe in invisible power; also they see sensible objects; an idol,
> however, is neither merely the one nor the other but a fusion
> of both.[12]

Thus mythology is the product of the intercourse between
humans and gods. Hume regards myth with as much despair as his
cool temperament can muster, but other writers, lacking Hume's
overall pessimism, used his insight in different ways. For instance,
the German romantics, while certainly not going along with him in
his general attack on religion, will agree that mythology is no set of
pretty tales but the fruit of humanity's deepest feelings about the
subjects nearest to its heart.

<u>4</u>

With the partial exception of Vico, all the writers reviewed to this point have had one thing in common, whatever their particular orientation—they all thought that the survivals from the mythopoeic age discernible in contemporary social institutions, especially religion, were lamentable and, fortunately, on their way out. The *philosophes*, like Bayle and Fontenelle, of course had no use for religion in any form, and especially disliked its irrational aspect. For Hume all religion was an unfortunate species of mania. For men like Turgot and Condorcet, who develop the doctrine of progress, myth and its survivals are hated reminders of the bloody and superstitious past; they envisage the day when the passions are everywhere vestigial, language has taken on the quality of mathematics, and reason rules the world. Even Vico, whose sympathy for primitives was real and deep, employed the concept of a cyclical return to savagery as a warning to his fellow men.

For our purposes it is safe to simplify and assert that none of the above held true for the German romantics. They opposed the rationalism of the Enlightenment heart and soul and completely inverted its scale of values; as might be expected, the new approach showed itself in the study of myth. It is convenient to use Johann Gottfried von Herder (1744–1803) as the representative figure here; prolific, exclamatory, open-hearted, ingenious, Herder was the greatest spirit of the first generation of German romanticism.

Herder was attracted to myth for precisely the same reasons that its enemies in the Enlightenment disliked it: it was ancient; it was irrational and frequently savage; it was natural. These were the "charges" against myth that he cheerfully, even exultantly, admitted, but he denied the conclusions that had been generally understood to flow from them. Myths, like dreams, were akin to mania, but mania too was an appropriate and worthwhile subject for investigation. Myth was natural, and therefore important, because Herder, an evolutionist, regarded myth as the first stage in the coming to self-understanding of each people (*Volk*). Since it was natural it was significant; like Vico, Herder thought history was the record of the action of divine providence through time, and therefore everything bore God's impress. It is necessary to sketch the main terms of

Herder's thought to provide a context for his ideas on mythology, which were immensely important for the romantic movement.

Herder begins with the notoriously untranslatable concept of the *Volk* (people, nation). He emphasized the conditions that differentiated one *Volk* from another, contrary to Enlightenment theorists of origins, who postulated a common experience for all primitive people.[13] The main differentia were two: *Klima*, the physical environment (geography and climate),[14] and the specific *genius populi*, the innate attributes of the *Volk*. The *Volk* struggled with the *Klima*, and this fruitful conflict organically generated their selfhood.

Herder's universal history began, like those of the rationalist philosophers, with a stage of terror through which all primitive peoples were supposed to have passed. This is a pre-*Volk* period, in which the individuating characteristics of the *Volk* have not yet emerged. Then physical conditions ameliorate somewhat and people get a chance to look around and ask questions about how everything—the world, the language, the *Volk* (which has come into being by this time)—began. During this interval each *Volk* answers these universal questions in its own way, depending on its character and its *Klima*. Although this stage docs seem to resemble that postulated by rationalist theorists—people as cause-seekers, "savage philosophers"— Herder, true to organicism, knows that remnants from the preceding terror-stricken age survive in this more rational age of explanation.

Mythology, then, was the earliest, and therefore the essential, expression of the spiritual being and the sense of beauty of each *Volk*. These first mythic effusions would be the greatest works ever created by the *Volk*, for they were spontaneously generated from the depths of the national spirit (*Volksgeist*). And because of the profundities from which these myths come, mythology is essentially religious. Herder inspected the earliest epics of many nations and duly found that they were deeply imbued with religious feeling. The archetype of all such early masterworks was, of course, the Hebrew Bible, but the pagan epics were repetitions, less well rendered, of the same divine revelation to humanity. The revelation took place whenever a *Volk* became aware of itself as a *Volk* and memorialized this crucial experience in poetry. Naturally, considering the dominant rationalist mythography of the time, Herder encountered widespread opposition. He persisted, however, in denying that myths were testimonies to barbarism, or allegories of wisdom, or anticipations of Christianity. The myths, when they were first composed, were the whole of the divine Revelation.

One of Herder's great contributions came from his new reading of the Bible. He was a pioneer in his willingness to approach the Old Testament anthropologically, and although he was no Semiticist, his emphasis on the Hebrew Bible as the repository of the Jews' most ancient and important traditions was extremely important inasmuch as it prefigured the approach of biblical criticism in the next century. His seminal influence in this area is to be seen more specifically in the work of his close friend Eichhorn, a pioneer in the Higher Criticism.

As might be expected, Herder promoted Greece over Rome, beloved by the Augustans of the Enlightenment. In this, of course, he was not alone, especially in Germany. One immediately thinks of the Hellenism of Winckelmann and Lessing. But these critics were basically rationalists who had enjoined men to return to the Greek spirit as it was reflected in the glories of Greek art, that is, in the achievements of the fifth century and later, a product of a relatively late Greek civilization. Herder on the other hand told his audience that to find true Hellenism they would have to go back to the spirit of the *Urvolk* out of which fifth-century Athens sprang. That the study of myth, as an aspect of the study of Greece, is necessary, flows from Herder's nationalism, for of course each *Volk* had its unique nature and purpose which could be realized only when it had attained full political and cultural identity. Certain societies had managed to realize their entire potential (pre-eminently ancient Greece) and therefore deserved the attention of all people in future ages. But for all that the sympathetic study and understanding of ancient Greece or any other culture could give us, there is nothing to be gained from a sterile attempt at copying the actions or manners of another time or place. So much for neoclassicism.

Turning to Herder's more specific ideas about myth, the first thing to say is that he was above all the prophet of process; for him everything was a becoming, not a being. Unlike Lessing and Winckelmann, who thought of the spirit of Greece as a series of works of art, a finished corpus, Herder thought of it as the power or urge that made these works possible. And as myth was the linguistic embodiment of the essence of the *Volksgeist*, it was itself a force. This idea, that myth was the verbal incarnation of the *Volksgeist*, was exceedingly influential on the later romantics and the nationalistic folklorists like the Brothers Grimm.

Perhaps Herder's most important specific contribution [following the philologist C. G. Heyne (1729–1812), with whom he corresponded actively] to the systematic (as opposed to the philosophic) study of myth was to classify myths into three groups:

> The mythology of the Greeks flowed from the fables of various countries: and these consisted either of the popular faith, the traditionary accounts that the different generations preserved of their ancestors, or the first attempts of reflecting minds to explain the wonders of the earth and give a consistency to society.[15]

This is the now familiar tripartite arrangement into (1) folk tales and folklore, (2) legends, or narratives conceived of as having a historical basis, and (3) myth proper. "But," Chase comments, "this salutary scheme of Heyne and Herder was too long neglected by mythologists who, like Herder himself, were concerned with nature worship and philosophy of nature, and who were consequently but too eager to see philosophy and science in myth."[16] Herder generally confined his observations to the philosophical level and never tried to show in detail the connections between myth and poetry or myth and society. These tasks fell to the philologists and historians of the early nineteenth century.

Two

Romantic Historicism and Philology

The study of the past—the primitive and primitive religion—in the nineteenth century took two main forms: the work of the earlier part of the century, inspired by romantic historicism, was mainly historical-archaeological-philosophical; that of the second half of the century, under the impetus of evolutionary biology, saw the development of the comparative anthropological approach. We shall use this as a framework for our discussion in the next two chapters, amplifying and correcting it when necessary.

We have reviewed several speculative reconstructions of primitive life and of the origins of religion carried out in the eighteenth century, emphasizing those with most resonance for future generations. The revolutionary break with earlier views implicit in the formulations of Herder and Vico has been made clear.

It has been suggested that the Enlightenment pursued its inquest into the pagan past largely so that the sources of the error embodied in religion might be discovered and reason made to rule once again. If one were to attempt an analogous simplification of the motives for the nineteenth-century historical inquiry, it would read very differently. For those who embraced the new way of seeing and relating humanity, nature, and time that is summed up in the word "organicism," the world was totally transformed. German romantic historians, theologians, poets, and philosophers were feeling their way toward the realization that mythology was not a disfiguring inheritance from the past that had to be overcome through reason, nor was it something that affected only those too benighted to know better, but rather that it was the result of a faculty or quality inherent in all human minds—even now, even the best minds—that had to be understood if the past—and therefore the present—were to be understood at all.

Intimately involved in the work of the historians and philologists to be surveyed is the impulse of German nationalism. By the time of the French Revolution, Britain and France had been nations for centuries; Germany was not to be one for another seventy-five years. It was the political and cultural project of German romanticism in the nineteenth century to create a nation; the theoretical basis for this movement had been enunciated in the speculations about the *Volksgeist* by Herder and those who followed him. So when evaluating romantic historicism, we must bear in mind the impetus supplied by the need to find analogues to the German experience in the past, and to plumb Germanic history to discern and elaborate an authentic and continuous German identity. Even when the ostensible subject of a work was the civilization of Greece or Rome, the work could often be read so as to yield some lesson for Germany, to refer in some way to German mythology, German poetry. If this was not the case, then there was the constantly felt analogy from medieval experience, particularly in a country like Germany that had begun to modernize itself only in the preceding generation. For instance, B. G. Niebuhr worked from the example of the *Niebelungenlied* as he attempted to achieve an intuitive understanding of the temper of republican Rome. This nationalism was the political framework and analogue to romanticism. Germany had the men, and it had the movement or idea necessary to give their work coherence and point.

Finally we must mention the giant fact of the French Revolution. Its outbreak, and especially its sanguine excesses, certainly must have daunted those who had dreamed of the imminent onset of the rule of reason. The Enlightenment theorists who had proclaimed myth to be a sign of the bloody and superstitious past must have seemed like pretty thin stuff after the Revolution. It is obviously silly to say that the Revolution occurred because the *philosophes* were unable either to develop a useful theory of myth or to elaborate a psychology and historiography founded on the unconscious and the unknowable. But the romantic insistence on the organic and the irrational may fairly be said to have been a decisive move toward a more adequate theory of human behavior and of a more adequate study of antiquity.

Romantic historicism completely transformed the idea of the past, and its relation to the present. "The basic thesis of historicism is quite simple: The subject matter of history is human life in its totality and multiplicity."[1] This dictum, already adumbrated by Vico and forcefully propagated by Herder, simply means that history will not be contained by clear and distinct philosophical ideas or categories. The job of the historian is to show how *everything* in human affairs is continually growing and transforming itself into something new, yet recognizable. History is now conceived as sending its taproot deep into the irrational depths from which spring many of the richest sources of human life. In order to study history in this new way, a new method must be used. Herder (naturally) was the first to characterize it when he used the verb *einfühlen* to describe how the historian feels his way into the alien past and makes it his own.[2]

By this definition and method, practically speaking there had been no useful history; the entire past had to be re-examined and understood anew. History had a whole new subject matter—now the organic connections between classes, languages, institutions, and the like would be emphasized rather than the record of battles and dynasties that had characterized the older history.

Some examples from this new tendency—Winckelmann's *Geschichte der Kunst des Altertums*—appeared as early as 1763. Although basically a rationalist critic, Winckelmann appears here because, as the title of his great work shows, he realized that ancient art *had* a history, which was a revolutionary idea at the time. Next is F. A. Wolf's *Prolegomena ad Homerum* (1795), a casually produced introduction to a school edition of Homer that turned the scholarly world upside down. For although he had not read Vico, Wolf was arguing in detail what Vico had suggested: that "Homer" was really a collective name for the spirit of the Greek people in a barbarous period. Wolf raised the "Homerische Frage" by asserting that the Homeric epics were in fact composites of lays that had been composed by var-

ious bards and stitched together by later editors. And finally in this
brief honor roll we must name one whose work had to some extent
been inspired by the critical spirit of Wolf, B. G. Niebuhr's *History of
Rome*, the first edition of which began to appear in 1811–12.
Niebuhr's was the first, and perhaps the greatest, monument of
romantic historiography.

Beginning with Machiavelli's *Discourses*, many men had attempted
to write on aspects of Roman history, but, as Gooch writes,

> no one before Niebuhr had regarded Rome as above all a great
> state, the institutions of which, political, legal, and economic,
> must be traced to their origin and followed through successive
> stages. . . . He had grasped the truth that the early history of
> every nation must be rather of institutions than of events, of
> classes than of individuals, of customs than of laws. . . . He
> painted a clear picture of the political issues at stake, and
> enabled the world to form a vivid conception of the state from
> its origins to the Licinian Laws.[3]

Niebuhr's sophisticated idea of his subject was matched by an
advanced critical methodology. His work is noteworthy for its exact-
ing examination of the sources of information on the earliest period
in Roman history. Niebuhr wrote his history about the Rome neglected by Gibbon, who was concerned with the greatness and decay
of the Augustan empire. Like all true romantics, Niebuhr was fasci-
nated by origins, and thus he was forced to deal with the problem of
myth. Like all his successors who would essay histories of the civilizations of antiquity, in his inquest into the earliest days of Rome he
had to confront the question of the relation between history and
myth. Was there anything to be gleaned by the historian from an
examination of myth? His own approach was moderate and eclectic,
neither discarding myths completely as some of his skeptical predecessors had done, nor accepting them fully as the euhemerists had
proposed. He sifted each story and was willing to take what he could
get wherever he found it. Methodologically he was creating as he
went, for no one had ever attempted a like undertaking. His specific
conclusions are not relevant here; Niebuhr's significance for our

subject lies in the fact that he forcibly brought myth forward as one of the problems that all historians of the ancient world would have to face.

In order to gain anything from mythology, however, the post-Niebuhrian historian would have to accept the axiom that the consciousness of each age is historically conditioned; no longer might he assume that, because the name of an institution or idea has come down to us from the ancient world, it meant to the ancients what it means to us. This idea in turn implies that the historian of an age distant from his own must gain an instinctive awareness of that civilization, or else his analysis and judgments will lack the all-important sense of organic life of his subject. In order that historians have ample materials from which to work, every aspect of ancient life must be studied afresh so that its connections to the rest of the cultural fabric of which it is a part might be determined. We have already seen that a start had been made in Winckelmann's attempt to chart the growth and decay of Greek art.

From the time of Winckelmann onward we see, especially in Germany but to some extent all over Europe, a swing away from Rome to Greece. Rome had of course been the model for the Augustans of the earlier eighteenth century, and Latin had been the language of intellectual life for more than a thousand years. For these two reasons Rome and Latin seemed, to the younger generation before and after the Revolution, to be symbols of pedantry. The earliest romantics of the Sturm und Drang movement associated Greek with radiant, organic natural beauty, as opposed to Latin, which stood for their stuffy forebears. Somewhat later, Goethe attempted to achieve the epic simplicity and objectivity he discerned in Homer. To him Greek culture was organic, but modern men were too specialized. They had to find their way back to the organicism of the ancients so that their spiritual malady might be cured.

1

The movement from Latinity to Hellenism reached its culmination in the German philological movement of the early nineteenth century. The philologists, moreover, were another expression of the deep interest in language as a phenomenon that was part of historicism. Language was felt to be the repository of the earliest, and therefore the deepest and most important, intuitions and emotions of the *Volk*; preserved in so much linguistic amber was not only what the *Urmensch* saw but also how he saw it and what he felt about it. Therefore, in this last pre-archaeological, pre-ethnographic period, philology seemed to offer the best hope for deciphering the riddle of the past in the sense that it permitted moderns to feel their way into ancient modes of consciousness. Furthermore, this investigation into the structure and interrelationships of languages seemed to offer a potent way of establishing an authentic Teutonic identity stretching back through the ages, and especially getting back before the time when the fatal Latin admixture was made to the pure German people and their language. (It is in such nationalistically inclined philological studies that we find the foundations laid for the "Aryan hypothesis," of infamous consequences and memory.)

German philology made crucial contributions to the study of myth in the nineteenth century. In establishing the kinship of the languages of the Indo-European speech area, it achieved the first great scientific triumph of the comparative method. But in its historical aspect it was at least as important. Today, when philology has been largely absorbed into linguistics (in the United States, at least) and exists vestigially in the titles of certain learned journals and professional chairs, it is useful to recall what its founders claimed for it and what it attempted to be. Holger Pedersen has written:

> One may define philology briefly as a study whose task is the interpretation of the literary monuments in which the spiritual life of a given period has found expression. This definition might seem to point in the direction of history, in so far as it is the understanding of spiritual life which is named as the ultimate aim of the work; and when the interpretation is not concerned with an individual monument, but seeks to derive all the information possible on an entire literature, then the philologist is on the way to encroaching upon the field of the historians. . . . Philology, then, can be regarded as a sort of linguistic activity which concerns itself with the interpretation of

the literary monuments of a given period; for this purpose it employs and itself produces aids of purely linguistic as well as historical kinds.[4]

Pride of place in any discussion of philology, particularly insofar as the study of mythology was concerned, must go to C. G. Heyne.[5] Although his commentaries on the *Aeneid* and the *Iliad* are still fundamental, it is not his scholarship but his vision that causes him to be mentioned here. For it was Heyne who first conceived of philology as the total science of antiquity. That is, he formulated the task of philology to be the historical study of ancient institutions, mythology, and religion. Moreover, he founded the first philological seminar, the students of which were to go on to provide the leadership of the philological movement that swept Germany.

But the advent of a more scientific attitude to myth in the person of Heyne naturally did not per se mark the end of the older points of view. The study of myth through philology also led to G. F. Creuzer (1771–1858), a man of yeasty imagination who used philology to support his idea that ancient myth represented the disguised embodiment of a great symbolic system. His main works, *Dionysus* (1808) and *Symbolik und Mythologie der Alten Volker* (1810–12), were embodiments of the romantic desire to find transcendental wisdom in the East. In these books Creuzer developed elaborate and far-fetched theories concerning Egyptian and Oriental influences on Greek civilization in general and on the legends surrounding Dionysus in particular.[6] Despite the eccentricity of his ideas, Creuzer did make the real contribution of calling attention to the Eleusinian mysteries, until that time neglected. We shall see that later nineteenth-century scholarship paid increasing attention to the irrational side of Greek life and religion.

An important result of Creuzer's mystical theories, which predictably elicited attacks from the dominantly rationalist scholarly community, was that to some extent they caused the erudite C. A. Lobeck to compose his encyclopedic *Aglaophamus* (1829) in reaction.[7] This work brought together in an objective fashion everything that was known about Greek myth and religion in that pre-archaeological, pre-anthropological era. *Aglaophamus* remained the standard text in the field for more than half a century and may be thought of as closing the first period of philological scholarship on the subject of myth.

The outstanding German philologist of the next generation who specialized in the study of myth was Karl Otfried Müller, whose premature death in 1840 at the age of forty-three was, according to Gooch, "the greatest loss that Greek studies sustained during the nineteenth century."[8] Müller showed how far one could go without the help of anthropology. Unlike some of his more ponderous fellow philologists whose works have just been noticed, Müller's *Introduction to a Scientific Study of Mythology* (1825; English translation, 1844) still holds the interest of the reader. One feels Wolf's example hovering before Müller as he writes. Wolf had maintained that Homer, and by extension all early Greek writing and therefore all mythography, had undergone all manner of alterations and emendations by the many priests, poets, scribes, and commentators through whose hands the texts had passed. Since this was the case it was necessary, if one wished to make sense of the myths, to subject them to the same process in reverse: to rid the narratives of the layers of extraneous accretion that had been deposited over the years. And this is what Müller proceeds to do. His method is linguistic and historical, with a large measure of common sense thrown in. He attempts in the case of each myth that he takes up to find some specific historical event to which it somehow may be traced or attributed—some war, or migration, or ritual, or some other important happening in the lives of the Greeks. Unlike scholars like Heyne (and nearly all others throughout the century), Müller does not begin with some a priori idea of what the mentality of mythmaking humans *must* have been. Especially does he deny that the proto-Greeks were little more than animals, and that the fantastic features in myths must be attributed to the native incapacity of their makers.

For Müller each myth is a mixture of two elements: the real and the ideal, or the actual and the imaginary. Thus in Chapter Fourteen, "Examples of the Method which has been laid down," he analyzes the myth of the bondage of Apollo to Admetus. He begins his discussion by asking: "What is here genuine ancient tradition, and what has been added by the authors who handed it down. . . ?"[9]

Müller then proceeds to discriminate various elements in the narrative: that bondage was a punishment for murder, that Apollo was obliged to serve Admetus because he had polluted himself as a result of killing the demon Python, and that however praiseworthy the motives for this killing, murder must be atoned for. He then shows how certain rituals surrounding the worship of Apollo at Delphi imitated the purification of the god. Having arrived at the "root idea" of the myth he gives a historical explanation of why Pherae was connected with the story. His main virtue is his relative flexibility regarding the kinds of explanations he is willing to adduce for the myths; although Müller is clearly a euhemerist, he is not unalterably committed to that theory. Admirable throughout is his avoidance of extreme positions, his willingness to admit ignorance, and his lack of polemic bitterness.

From Pedersen's definition of philology given above it is plain that philology had two aspects, one linguistic and the other historical. (These tendencies prefigured what was to happen to philology in the twentieth century: it has split into two parts and has largely been absorbed into the disciplines of linguistics and history.) We have already seen how the historically minded philologist, inspired by exciting advances in more properly historical research, made important contributions to the study of myth. The work of the other group (of course these groups were in no sense insulated from one another) also influenced the course of myth study, in a more indirect, but more important, fashion. To understand the effects of their work a brief summary is in order.

Two main periods may be discerned in what came to be called comparative philology (to distinguish it from historical philology and to denote its methodology). The earlier concentrated on establishing the basic proposition that the Indo-European languages were in fact related genetically and structurally. Many philosophers and writers on language (Vico, for one) had suspected this for a long time, but until the nineteenth century no one had worked out a method for comparative linguistic study any more reliable than that of comparison of vocabulary, which led to predictably haphazard results. However, when the Dane Rasmus Rask in his *Investigation into the Origin of the Old Norse and Icelandic Tongues* (1814, 1818), came forth with a workable method—comparison of inflectional systems, and especially endings—philology was fairly launched. Rask wrote what "may be called a comparative Indo-European grammar in embryo."[10] In a brilliant insight he saw that most of the European languages were connected and that they were the descendants of some common pre-existent language.[11] The next pioneer, Franz Bopp, made the great advance of adding Sanskrit to the linguistic network that Rask had proposed. And in 1833 Bopp published the first edition of the first comparative Indo-European grammar. Bopp's work was augmented by August Pott and Jakob Grimm,[12] who redressed the grammatical (morphological) bias of their predecessors by showing that sound shifts too might be described systematically. The second period of comparative philology, beginning in the 1870s and lasting until the First World War, consolidated what the earlier workers had begun and conclusively demonstrated the universality and invariability of phonological laws.

2

Comparative mythology was the offspring of comparative philology. Its chief exponent was the Right Honourable F. Max Müller (1823–1900), a German (son of the romantic poet Wilhelm Müller) who had studied with Bopp and then learned Sanskrit. In 1849, at the age of twenty-six, he had come to England to translate the Hindu scripture known as the Rig-Veda and oversee the publication of an edition of Hindu sacred texts. He settled in Oxford, where he remained for the rest of his life (becoming professor of comparative philology in 1868), supervising the edition of the famous series called "Sacred Books of the East." In 1856 he published an epoch-making essay, "Comparative Mythology."[13] In it he advanced the theories that were to become synonymous with his name and make him one of the leading writers on myth both in Britain and throughout Europe for the rest of the century.

Effectively, Müller turned the method and results of the discipline in which he was trained, comparative philology, to the study of myth. He began with the idea, advanced by the earlier comparatists, that most of the European languages along with Sanskrit were descendants of some now-extinct common tongue that had been spoken by the shadowy Aryans, the early invaders of India. This so-called Aryan hypothesis, generally accepted by the 1850s, postulated that what we now know as the basis of Western culture had been brought from India to Europe by the successive waves of Aryan-descended peoples who poured out of Central Asia. Applied to myth, this meant to Müller that Greek myths were in fact variants of Indic originals, and that these originals and their relationships might be recovered through an exclusively philological analysis, based on the known laws of linguistic change. Müller next asserted that these primitive Aryans (about whom nothing besides their reconstructed language was known) worshiped the transcendent power manifested through nature. The language of these children of nature had a curious feature, however, that later brought about endless difficulties. It seemed that these Aryans, by the peculiarity of their language, were doomed never to be permitted to worship their nature gods directly but instead were forced into the most elaborate periphrases to voice their piety. The reason for this state of affairs was that Aryan was a truly primitive language in that it consisted solely of words that expressed action; its speakers could not therefore use it to express abstraction. All these "roots," as Müller called them, were examples of the primitive mind acting to animate the inanimate world: "the creation of every word was originally a poem, embodying a bold metaphor or a bright conception."[14] The result of this extraordinary limitation was remarkably "poetic."

> Every word, whether noun or verb, had still its full original power during the mythopoeic ages. Words were heavy and unwieldy. They said more than they ought to say, and hence, much of the strangeness of the mythological language, which we can only understand by watching the natural growth of speech. Where we speak of the sun following the dawn, the ancient poets could only speak and think of the Sun loving and embracing the Dawn. What is with us a sunset, was to them the Sun growing old, decaying, or dying. Our sunrise was to them the Night giving birth to a beautiful child; and in the Spring they really saw the Sun or the Sky embracing the earth with a

warm embrace, and showering treasures into the lap of nature.[15]

Thus because of the entirely metaphoric nature of Aryan, its speakers could not successfully express the intimations of the infinite that Müller believed lay at the heart of their religion. As a result, myth, which is really a degradation of meaning, or as Müller put it in a famous phrase, "a disease of language," appears. Myth was thus a stage of development (or degeneration) through which all languages and peoples had to pass, which accounts for its universality.

This "explains" the genesis of Aryan myth. But there is more. As the Aryans moved into Europe and as their language changed into the prototypes of the various modern European languages, these remarkable idioms that had expressed, however inadequately, the primitive Aryans' feelings about the infinite, nature, the heavens, and the gods, became misunderstood. Their meanings were forgotten but the metaphors, which were beautiful and suggestive, lived on. Thus, what we today call myths were stories that arose to explain these free-floating metaphors. And because most of these metaphors had to do with the sun, Müller and his disciples found, after laborious philological investigation, that nearly all myths turned out to be misunderstood ancient Aryan statements about the sun,[16] with the result that Müller and his followers were often called "solar mythologists."

As Andrew Lang remarked, "Between 1860 and 1880, roughly speaking, people who became interested in myth and religions found the mythological theories of Professor Max Müller in possession of the field."[17] Solar mythology became generally accepted, at least in the popular mind, and it was only over the corpse of solarism that the anthropological view of myth established itself.

Three

The Rise of Anthropology:
Lang, Tylor, and Smith

The third quarter of the nineteenth century in Britain saw the resolution of a conflict between two different ideas of the use and value of the past. The first, deriving from Coleridge and of which the main proponents were Carlyle, Newman, and Ruskin, may be termed romantic, religious, organic, and reactionary. This view presented the past—or certain select parts of it—as a touchstone by which the decay of the present age might be measured. The past, whether it was medieval Catholic or Reformation Puritan, was held up as a model in terms of both social organization and individual conduct. The other approach, progressivist, rationalist, secularist, and evolutionist, was espoused by the scientists and the rationalist philosophers like the younger J. S. Mill and Spencer, and groups like the Philosophical Radicals and the positivists. Its basis, the Benthamite dream, was the assumption of a "science of society"—the idea that social organization and social relationships could and should be analyzed and reformed on rational grounds. For this group the past provided the base line from which one might measure not man's degradation but his ascent; the future and not the past contained the ideal society. The development of a new ethnographic approach to myth and ritual—the subject of this chapter—was one result of this warfare between romantics and rationalists.

The main figures in this pioneering British Rationalist school of anthropologists were Andrew Lang, Edward Burnett Tylor, and William Robertson Smith. Lang succeeded in exposing the inade-

quacies of the philological approach to myth; Tylor laid the theoretical foundations for the evolutionary study of human culture; and
Smith argued that ancient religion was a tissue of rituals, not beliefs,
so that any future study of primitive religion would have to account
for ritual as well as myth. Together they made possible the work of
Frazer and the Cambridge Ritualists.

Before we turn to these founding fathers of British anthropology,
some consideration seems appropriate of the reasons why evolutionary social thought of all sorts prevailed so completely in the third
quarter of the nineteenth century in Britain. For the growth of
anthropology was only part of the general surge of such evolutionary theorizing in all the social sciences. Accordingly, our discussion
begins with Darwin.

The antepenultimate paragraph of *The Origin of Species* calls for
the application of evolutionary principles to the study of mankind
("Much light will be thrown on the origin of man and his history").
And fifty years later, in 1909, Jane Harrison, writing on "The
Influence of Darwinism on the Study of Religion" in a volume issued
to commemorate the centenary of Darwin's birth, began her paper:
"The title of my paper might well have been 'the creation by
Darwinism of the scientific study of Religions,' but that I feared to
mar my tribute to a great name by any shadow of exaggeration."[1] But
here as elsewhere Harrison does tend to exaggerate; it is an over-
simplification to assert that the scientific study of religion, in social-
anthropological terms, came into being as a result of Darwin's call.
In fact the leaders of evolutionary social thought—Herbert Spencer,
Henry Maine, J. F. McLennan—had been airing their characteristic
views in print for at least a decade by 1859. John Burrow has put it
neatly: "In this context, Darwin was undoubtedly important, but it
is a type of importance impossible to estimate at all precisely. He was
certainly not the father of evolutionary anthropology, but possibly
he was its wealthy uncle."[2] There can be no doubt, however, that *The
Origin of Species* gave a mighty impetus to the stream of evolutionary
theorizing that is to be found throughout Europe during the
decades following 1859.

It will not do, then, merely to invoke the great name of Darwin
and pass on; rather one must inquire into the reasons why the

stream of evolutionary social thought, although undoubtedly quickened by the appearance of *The Origin of Species*, was able so completely to sweep the field in the second half of the century.

There are several factors that contributed to this decisive turn in British social and scientific thought. First, the nineteenth century in general is characterized by its passionate concern with the search for origins, which has been noted in the brief discussion of romantic historicism above. Jerome Buckley has written:

> Evolution rather than revolution seemed to be the true way of history. . . . Evolution . . . meant an organic growth of all things in time, a development in which the past, though never repeating itself, would persist through each successive modification. The past accordingly became the subject of solicitous regard; the present could not be cut from its history; civilization was a branching plant which could droop and wither if its roots were neglected or dislodged. The organic image, applied both to nature and human culture, replaced the standard eighteenth-century mechanistic analogy; the world was no longer a machine operating on a set cycle, but a living body fulfilling itself in constant adaptation to new conditions.[3]

In this regard it should be remembered that "the past" literally meant something new in the second half of the nineteenth century. By the 1860s few British intellectuals continued to accept the Mosaic cosmogony and timetable. First in the 1830s and 1840s it had been the "dreadful hammers of the geologists," in Ruskin's phrase, whose findings had forced thinking people to agree that the Creation, if divinely ordered, had not taken place over six twenty-four-hour intervals. Then Boucher de Perthes in France in 1859 had convinced leading British scientists that the flints he had excavated were indeed implements that had been fabricated by humans, which forced a further revision in thinking: now it was not only the earth that was immensely old but human life on the planet had a much longer history than had been supposed. With the advent of human prehistory it became feasible to attempt to extrapolate backward into the dim reaches of time so that some evolutionary developmental schema for man might be established.[4] Prehistory gave the evolutionists the time needed for man to evolve.

Second, Britain was passing through what may be called an ideological crisis. The only reasonably systematic theory of society was utilitarianism and its offshoot political economy, and these had sustained some powerful attacks around the middle of the century. Both Macaulay and Mill had struck at the weakest point in the Benthamite argument—the assertion that all people in fact are solely motivated to increase their pleasure and decrease their pain.[5] The result was a dominant rationalism increasingly without an ideology. John Burrow has suggested that evolutionary social theories were so successful in the third quarter of the century because they seemed to breathe new life into a faltering rationalism.

> The specific attractiveness of evolutionary theories was that they offered a way of reformulating the essential unity of mankind, while avoiding the current objection to the older theories of a human nature essentially the same. Mankind was not one because it was everywhere the same, but because the differences represented different stages in the same process.[6]

These theories were then frequently moralized by calling evolutionary development progressive, so that the inevitable became a built-in universal striving toward the good. One may view the burst of late Victorian progressivist social theorizing as a way for some intellectuals to avoid facing the dangerous relativistic implications of historicism. When one thinks of how hard it must have been for people to hold on to any certainties in a world in which the loudest sound was the "melancholy, long, withdrawing roar" of the Sea of Faith, such reluctance is entirely understandable.

Third, it should be recalled that Anglo-Saxon philosophy, unlike German, had experienced nothing like the great transformation that had occurred in historiography. The historicist outlook itself was basically a foreign import, not well established compared with the sturdy native rationalism of Philosophical Radicalism, which was very much a creature of the Enlightenment in its ahistorical outlook. Nor had any British thinkers—not even Coleridge or Carlyle, most attuned to German romantic philosophy—developed a doctrine concerning the relationship of myth to national consciousness, as had occurred in Germany. So myths were still classical, and folklore (a term coined in 1847) was still a subject for discussion in anti-quarian societies. It is not surprising, therefore, that writing about myth in mid-Victorian England was extremely eclectic and without urgency.[7]

A handy way of surveying the progress of mythological study in mid-Victorian England is to compare the articles on "Mythology" in the eighth and ninth editions of the *Encyclopaedia Britannica*, pub-lished respectively in 1853–60 and 1875–79.[8] The earlier article, by "D. D.," reads as though it could have been written at any time in the century (although he cites both Otfried Müller and Max Müller); it is an incoherent jumble of conjectures. He characterizes his subject as synonymous with "any kind of fabulous doctrine" (759). Mythology arises because the human race, in its infancy, has an instinct "for the new and surprising." Ancient priests, legislators, poets, etc., used fable to impart their teachings. Mythology is the wreckage of a superior knowledge that has become garbled as a result of the many centuries sinful mankind has passed on this earth since the Creation. By comparison, the article in the ninth edition, by Andrew Lang, is a long, well-argued polemic, arguing the superi-ority of anthropology to philology as the best approach to myth. In it we reach something like the modern world.

1. Andrew Lang

When Andrew Lang (1844–1912) went up to Oxford to read classics in the mid-1860s, solarism was everywhere in the ascendant. Lang read but was not convinced. After taking his degree, he tells us in an autobiographical aside in *Modern Mythology* (1898), he read more deeply in the myths of all nations, savage and civilized. He found that myths from such exotic cultures as the American Indians, the Kaffirs, and the Eskimos closely resembled Greek myths that Müller had explained as the products of the disease of language working according to the known and inexorable laws of specifically Indo-European philology. He then asked himself: "Did a kind of linguistic measles affect all tongues alike, from Sanskrit to Choctaw, and everywhere produce the same ugly scars in religion and myth?"[9]

His deepening distrust of solar mythology issued in his first essay on the subject, "Mythology and Fairy Tales," published in the *Fortnightly Review* in 1872. The article, a lightweight piece, was mainly notable because it was the opening shot in a twenty-five-year running battle with Max Müller on the origin and meaning of mythology.[10] Although the men were friendly enough to each other in person, on the printed page they were sworn enemies. Each time Müller or one of his many disciples brought out a book or published a series of lectures, Lang could be counted upon to contribute a mocking review in one or more of the many journals for which he wrote. After 1884, once Lang had become expert enough in the field to begin writing books himself, he could count on a polemic rejoinder from Oxford within a matter of months.

The controversy between Müller and Lang is a good example of the romantic-rationalist confict sketched earlier. Müller's solarism had postulated a mythopoeic age, in which the original sublime ideas of the Aryans had been conceived. Since then mental and linguistic devolution had set in, and the result—myth—represented the detritus of a glorious past. In this sense solarism is a linguistic variant of the old theory that pagan mythology embodied the pitiful remnants of a vast trove of arcane wisdom that had been the possession of antiquity, which is in turn a version of the myth of the Golden Age.[11] The degenerationist position was widely held in the nineteenth century by moralists, who used it to explain a great deal besides mythology, for it sorts well with Christian pessimism.

Lang, by comparison, had adopted the doctrine of uniform mental development advanced by E. B. Tylor in his epoch-making *Primitive Culture* (1871).[12] This meant that humanity necessarily passes through certain predetermined stages in its evolution, and the myth-making mind characterized one of these. First gradually, then radically, he modified his position, to some extent as a result of the criticism he received from Müller, but more because at the end of his life he returned to the Christianity he had abandoned as a young man. By the end, in a striking deconversion, he had totally renounced evolution and all its ways.[13]

But even when Lang was a convinced evolutionist it should not be thought that he had his own way from the start. Müller, possessor of a lucid style and great erudition and industry, soon began to give as good as he got, and his criticisms of Lang anticipated the general critique of evolutionist anthropology around the time of the First World War.[14] For example, he saw that contemporary savages were not the same as primitive peoples, and he criticized the indiscriminate use of data gathered by a mixed bag of explorers, missionaries, and traders, many of whom could not speak the language of the "natives." Again and again he came back to language, advising Lang and his fellow folklorists to stay out of a field in which they were unqualified because they lacked philological expertise. Although solarism had many followers who were neither as learned nor as scrupulous as their master, Müller himself always took pains to restrict himself to the Indo-European speech area. He never doubted that the disease of language had infected the speech of non-Aryan-descended peoples, but he never deemed himself expert enough to pronounce on these exotic folk. It therefore angered him that Lang and other folklorists blithely sallied forth to adduce parallels from all over the world, cutting across and mixing up widely diverse speech areas with impunity.

Finally it came down to the question of which theory accounted for more of the facts. Müller's self-imposed linguistic limitation left him at a loss while Lang ransacked the world's mythology for materials. Again and again Lang would bring in new African or Polynesian versions of stories that closely reproduced myths that Müller had derived by the strict laws of Indo-European philology. How could this universality of folk motifs be explained among peoples who had had no historical or linguistic connections with one other? Müller was gradually forced back on the defensive, although he never yielded on his basic position.

Another of Müller's problems was that Lang was so versatile and prolific and wrote in so many different magazines (often anonymously) that his strength was as the strength of ten men. He peppered Müller, and especially Müller's much less knowledgeable disciples, from all sides. Added to this, of course, was the overwhelming acceptance of evolutionary explanations by the end of the century,

and the story is complete. When Müller died in 1900, Queen
Victoria sent his widow a telegram of sympathy, royalty around the
world added their condolences, but no one succeeded him.[15]
Solarism was finished.

2. Edward Burnett Tylor

Edward Burnett Tylor (1832–1917) was born into a wealthy London
Quaker family, which explains why he never attended university.
Feeble as a young man (he lived to be eighty-five), he was advised to
travel for his health. Instead of making the standard tour of Europe,
he went to Mexico. The result of his trip was his first book, *Anahuac*
(1861), written before its author had read Darwin. In it he already
brings up, in a rather scrappy way (it is, after all, a travel book and
he was a young man), many of the ideas and issues to which he
would return in his later work: for example, the meaning of survivals,
the assumption of the uniformity of human nature, and the question
of whether culture evolved independently in several places or diffused from a single center. Moreover, as might be expected from a
person of his religious background, *Anahuac* shows him as staunchly
anti-Catholic, with a deep antipathy to what he regarded as empty
display in religious observance. The likely effect of this unfortunate
prejudice, so far as the study of primitive religion was concerned, was
to emphasize his tendency to value the cognitive component of religion (beliefs and intentions) at the expense of the performative
(rites and ceremonies).

Tylor's is an anthropology of origins. His self-assigned task was to
recover the prehistory of mankind. He starts from the premise that
a fundamental unity exists among people, and that the similarities
and continuities in human culture far outweigh the differences and
discontinuities. His work thus reflects the rising tide of democracy
all over Europe, for comparative evolutionary anthropology may be
thought of as a scientific, "objective" demonstration of the unity of
man that philosophy and "enlightened theology" had already been
proclaiming since the French Revolution.

Tylor asserts that an organic law of development and progress
operates in the growth of human institutions. This meant that

change was gradual and orderly, much the same the world over, and that human institutions, once simple and confused, had become complex and highly coordinated over the passage of time. His problem, obviously, is one of evidence. In his day even archaeology was not yet much help, for when his major work, *Primitive Culture*, appeared in 1871 the great burst of excavations in the Mediterranean world had not yet begun, much less the digging in less well-known areas.[16] How then was Tylor to make his case that human society had evolved like everything else in the natural world? How to secure anything firm on which to base developmental schemes charting the growth from undifferentiated savagery to complex, advanced European societies? He solved this problem by the use of the comparative method and the doctrine of "survivals."

Tylor (and the many who followed him for half a century) assumed that, human nature and development being relatively homogeneous, one might legitimately discover, in the behavior of contemporary primitive peoples (with many of whom the growing British Empire was then coming into contact), living links in the evolutionary chain. Despite the fact that there was no evidence that their histories were any shorter than those of their European observers, these "savages," then, were assumed to show humanity as it was many thousands of years ago, before some or all of the great cultural advances occurred that had led up to the societies of nineteenth-century Western Europe. Once this step was taken, it was not much further to the next: that to secure the needed dynamic view of prehistoric development, one might string together items of culture taken from the most diverse "primitive" societies if in their totality they showed the steady upward movement of human development. And thus it was that the burgeoning ethnography of the time (which was made possible by the fact that traders and missionaries followed the Union Jack into the farthest corners of the world and, through their extended permanent residence in Malaya or Nepal or Uganda, were enabled to observe the native societies over long periods of time) was levied upon to provide comparative examples of all the various "stages" of human behavioral and social development.

Any argument from a series of artifacts necessarily must demonstrate that in fact each of its items evolved from the preceding one—

that the series was indeed evolutionary. To this end, Tylor adapted the notion of "survivals." These were objects or traits or attitudes with a *raison d'être* in one developmental stage that had become obsolete or misunderstood because they had, through social conservatism, "survived" into a new, higher stage in which they were nonfunctional. Thus the magician's rattle and the warrior's bow and arrow become children's toys; Tylor gives many examples. This device of survivals made it possible, Tylor and other evolutionists thought, to reconstruct the way of life of bygone eras. The similarity to the argument of Herder and then later of Max Müller and the comparative philologists—that language provided a repository of archaic attitudes, that is, linguistic "survivals"—is striking.

But all this was not enough. Savages could provide all the material artifacts imaginable and Europe would not be satisfied. For the most absorbing subjects, humanly speaking, were the development not of agriculture or smelting but of religion and morality. Late Victorian Europe was facing a spiritual crisis, not a technological one, and any evidence whatever that could be construed to undermine or buttress religion was sure to secure a deeply interested audience. Thus Tylor had important chapters in *Primitive Culture*, and later in his textbook *Anthropology* (1881), on the origins and development of these sensitive social and "spiritual" institutions—art, language, religion, and mythology.

For Tylor religion and myth arise from the same source, although "error" would perhaps be closer than "source" to what he had in mind. This source is exclusively mental, inherent in the functioning of the savage mind, which is postulated to be qualitatively different from our own. This mentality is radically subjective and is characterized by an inveterate habit of animating nature, which survives in the vivid fancy of children.[17] The savage animates nature, or as Tylor puts it, "transfigures into myths the facts of daily experience," as the result of his application of a "broad philosophy of nature, early and crude indeed, but thoughtful, consistent, and quite really and seriously meant."[18] The "savage philosopher" (memorable phrase) founds his theory on the notion of souls. Souls in turn are thought to exist because it is well known that the (spirits of the) dead appear in dreams and visions to the living; ergo, some part of them must still live. And from this the primitive savant proceeds to expand the scope of the doctrine, attributing souls of some kind to nonhuman objects—animals, plants, and even stones.

For Tylor, the question to ask of myth was whether or not it was true. This followed from his premises, for myth (like its vehicle religion) was a product of primitive ratiocination, and therefore ought to be judged like any other cognitive effort. Although most of it was patent nonsense by this standard, Tylor adjures his reader to take it seriously notwithstanding, for it can help us to understand much, especially concerning that dim prehistoric period about which we know so little. As he wrote in *Anthropology*, "Myth is not to be looked on as mere error and folly, but as an interesting product of the human mind. It is sham history, the fictitious narrative of events that never happened."[19] It is reasonable to inspect myths and extract whatever factual content they may have, discarding the great amount of rubbish one finds. The study of myth permits us, he says, to lay bare ancient connections between peoples that have been totally effaced in memory and of which we have no material evidence. Tylor thus resembles Otfried Müller, who tried to educe from myths evidence of migrations and other events in Greek tribal prehistory, in his basic orientation toward myth and in his idea of their utility, except that Tylor has the advantage of a wealth of ethnographic data, whereas Otfried Müller was working solely from philological evidence.

3. William Robertson Smith

We have observed how the data from anthropology, philology, and archaeology, interpreted comparatively, had been used to illuminate the prehistoric past. More light was to be shed on mythology and primitive religion as a result of students of these three disciplines working in a related area—Near Eastern and biblical studies. For our purposes the most important of these was William Robertson Smith, who along with Tylor was a primary influence on Frazer; Frazer in turn was, if not the father, then the "wealthy uncle" of Cambridge classical anthropology.[20]

William Robertson Smith was a brilliant Scottish theologian and

Semiticist who, more than any other single person, succeeded in interpreting for Britain the results of a century of German biblical "higher criticism."[21] For his pains, Smith was prosecuted in the last great heresy trials in Scotland, the protracted strain of which ordeal undoubtedly shortened his life (he died at the age of forty-seven in 1894) and prevented him from completing what would have been his masterwork, *The Religion of the Semites*.[22]

Smith built on the foundations laid by German Higher Criticism, which began in the pioneering efforts in the seventeenth and eighteenth centuries of Spinoza, Astruc, and Simon, who argued that the Hebrew Bible was a collection of books written by human beings (rather than the revealed word of God) that could, and should, be criticized by the same criteria suitable for any other ancient, difficult text. Working on this assumption, a series of distinguished German scholars most notably concluded that the Pentateuch we have today, far from being the monolith of orthodox belief, was the result of a long series of extensive redactions of ancient traditions and that the Deuteronomic histories had likewise been extensively edited by later hands. In short, the Higher Criticism illustrates the same de-allegorizing and historicizing tendencies already noted in connection with secular historiography in the study of the pagan past.[23]

The enlightened view of the Bible was not solely the result of the critical and analytical labors of the German Higher Critics. The rest of the Near Eastern past was being opened up as well, with impressive results. First had come the discovery and decipherment of the Rosetta Stone, which permitted scholars to read hieroglyphics, a task that occupied them for the rest of the century. Then Layard and Rawlinson had discovered and finally deciphered cuneiform, and the vast Babylonian and Assyrian archives were made accessible. The light they shed on the understanding of the Bible was immense. But beyond any specific biblical reference that they clarified was their cumulative effect of forcing Protestant Europe to see that the people and events of the Bible had a new, denser kind of historical reality and did not exist in some special never-never world compounded of piety and revelation, wholly unlike the everyday world of antiquity.

William Robertson Smith was the first scholar-theologian to attempt to study Semitic religion from the comparative anthropological point of view. This had not been done earlier because until then (the 1870s and 1880s) the Semitic religions were felt to be unique and therefore incomparable, which is to say that any comparative study of them was thought to be both futile and sacrilegious. Furthermore, until Smith's time simply not enough work had been done on primitive religion to make such an undertaking possible: that is, the analysis of social systems in general and of religion in particular had barely begun.

No armchair scholar, Smith began by traveling to the Near East, where he spent several years, mostly in Arabia. Of course others had traveled among the Arabs and studied their way of life. But Smith, a reader of Tylor and an evolutionist, extrapolated backwards from contemporary Arab life in an effort to understand the life of the people of the Old Testament. In *The Religion of the Semites* Smith attempted a reconstruction of the "Semitic world picture" out of which were born the historical Semitic religions. And here he parted company with the rationalism so well exemplified by Tylor. Whereas Tylor began with the idea of a primitive philosopher who elaborated religion and then, in its final stage, myth in an attempt to understand and answer questions about the natural universe in the same way Edward Burnett Tylor would have if he had been a primitive man, Smith somehow intuited that primitive religion arose from something else entirely. Unlike modern religion, and especially modern Protestantism, primitive religion to Smith was primarily a matter of things done, not things believed, of rituals, not creeds. He understood that ancient religion was not something that happened in a certain building on a certain day of the week, but an attitude toward life that penetrated every aspect of existence. He saw that our distinction between the "sacred" and the "profane" simply does not agree with ancient ideas and practice.

Unlike rationalists like Tylor (and later Frazer), who offer psychological (that is, cognitive) explanations for the genesis and perpetuation of religion, Smith's is fundamentally a sociological approach: significantly, his ideas were to be immensely influential on Emile Durkheim, and therefore on twentieth-century sociology, whereas the triumphant rationalism of the late nineteenth century is now of interest largely to historians of anthropology. Smith found the origins of ancient religion in the *structure* of the worshiping community. In the same way that political institutions antedate the political theories that explain them (as Vico saw), so religious practices precede the doctrines that grow up to explain them. What the ancient religious community really worshiped, Smith believed, and therefore what the gods represented, was the social order—society itself—idealized and divinized. That is, ancient religion provided what we should call supernatural sanctions that legitimized the existing order of things, an order which seemed to the primitive person to be natural and inevitable and therefore divinely ordained.

Because "ancient religions had for the most part no creed; they consisted entirely of institutions and practices,"[24] we should take the basic religious unit to be the worshiping group, not the individual (as it was "naturally" taken to be, considering the largely Protestant character of the nineteenth-century inquiry into the origin of religion). This group, Smith theorized, was linked by blood. Members were totemic brethren, the totem group including gods and animals as well as men. Socially, the human members of the group performed the rites necessary to preserve the world; psychologically, the group was a prime means of establishing the identity of its individual members.

The main religious ritual of the Semites was sacrificial in character, and most of *The Religion of the Semites* is devoted to an examination of the many sacrifices prescribed and described in the ancient Semitic records. In the most notable form of such sacrifice, the totemic brethren entirely consumed the sacrificial animal victim, which was their divine totem-brother god. This totem animal was ordinarily taboo to the tribe, but at certain solemn days of the year, and in times of emergency, the tribe killed and ate the forbidden animal. In Frazer's words, "Smith was the first to perceive the true nature of what he has called mystical or sacramental sacrifices," the peculiarity of these being that in them the victim slain is "an animal or a man whom the worshippers regarded as divine, and of whose flesh and blood they partook, as a solemn form of communion with the deity."[25] Smith's idea of the dying god was immensely and directly influential: as Frazer acknowledges in the preface to the first edition of *The Golden Bough*, "the central idea of my essay—the conception of the slain god—is derived directly, I believe, from my friend [William Robertson Smith]."[26]

We must resist here the temptation to pursue further Smith's complex ideas or to assess his importance for the study of comparative religion, but instead focus on his contribution to literary criticism. Smith's importance for the Ritualists is sizable and clear. As mentioned above, it was his organic, sociological approach to religion that inspired Durkheim, and it was the Durkheimian vision of the perfusion of society by religion that provided the theoretical framework for Jane Harrison's *Themis* and Cornford's *From Religion to Philosophy* and *The Origin of Attic Comedy*. More immediately, it was Smith who placed the study of ritual in primitive religion in the forefront of scholarly consciousness by arguing that the rite in antiquity took the place of the creed. This was all the more remarkable in that Smith was brought up in the puritanical Free Church of Scotland, which had denigrated, more than most of British Protestantism, the importance of ritual as "Romish" and therefore the work of the devil.

Smith, however, saw the distortion that had been introduced by the attempt on the part of Protestant missionaries, or students of ancient religion brought up in Protestant countries like Britain or Germany, instinctively to search out and focus on the creed of the religion in question. When they found no proper creed (for there was none to be found), they took as second best the stories about the gods contained in the mythology. They then concluded that no sane person could believe the sordid and contradictory accounts furnished by these myths, and thus were reinforced in their beliefs that the primitives and ancients had nothing worth gracing with the name "religion."

To Smith this approach was pointless; instead, he argued, historians and anthropologists should study the rites of the community as the significant acts, and regard the myths as secondary developments. It was his explanation of the relation between ritual and myth that provided the theoretical foundation for the Cambridge Ritualists and all later myth-and-ritual criticism. Rather than attempt to use the myths to shed light on the rites, Smith asserted that the true relation would be found to be the other way round. The myths only offered explanations of what the worshiping community was doing in its rituals but were not binding in a creedal sense on the worshiper, and therefore the worshiper was not disturbed by varying narrative accounts of the same rite. Belief was not obligatory in such a community: "What was obligatory or meritorious was the performance of certain sacred acts prescribed by religious tradition."[27] And here is the key sentence: "So far as myths consist of explanations of ritual, their value is altogether secondary, and it may be affirmed with confidence that in almost every case the myth was derived from the ritual, and not the ritual from the myth; for the ritual was fixed and the myth was variable, the ritual was obligatory and faith in the myth was at the discretion of the worshipper."[28]

Smith agreed that some myths do indeed answer to Tylor's concept of abstract quasi-scientific speculations about natural phenomena, but he says that these constitute only a small minority. Basically, he asserts, myths have grown up as elaborations upon rituals, and only when the original sense of these rituals has been misunderstood or forgotten. It follows, then, that the only useful way to understand a myth is to examine the ritual it attempts to explain, or if the ritual no longer exists, then to read backwards through the myth and attempt to reconstruct the ritual.[29] This, of course, is exactly what the Ritualists and their followers were to adopt as their method, and it is therefore fair to say that Smith, although no literary critic, was one of the forerunners of myth-and-ritual criticism.[30]

Four

J. G. Frazer

By 1870 European classical scholarship had absorbed the great contributions of comparative philology. Schliemann's announcement of the discovery of the site of Troy in 1871, however, completely shattered the calm of Greek studies, and the task of the next half century for classicists was to assimilate and make sense of the masses of information that resulted from a host of archaeological excavations all around the eastern Mediterranean. Equally destructive of old notions were the several attempts by scholars, chiefly British, to employ comparative evolutionary anthropology in understanding the past. The work of the two best known of these—Tylor, who mainly treated "savages," and Smith, whose field was Semitic antiquity—has already been noted. The heir to the work of both was (Sir) James George Frazer, who extended the ethnological approach to the classical past.

1

Neither the work nor the reputation of Frazer has weathered well. Despite a notable (and I believe misguided) attempt in 1959 on the part of Theodor H. Gaster to revise *The Golden Bough* by drastically abridging it and bringing some of its "facts" up to date, one may safely say that the work today is regarded as a monument of industry by the few more magnanimous historians of anthropology and as a colossal waste of time and effort by the many less charitable.[1]

This disdain is largely the result of the great theoretical reorientation that has taken place in anthropology since Frazer. For *The Golden Bough* is both the culmination and the swan song of old-style evolutionary anthropology. Nineteen eleven, when the third edition (in twelve volumes) began to appear, was one of the last years in which such a book could have been greeted with enthusiasm by (some of) Frazer's colleagues and the general public. For immediately after the First World War his kind of naive, belletristic, philosophical evolutionism began to be replaced by the more pragmatic, functional, and professional approach associated with the names of Malinowski, Radcliffe-Brown, and Boas. Indeed, as 1911 has receded, *The Golden Bough* looms more and more like a beached whale, and Frazer (despite the influence of Tylor and Smith) increasingly shows his true affinities to be with the seventeenth- and eighteenth-century polyhistorians, each of whom summed up in his turn what was then known of the origins of religion, rather than with modern anthropology.

In the decade following the First World War, evolutionism in general and Frazer in particular were subjected to searching and thoroughgoing criticisms: (1) grave doubts were expressed about the validity of the comparative method (at least in the uncritical way that Frazer used it), in which items of culture were lifted out of the physical and social contexts that alone gave them meaning; (2) Frazer's claim that everywhere magic (understood as a worldview rather than a technique) was the first stage of human mental evolution, to be followed necessarily by religion and then by science, and that each stage was clearly distinguishable from the others, was shown on the facts to be false; (3) social function and social structure replaced mental states as the central concerns of the student of primitive culture; (4) and further, Frazer was especially attacked on the ground that his use of evidence was uncritical, in that he indiscriminately employed data furnished by missionaries, explorers, and traders whose naive, prudish, and ethnocentric assumptions seriously distorted their accounts of the "natives" they described.

All this notwithstanding, however, many of these same critics admit that Frazer was one of the giants; many would agree with Stanley Edgar Hyman that Frazer should primarily be thought of, along with Marx, Freud, and Darwin, as (appropriately enough) a modern mythmaker, in the sense that he and his illustrious companions have provided basic metaphors and ways of understanding the world that have permeated the modern consciousness.[2] Indeed, the four have shared the same fate in that they all have been roughly handled (although none nearly so harshly as Frazer) by "revisionists" and modernizers who have freely discarded important parts of the teaching and canon of the master. The work of all four has become a central part of the humanistic legacy of nineteenth-century science in that all have provided key images and concepts for the twentieth century, and therefore their achievements will remain valuable for cultural historians, literary critics, and theologians, no matter how they fare in the hands of their professional descendants.[3] The reason is simple: history, criticism, and theology are not positivist in their attitudes toward knowledge, valuing a theory only for its factual correctness. Rather they are concerned with the spiritual effects and moral residues that all powerful images possess and express about the tenor of an age; considered in this perspective, Frazer is of inestimable importance.

<u>2</u>

James George Frazer (1854–1941) was an unknown classics don when in 1890 he published the first edition, in two volumes, of *The Golden Bough*. A fellow of Trinity College, he had written his fellowship essay on Platonic epistemology and seemed about to embark on a routine Cambridge scholarly career, editing classical texts. But a friend, the psychologist James Ward, urged him to read Tylor's *Primitive Culture*, which got him interested in primitive peoples. Then in 1884–85 he met and became friendly with William Robertson Smith, who had just arrived at Trinity as the new professor of Arabic, having been driven into "exile" from Scotland as a result of his heresy trials. Smith's books and conversation caused the young Frazer to see that the study of primitive peoples might shed some light on classical literature, at least insofar as Greek and Roman ritual practices bore amazing resemblances to certain ceremonies observed among "savages." Smith, who was also the editor of the ninth edition of the *Encyclopaedia Britannica*, nurtured Frazer's anthropological interest by assigning him several articles to write, among them those on "Taboo" and "Totemism." Frazer never looked back.

The first edition of *The Golden Bough*, as its author acknowledges, bears the impress of two men: William Robertson Smith and Wilhelm Mannhardt. As Frazer plainly says in the preface, "I have made great use of the works of the late W. Mannhardt, without which, indeed, my book could scarcely have been written." Mannhardt began his study of primitive folklore as a Müllerian solarist but became disillusioned by the sharp disagreements he found among practitioners of an allegedly scientific method. He turned to fieldwork instead, collecting thousands of "popular superstitions and customs of the peasantry," as Frazer puts it, because he understood that these would furnish "the fullest and most trustworthy evidence we possess as to the primitive religion of the Aryans."[4]

For Frazer in 1890 the problem is still the same as it was for Max Müller in 1856: the nature of "the primitive religion of the Aryans." But Frazer explains why Müller's essentially literary method of examining and analyzing ancient texts is defective: because "the primitive Aryan, in all that regards his mental fibre and texture, is not extinct. He is amongst us today."[5] The reason is that the descendants of the Aryans, the illiterate peasantry of today, have been untouched by the modern world and thus still essentially participate in a mental universe that is unchanged from that of the earliest humans. Therefore scrutiny of texts must give way to inspection of what these contemporary primitives actually do. Mannhardt had taken it upon himself to collect and classify as many as he could of the countless rites and customs of the farmer and woodsman. These findings he presented in a series of works, the most important of which being *Der Baumkultus der Germanen und ihrere Nachbarstämme* (1875) and *Antike Wald- und Feldkulte* (1877). Briefly, Mannhardt found that most of these modern peasant rituals were of a magical character, primarily intended to ensure fertility of man, beast, and field. To Mannhardt, Frazer owes the key conception of "vegetation spirit" or "corn demon," that is, the divinity believed to be indwelling in growing things whom the rite is supposed to placate or gratify.

Further, he took from Mannhardt as well one of his cardinal methodological tenets, which he calls "the law of similarity": when customs are similar in different societies, we may then infer that the motives of the people performing them are also similar. This follows from the Tylorian assumption of uniformity of mental functioning and illustrates Frazer's penchant for psychological explanations: the main value of any rite or ceremony is that it exemplifies some otherwise inaccessible mental state.

3

Northrop Frye, of modern literary critics the one owing most to Frazer and the Ritualists, asserts that "all literary genres are derived from the quest-myth."[6] From this it follows that the *ur*-genre is the epic, in which the hero travels on a divinely ordained mission. By these standards, certainly, *The Golden Bough* is a super-epic, in which the quester, the human race, wanders through history seeking its own true identity by the progressive exercise of reason. Here is Frazer's characteristically metaphoric statement of his theme:

> we may illustrate the course which thought has hitherto run by likening it to a web of three different threads—the black thread of magic, the red thread of religion, and the white thread of science, if under science we may include those simple truths, drawn from the observation of nature, of which men in all ages have possessed a store. Could we then survey the web of thought from the beginning, we should probably perceive it to be at first a chequer of black and white, a patchwork of true and false notions, hardly tinged as yet by the red thread of religion. But carry your eye further along the fabric and you will remark that, while the black thread and the white chequer still run through it, there rests on the middle portion of the web, where religion has entered most deeply into its texture, a dark crimson stain, which shades off insensibly into a lighter tint as the white thread of science is woven more and more into the tissue. To a web thus chequered and stained, thus shot with threads of diverse hues, but gradually changing colour the far-

ther it is unrolled, the state of modern thought, with all its divergent aims and conflicting tendencies, may be compared. Will the great movement which for centuries has been slowly altering the complexion of thought be continued in the near future? Or will a reaction set in which may arrest progress and even undo much of what has been done? To keep up our parable, what will be the colour of the web which the Fates are now weaving on the humming loom of time? Will it be white or red? We cannot tell.[7]

The three colored threads aptly figure Frazer's concept of three necessary stages of human evolution. As already noted, this resembles nothing so much as Vico's tripartite division of each age, to which has been added the element of progress by the French perfectionist thinkers. This scheme, publicized by Comte as the triad of theology, metaphysics, and positive science, has been anthropologized by Frazer, who asserts that the comparative ethnological study of the evolution of human culture illustrates that humankind must pass through the stages of magic, religion, and science—each of which is superior to its predecessor because it marks a better use of reason.[8]

The Golden Bough shows, as its author scours the world for examples in a staggering exhibition of erudition, that most of the human race has not yet attained the stage of science but is still mired at either of the preceding, more irrational levels. Even we of the West, who have achieved enough positive knowledge and self-consciousness to make an inquiry (like *The Golden Bough*) possible into our own mental origins, still display a multitude of traits that point back down the long road we have come: survivals of the primitive past. As Herbert Weisinger has noted, the theme of *The Golden Bough* is human survival in the face of the forces of gigantic unreason. "Like the dying-reborn god of his own making, he [man] engages in conflict with the powers of darkness, death, and evil; he is defeated; he suffers; he dies; he is reborn triumphantly; and he celebrates that victory in a new vision; and then the cycle is repeated on ever higher levels of achievement."[9]

The leading ideas of the third edition of *The Golden Bough* are sufficiently simple that a brief synopsis will be adequate for the purposes of discussion. In Part One (the two volumes called "The Magic Art"), Frazer notes that the priest in the grove at Aricia (or Nemi) in ancient Italy was called "the king of the woods." This indicates that he was thought of as an embodiment of the spirit of the woods. His function was to ensure and control fertility. Such priest-kings are known throughout the primitive world. They use magic to achieve their ends; magic, analyzed, has two main principles: (1) homeopathy—"like produces like"—and (2) contagion—things or persons that have once been in contact continue to influence one another ever after.

In accordance with the principle of homeopathy, the king is also the bridegroom of a female spirit; their union is necessary to produce fecundity. Such "sacred marriages" illustrate the idea that sexual intercourse causes vegetation to grow (whence we get the many primitive seasonal festivals of an orgiastic character).

Part Two ("Taboo and the Perils of the Soul"): As fertility incarnate, the priestly king is a human god, and therefore special pains must be taken to ensure that his soul (or vital power) remains undamaged. He is therefore hedged about by an abundance of prohibitions (taboos) so as to prevent this disaster from occurring.

Part Three ("The Dying God"): If, however, despite every care, the priest-king begins to weaken in the performance of his vital functions, then he must be killed or deposed, so that his power might pass undiminished to another. This explains why the priest-king at Aricia succeeded to his position only through killing the incumbent.

Part Four ("Adonis, Attis, Osiris"): The concept of the death and resurrection of the embodiment of fertility is illustrated not only in ritual and folklore but in myth as well. The most noteworthy examples in the ancient world are to be found in the myths of Adonis, Attis, and Osiris.

Part Five ("Spirits of the Corn and of the Wild"): Sometimes the spirit of fertility is thought of in more specific terms: as the spirit indwelling within the corn (grain). This is exemplified in the myth of Demeter and Persephone as well as in the figures, familiar in European folklore, of the Corn-mother and the Corn-maiden. Sometimes this spirit is embodied in a human being, who is, among primitive peoples, occasionally killed at harvest time. Lastly, the spirit can be conceived of as an animal, the best example of this type being Dionysus in his bull or goat aspects. This explains why animals are so frequently sacrificed in the rituals of agricultural festivals.

Part Six ("The Scapegoat"): The old king's death or deposition must be accompanied by the expulsion of all harmful influences that might impair the life and prosperity of the people and the assurance of a successful rule by the new monarch. This is done by concentrating all such baneful tendencies in a scapegoat, either human or animal, who is then driven from the community, taking all evil with him. Between the death of the old king and the installation of his successor normal life is suspended. The reflection in folklore of this interregnum is the period of license during which the social order is inverted and a slave or convict is crowned as ruler (for example, the Saturnalia).

Part Seven ("Balder the Beautiful"): Every aspirant to the title of king of the wood at Aricia had to pluck a golden bough that grew high on a sacred tree. This tree is identified as the oak and the bough a sprig of mistletoe. The point of plucking the bough was to ensure that the resident fertility spirit "survives" when, as in the original form of the rite, the tree was burned. There is a possible analogy in the rites and myths surrounding the Scandinavian god Balder.

The foregoing epitome of *The Golden Bough* is adequate for purposes of discussion but gives no sense of what one encounters in actually reading the book. For Frazer's argument is extraordinarily attenuated (especially in the third edition). Customarily he begins each section with a brief introduction sketching what is to be proved or demonstrated, and then he proceeds, slowly, painstakingly, by making an assertion and then backing it up with mountains of "evidence." I write "evidence" because its relation to the point at issue is often only dimly "evident." This evidence is typically a mass of customs, taken from all over the world and throughout history, that Frazer thinks are analogues which, by the law of similarity (that is, like acts bespeak like motivations), can be said to illustrate his contention. Many of these data have little or no intrinsic interest and are impressive only in their quantity. All too frequently some feature of a rite or myth that has been cited will lead Frazer into a digression or elaboration that is gratuitous (like a Homeric simile) and unconnected with his immediate, not to mention his ultimate, object. If the reader decides to read for the argument alone, it is therefore possible to go through the many thick volumes of *The Golden Bough* with surprising rapidity.

The distinctive shape and quality of Frazer's argument are in a sense a function of his epistemology. For he was perhaps the last great exemplar in English of the trend, widespread around the turn of the century, to apply purportedly "scientific" standards to social studies and thereby to raise them to the standards already achieved in the natural sciences. This tendency, perhaps best observed in historiography, is associated with the several late-nineteenth-century attempts to write "objective history." In Frazer this takes the form of frequent assertions like the following: "Hypotheses are necessary but often temporary bridges built to connect isolated facts. If my light bridges should sooner or later break down or be superseded by more solid structures, I hope that my book may still have its utility and its interest as a repertory of facts."[10] That is, the facts stand by and for themselves. This is not to say that Frazer lacks theories. On the contrary, his work is a tissue of conjecture (as extended arguments by analogy must be), which is why he felt compelled to support it as strongly as he could by such copious use of analogies.

The problem arises from the frequency with which Frazer changed his mind in print.[11] When he did so, however, he neglected to delete the theoretical statements in which he no longer believed, but simply buried them under his new speculations. The result, in its curiously layered effect, is something like the medieval palimpsest that is one of Frazer's favorite figures for the human mind. Indeed, it is fair to say that *The Golden Bough* is a history of the development of Frazer's own mind over a quarter of a century—a history in the best nineteenth-century manner: filled with fossils embodying stages in the growth of an organically evolving consciousness.

On no matter did he change his mind more often than on the nature and origin of myth and its relation to ritual. One can find, strewn through the many volumes and editions of *The Golden Bough*, statements by Frazer supporting at least three different and incompatible theories concerning myth: euhemerism, intellectualism, and ritualism.[12] The first we have encountered in the discussion of ancient and Enlightenment ideas: that myths are based (however loosely) on real events in the lives of real heroes and kings, who are the originals of the gods. Frazer inclined toward euhemerism especially in his frequent and heavy-handed anticlerical moods, because this approach naturally falls in with any attempt to show up religion as an error founded in imposition and fraud. The second, intellectualism, is Tylor's doctrine that myths arise from the attempt made by primitive people to reason. The result is aetiological tales that explain how the world came to be the way it is and how it operates now. Intellectualism means that myths are mistaken efforts at scientific explanation, and probably was most congenial to Frazer's thoroughgoing rationalism.

The third, ritualism, with which Frazer is most prominently connected (although ambivalently, as I shall argue), begins with two assumptions. The first is his notion, already mentioned, that religion originated in man's attempts to control the world by aiding the gods to do his bidding magically (that is, by means of ritual). The second, derived from his early mentors Smith and Mannhardt, says that man worshiping is first (and foremost) an actor. He *does* something to cause his gods to shine their countenances upon him; he may sing or chant and he will certainly dance.[13] When he moves he acts out what he wants the gods to do for him: assure him a plentiful catch or a good hunt, cause his enemies to fall before him, make his women or his fields or his cattle bear. Myth arises when, for some reason—a religious reform, or the passage of time that brings with it forgetfulness and/or misunderstanding—the ritual falls into disuse, with the result that the words, which had been only (or mainly) accompaniments to the essential ceremonial actions, now take on an independent life of their own.

What do these words say? They originally came into being as a description of what the performers or dancers were doing as they imitated the gods enacting something desirable; they now become the stories of the gods' actions themselves—myths. Thus behind the myth is the archaic, superseded ritual, and it is the ritual that permits us to examine how primitive people truly thought of themselves in relation to the universe. Myths, then, are secondary elaborations of the basic rituals, and are in that sense less important than those rituals. And of course rituals are more reliable (for the study of the history of religion) than myths because they are more conservative, whereas myths, made of words, have all the possibilities for textual corruption that classically trained scholars knew so well.

We have already noted the primacy of ritual over myth in Smith, and Mannhardt likewise cites hundreds and hundreds of rites, from which, by patient induction, he elucidates and expounds his basic ideas. It is not surprising, therefore, that Frazer seems in general to have inclined more to the ritual theory of mythogenesis in the earlier part of his career (that is, the first edition of *The Golden Bough*), when the influences of Smith and Mannhardt were strongest. It is noteworthy, therefore, that Frazer was at pains to disavow Smith's influence especially in later years, explicitly rejecting any central place for ritualism. This is clearly implied in the striking passage in the preface to the second edition in which he states that the eminent French sociologists Henri Hubert and Marcel Mauss

> have represented my theory of the slain god as intended to supplement and complete Robertson Smith's theory of the derivation of animal sacrifice in general from a totem sacrament. On this I have to say that the two theories are quite independent of each other (xxii).

A much more remarkable instance of Frazer's desire to reject any affiliation with Smith on the matter of the origin of myth is found in an exchange of letters between Frazer and his younger contemporary, the already eminent anthropologist R. R. Marett.[14] In a letter of 11 May 1911 (that is, just when the third edition of *The Golden Bough* was beginning to appear), Frazer, apparently commenting on a recent conversation with Marett, rejects the latter's contention that Smith believed ritual to precede myth. He states that this is not a fair statement of Smith's position and that in any case he certainly does not agree with it. Ritual rather than myth or creed is to be studied *not* because it is antecedent ("that I regard as absolutely false"), but because it is more conservative and thus changes less. He says that others, inexplicably, have misunderstood Smith's work in the same way and indeed have attributed such views to himself as well, "who repudiate[s] them as an absurdity." "Savage ritual, so far as I have studied it, seems to me to bear the imprint of reflexion and purpose stamped just as plainly as any actions of civilised man."

In reply to this extraordinary letter, Marett adduces the passages from Smith already quoted here and shows that Frazer's version of Smith's views on this question is much distorted. Marett likewise denies that savage ritual is "just as" much a product of ratiocination as that of more civilized peoples.

> All that some of us—McDougal, for instance, and Lévy-Bruhl, etc., in France—have been trying to do is to emphasize the mobbish character of primitive religion and primitive life. . . . You, on the other hand, have Howitt and Spencer behind you when you insist that in Australia a primitive legislator was capable of organising the marriage system, etc. (letter of 13 May 1911).

Frazer, in his response, after having reread parts of *The Religion of the Semites*, backed down somewhat on his characterization of Smith but still upheld the intellectualist views of the origins of mythology expressed in his earlier letter (letter of 17 May 1911).

These repudiations of Smith do not gibe with Frazer's statement from the first edition (1890), already quoted, acknowledging the inestimable debt he owed Smith. They obviously bespeak a vast change in ideas and convictions, and it is tempting to see in them the disavowal of the intellectual "father," which Smith truly was. Stanley Edgar Hyman persuasively suggests that such changes in attitude betray a continual, never-ending dialogue taking place within Frazer's mind about religion:

> There is a sense in which no one and no evidence ever convinced Frazer, but in which his ambivalent and shifting mind each time found statements and evidence to reinforce positions it had already reached. Thus Mannhardt and Smith

appear when Frazer is moving away from the Trinitarian Christianity of his Presbyterian upbringing, Roscoe and Budge [euhemerist anthropologists] when he is moving back to a Unitarianism of his own devising.[15]

Whether or not Hyman's interpretation is right, there is no doubt that although Frazer never wavered on evolution or the comparative method, he changed his mind (in print) about almost everything else.

To speak decisively about Frazer's ideas on the origin and meaning of myth and ritual at any one moment during the quarter century represented by the writing of *The Golden Bough* is therefore impossible because of the theoretical confusion that prevails. Only if one were prepared to cull what must be hundreds of utterances on the subject scattered through the work, and then to collate and compare them chronologically, could one be sure exactly how and when Frazer's views changed (and whether he knew they did). And even then one's result would be problematic because of Frazer's seeming indifference to self-contradiction. To put it kindly, the strength of Frazer's mind lay in its power to synthesize vast quantities of data into a small number of manageable categories; to put it more bluntly, Frazer seems to have lacked nearly completely the analytic rigor required for such a sweeping investigation into the deepest springs of human behavior.

Not having compiled this variorum *Golden Bough*, I can only chart Frazer's movements approximately: from ritualism through cognitionism to euhemerism, to which he gives the palm, as already noted, in the last volume of the third edition, written in late 1913. But even this statement did not mark the end of his thinking about the question. In what was to be his last pronouncement, in his first work to appear after the War—an edition of Apollodorus's *The Library* (1921)—we have:

By myths I understand mistaken explanations of phenomena, whether of human life or of external nature. Such explanations originate in that instinctive curiosity concerning the causes of things which at a more advanced stage of knowledge seeks satisfaction in philosophy and science, but being founded on ignorance and misapprehension they are always false, for were they true, they would cease to be myths.[16]

A better enunciation of intellectualism may not exist even in the works of Tylor. But the point surely is that this passage marks no real change in Frazer's views. He was always a rationalist, even in his ritualist moments. Even when he saw the primitives engaged in re-enacting the stages in the sacred life of the god, in which the ritual was primary and the myth secondary, he still conceived of the myth as being "devised" later to explain the rite fallen into disuse. And of course euhemerism is fundamentally just as rationalistic as intellectualism in that both explanations discern in myth some form of conscious mental activity, either of a speculative-philosophical or of a historical-allegorical kind.

But Frazer was not content to rest with the ringing affirmation of intellectualism just quoted. In a footnote appended to this very passage he took pains to attack those in the next generation—the Cambridge Ritualists—who had carried on the ritualist view that he had championed, if uncertainly, at times during the early part of his career:

> By a curious limitation of view, some modern writers would restrict the scope of myths to ritual, as if nothing but ritual were fitted to set men wondering and meditating on the causes of things. No doubt some myths have been devised to explain rites of which the true origin was forgotten; but the number of such myths is infinitesimally small, by comparison with myths which deal with other subjects and have had another origin.
>
> It might have been thought that merely to open such familiar collections of myths as the *Theogony* of Hesiod, the *Library* of Apollodorus, or the *Metamorphoses* of Ovid, would have sufficed to dissipate so erroneous a conception; for how small is the attention paid to ritual in these works!
>
> The zealous student of myth and ritual, more intent on explaining them than on enjoying the lore of the people, is too apt to invade the garden of romance and with a sweep of his

scythe to lay the flowers of fancy in the dust. He needs to be reminded occasionally that we must not look for a myth or a rite behind every tale, like a bull behind every hedge or a canker in every rose.

The utilitarian creed is good and true only on condition that we interpret utility in a large and liberal sense, and do not restrict it to the bare satisfaction of bodily instincts on which ultimately depends the continuance both of the individual and of the species.[17]

In short, Frazer's epistemology has led him up a blind alley, and he seems to despair of making any sense of the fantastic diversity of myth and ritual he has so successfully displayed to the reader.

One may now ask why Frazer is generally thought of today (especially by literary people) as the father of the ritual approach to myth, although he was at best a qualified ritualist and that only at the beginning of his career, when he was obscure, and not at all when his work became well known among the general public. The answer lies partly in ignorance; few have had the interest or patience to trace the convoluted and disorderly growth of Frazer's ideas, so that his reputation of being the "onlie Begetter" of the Cambridge Ritualists is in one sense simply a vulgar error. There is little doubt that his ideas hardly changed at all after about 1907, and that for the last twenty-five years of his career (that is, after the completion of *The Golden Bough*) he continued to pour out a series of books that merely elaborated his older ideas in new or slightly different settings.[18] These continued the encyclopedic and taxonomic tendencies shown at such length in *The Golden Bough*. The other side of Frazer's scholarly career—classical scholarship—which had been represented in the earlier period with his masterful translation and commentary (still the standard) in six volumes on the travels of Pausanias (1898), continued in the postwar years with editions of Apollodorus's grab-bag of myths called *The Library* and (in five volumes) of the *Fasti*, in which Frazer amplified and enriched Ovid's narrative with many ethnographic parallels drawn from all over the world.

But for all that, there is a real sense in which Frazer, despite his many and drastic changes of mind, can rightly be called the *fons et origo* of the ritualist school. First, he did comment, albeit passingly, on the question of the origins of the drama, although the structural analysis of tragedy and comedy to be made by Murray and Cornford was beyond his purview of interest. Typically, when in his discussion of saturnalian dramatic rituals, he does speak of the origin of such rites, it is in terms of the motivation of the participants.

> For it seems probable that the masked dances and ceremonies, which have played a great part in the social life of savages in many quarters of the world, were primarily designed to subserve practical purposes rather than simply to stir the emotions of the spectators and to while away the languor and tedium of idle hours. The actors sought to draw down blessings on the community by mimicking certain powerful superhuman beings and in their assumed character working those beneficent miracles which in the capacity of mere men they would have confessed themselves powerless to effect. In fact the aim of these elementary dramas, which contain in germ the tragedy and comedy of civilised nations, was the acquisition of superhuman power for the public good.[19]

And a few pages later he remarks of the Greeks:

> Certainly the Athenians in the heyday of their brilliant civilisation retained a lively sense of the religious import of their dramatic performances; for they associated them directly with the worship of Dionysus and allowed them to be enacted only during the festivals of the god.[20]

But there is something more, something that will be employed by later, more literary analysts, even though Frazer was not especially interested in its literary value. I refer here to what might be called "the tragic rhythm." By this I mean the common pattern discernible (at least by Frazer—many scholars today would disagree, especially about Osiris) in the myths and rituals of Attis, Adonis, Osiris, and Dionysus, the gods Frazer examined most closely. For these deities are the main examples of the type of the vegetation god, or corn spirit, that Frazer found throughout the religions of the eastern Mediterranean and Asia Minor, the cradle of Western culture. Frazer, always looking for similarities rather than differences, emphasized that all four gods have the same "life story": their myths narrated (and their rituals showed) how the god suffered a wound as the result of a combat with either a wild animal or a human adversary, died and was buried in the earth to the accompaniment of universal mourning—only to revive and show himself again in the rebirth of green and growing things.

And further, these "hieratic" sacred stories and performances stand in paradigmatic relation to the thousands of examples of "demotic" folklore collected by Frazer from all over the ancient and especially the modern world. These ceremonies, typical of seasonal festivals so late as the nineteenth century (this is the debt especially owed to Mannhardt), all turn on the idea of renewal, or *renouveau* as Jane Harrison called it. They were, of course, magical rituals designed to bring to pass that which was enacted, namely, that fertility be ensured and blight and drought be banished. These rites will be more fully discussed in the next chapter in their relation to the origins of drama; here it suffices to name them. They are of several kinds and frequently are found mixed up with one another. (1) The expulsion of the old, often in the shape of the deposition of a king, or of death, or of evil, which is followed by the installation of a new king (king of the May, or sometimes the Maypole itself, another incarnation of the spirit of generation). (2) The ritual combat between antagonists embodying the new and the old in seasonal form—winter versus summer—or else as life against death. The winner of the battle is then crowned as king and often there ensues a sacred marriage with a bride—the May queen—in order to ensure fertility. (3) Sometimes fertility is attained by performing a mock death and burial of the old, followed by his revival and restoration as the new.

These gods and the repetitive rhythmic pattern that constitutes their myth lie at the heart of the third edition of *The Golden Bough*. In the most literal sense, the reader encounters them right in the middle of the work, *Adonis, Attis, Osiris* being the title of volumes five and six and Dionysus being considered at the beginning of volume seven, *Spirits of the Corn and of the Wild*. This central placement is symbolic of their importance, for their sufferings and resurrections furnish the models for the rites to be enacted by their surrogate in this world, the (divine) king. Their rituals are, in turn, the central acts by which the primitive worshiping community affirmed its oneness with its god and the world order he represented and, most importantly, magically assured itself of that best evidence of divine favor, fertility of the earth. And although the worship of the dying and reviving god, being sacramental in nature, was marked (even in historical times) by sacrifices of human scapegoats and other bloody and obscene rites, nevertheless the pattern of death and resurrection had the potential to be transformed into "higher," "more spiritual" kinds of religion—most especially, Christianity. Despite the fact that Frazer is anticlerical, he is also progressivist, and he is willing to admit that Christianity does mark a humanizing advance over what preceded it.

Because of their central placement, and because of their obvious relevance to Christianity, and because of the fullness with which Frazer discusses them, these gods seem to have made the strongest impression on readers of *The Golden Bough*. Although this essay is not a study of the literary effects of the myth-and-ritual approach, the large number of references to the figure of the dying god in the literature and letters of postwar Britain eloquently testifies to the impact of Attis, Adonis, Osiris, and the rest of their tribe on the most sensitive readers of the time.

More importantly, we can say that Frazer and the other British rationalist anthropologists of the time had a salutary effect on classical studies in that they acted as a counterweight to the romantic exaltation of the Greeks that so characterized the nineteenth century, especially the aesthetic movement in the 1880s. The comparative approach emphasized how much the great achievement of Greece had been overlaid on the darkness of the old brutal pre-Olympian religion, and also how close the ancient Greeks were to European peasants of the nineteenth century. In retrospect there can be little doubt that this deflationary movement was salutary in permitting us to see better who the Greeks truly were and what in fact they accomplished. But it was also true that by its nature the comparative method, of which Frazer is the practitioner par excellence, tends to place greater emphasis on the lower rather than on the higher, to focus on the potential rather than the actual. And since the Frazerian schema held that the first stage of mental evolution was characterized by magic, there is a built-in bias toward rituals (magical acts) that no amount of theoretical vacillation on Frazer's part could efface.

4

It remains to indicate the connections between Frazer and his successors the Ritualists. The most immediate and important similarities, or affiliations, are two: neither Frazer nor the Ritualists ever doubted either that evolution was the dynamic of human culture nor the validity of the comparative method in studying it. In addition, the reader of Frazer who comes to Jane Harrison's books, or those of her coworkers, will immediately recognize certain key concepts, popularized but not originated by Frazer, like divine kingship, taboo, the dying god.

But the differences are at least as important. They are in the areas in which Frazer was weakest: sociology and psychology. Frazer's sociology is completely implicit, for he seems to have had neither interest in, nor feeling for, any systematic analysis of society and its institutions. His ideas, predictably enough, are those of the social contract, which corresponds to Tylorian intellectualism. That is, the social organization of the primitives, like their mythology, was originated by "primitive philosophers," and thus one may appropriately criticize primitive institutions by modern rational criteria. Frazer seems to have had no sense of the social matrix, the interconnectedness of things, that gives artifacts or customs whatever meaning they may possess. That said, it should also be said that his rationalism was not particularly reactionary. No one in his generation, with the exception of Smith, had any better sense of the organic and unplanned nature of human society; indeed Émile Durkheim and the *Année Sociologique* school, whom we now think of (along with Max Weber) as the founders of modern sociological thought, did not begin to publish their work until the last three years of the nineteenth century, long after Frazer had made up his mind on the important questions. And insofar as psychology is concerned, the situation is completely analogous. Frazer's is a faculty psychology; the mind is a machine that acts by the mechanism of association. The Ritualists realized that such an approach was futile and sought for some method that would go beyond rationalism. Turning away from empiricism, they were fortunate enough to be the beneficiaries of great advances in psychology just then being made by Freud, Bergson, and later Jung.

Frazer seems several times to have changed his mind as to exactly what he thought the subject of *The Golden Bough* was, but one of his last formulations, taken from the preface to the final volumes of the third edition, dated 1913, is instructive: "If there is one general conclusion which seems to emerge from the mass of particulars, I venture to think that it is the essential similarity in the working of the less developed human mind among all races, which corresponds to the essential similarity in their bodily frame revealed by comparative anatomy." It was this kind of intellectualism—*The Golden Bough* as a comparative anatomy of the human mind—that prevented him from attaining any organic theory of society; his epistemology, with its disfiguring empiricism, likewise discouraged him from going beyond the merely classificatory (even if he were so inclined) in dealing with his data, or in any case from attempting to make his argument intellectually more coherent. His style was the direct outgrowth and expression of his viewpoint, frequent heavy irony being his response to the endless panorama of human aberration that lay spread before him as he regarded humanity struggling so painfully toward rationality.

The Ritualists, then, dissatisfied with the atomizing results of Frazerian rationalism turned upon ancient and primitive religion, looked elsewhere for a more comprehensive theory of mental functioning and a better view of the connection between religion and the rest of society. They found what they were looking for in psychoanalysis and vitalism and in the sociology of their exact contemporary, Émile Durkheim. (Ironically enough, Durkheim had been inspired by the work of Smith.) The Ritualists likewise rejected Frazer's idea of a lockstep progress for humanity from magic through religion to science. With the key idea of the organic inter-relationship of social institutions, they did not content themselves with exposing folly, as Frazer so often did (especially in his barely veiled attacks upon Christianity in the guise of analyzing paganism), but in understanding what function primitive religion had for its practitioners, what needs it satisfied. Without Frazer's overdone facticity, they also lacked his universalist encyclopedic qualities; at most they studied Greek religion. The result, predictably, is much greater clarity and coherence; the reader has a sense that the data truly support the argument rather than that they have been chosen arbitrarily to suit preconceived ideas.

Five

Jane Ellen Harrison: The Early Work

The Cambridge Ritualists were Jane Ellen Harrison, Gilbert Murray, Francis Macdonald Cornford, and Arthur Bernard Cook; from about 1900 to 1915 they worked together on the origins of Greek religion and Greek drama. For me the group is best approached by focusing on the career of Jane Harrison, with Murray, Cornford, and Cook considered in their relationship to her. Since each member of the group was a considerable scholar in his own right, this decision calls for comment.

To understand in what way the Ritualists *were* a group, one must know something of Jane Harrison's life and temperament. She was one of that talented first generation of women admitted to English university education, entering the recently established Newnham College, Cambridge, in 1875. She and others like her (one thinks of her contemporary fellow Yorkshirewoman Beatrice Potter Webb) showed that women, given the chance, could pursue and attain the highest goals in intellectual life. She was born in 1850 (four years before Frazer) into an upper-middle-class Nonconformist family and, like all women of her time and class, educated at home by a series of governesses. After some struggle on her part, her exceptional gifts caused her to be sent away to school (Cheltenham) in 1867 and then on to Newnham. Nevertheless, she suffered throughout her life from having begun the study of Greek relatively late, and despite her obvious *Sprachgefühl,* she never was as competent a philological scholar as she would have wished to be.[1]

This matter of the adequacy of her scholarship had important consequences throughout her life. Ms. Harrison was, at every period of her adult life, always connected in a deeply emotional way with some male scholar of superior philological attainments who acted as a technical adviser and, just as importantly, as an essential emotional support. First it was D. S. MacColl, and then Francis Cornford, with both of whom she seems to have been in love;[2] and by no means least there was R. A. Neil (to whom *Themis* is dedicated) and whom she seems to have been about to marry when he died suddenly. There were as well older (married) men with whom she was likewise close, although probably not in love: as an undergraduate it was her teacher A. W. Verrall (to whom *Prolegomena* is dedicated); and then there were A. B. Cook and, pre-eminently, Gilbert Murray, both younger men, to both of whom she was deeply attached. And of course each of these men, in his own way, returned her affection. In a sense, then, the era of the Ritualists may be seen, biographically speaking, as a particularly happy time in Jane Harrison's life, when her emotional and intellectual energies were most closely unified. In one sense, then, the reason for the group's coming-to-be was that Jane Harrison had a need for making passionate intellectual friendships.

If this reading is generally correct, it may explain how and why each of the members of the group was close to Jane Harrison but not how or why they were a group. Here we might de-emphasize sentiment and point to the fact that she was the center of the group because she always seems to have had a broader conception of their common subject matter than any of the others. For this reason she was able to afford each of the others an important intellectual stimulus just as she had with men like Verrall and MacColl, who were in no sense members. (The exception here is Cornford, who met her at the outset of his career; I am sure that their intense personal relationship was instrumental in determining the direction and tone of Cornford's scholarly work.)[3] Although each man had independently been attracted to the anthropological approach to classics, she was able to broaden each of them by introducing them to material to which they were largely strangers. Specifically, she was able to offer a wide and deep knowledge of Greek art and archaeology, and later of contemporary work on religion, psychology, sociology, and philosophy, that was invaluable to Cook, primarily a classical folklorist; to Murray, primarily a literary and textual scholar; and to Cornford, primarily a student of ancient philosophy. And reciprocally their work extended her own areas of interest and competence, so that their collaboration must have been deeply satisfying and exciting in an intellectual sense. As Gilbert Murray wrote in retrospect to Jessie Stewart, "We were as you say a remarkable group; we somehow had the same general aim and outlook, or something, and the work of each contributed to the work of the others. We were out to see what things really meant, looking for a new light our elders had not seen."[4]

And this reading of Harrison's life also explains certain social facts otherwise perhaps difficult to account for: for example, how it was that around 1905 Francis Cornford, then a newly elected fellow of Trinity College, and Gilbert Murray, former professor of Greek at Glasgow, nearly ten years his senior, and without a college affiliation at Cambridge, should have become close friends and co-workers. This is not impossible on its face, but given the rigidly stratified social and academic world of British universities at the time, it is unusual, to say the least. The answer is that they, along with Cook, first came together in their affection for Jane Harrison. It is difficult to be certain now because the only letters that have survived in any appreciable numbers are Harrison's to Murray, but it is likely that each man in the group, especially in the early years, was closer to her than to any of the others.

The evidence for this interpretation of Harrison's life is abundant but difficult to summarize. The main document is the biography of Jessie Stewart, first Harrison's student and then her good friend from 1900 onwards. This work, subtitled "A Portrait from Letters," is based on the more than eight hundred letters from Harrison to Gilbert Murray that date from 1900 to the end of her life. The letters naturally permit unequivocal judgments only about Harrison's relationship to Murray, but Stewart supplies a great deal more from her own memory and the memories (and some letters) of others; she makes it clear (without being indiscreet) that Harrison's life really consisted of a series of these passionate scholarly collaborations. Harrison herself alludes to this in her own memoir, characteristically entitled *Reminiscences of a Student's Life.*

By what miracle I escaped marriage, I do not know, for all my life long I fell in love. But, on the whole, I am glad. I do not doubt that I lost much, but I am quite sure that I gained more. Marriage, for a woman at least, hampers the two things that made life to me glorious—friendship and learning.[5]

Stewart as well provides specific evidence concerning the profound depression that settled over Harrison's life when Francis Cornford married. Cornford's young wife, Frances Darwin, sensed that Harrison—"Aunt Jane," as they called her—was in love with him even though she was old enough to be his mother. (Needless to say, Cornford seems to have had no idea of this.)[6]

1

Reading anything by or about Harrison, one is struck forcefully by her intellectual power and her passionate nature. From without, she lends herself to easy paradoxes: a tough-minded sentimentalist,[7] a woman who could speak of "falling in love" with Greek or Russian and becoming excited about grammar, an intellectual who always kept an engaging childlike quality. But these are mere paradoxes; they resolve into a unified being, one of those rare and fortunate persons who recognize no barriers between specialist knowledge and everyday life, and who bring to both an extraordinary energy and integrity.

One of the keys to understanding Harrison's life and achievement is perfectly obvious, but bears naming nonetheless—she was a woman. That is, if one may deal in generalizations, as a female she had not been brought up to stifle feeling or the expression of emotion, as had the majority of her male colleagues. After all, women in Victorian England were supposed to be repositories of emotion, if little else. Likewise she was not constrained as were her fellows by existing models of proper scholarly behavior. This is not to deny her male friends and colleagues their individuality nor to assume that they were all conformists. (Indeed, Murray was regarded as a dangerous radical in his youth, and Cornford was a lifelong Fabian socialist.) I merely allude to the obvious fact, true then as now, that in Britain (or anywhere else) men were not permitted the same range of emotional expression as women. Nor am I arguing that once her gender is noted everything about Harrison becomes clear. But nothing can be understood without starting from that point.

Because she was a woman I am sure (without being able to prove it) that to some extent at least her world found her behavior charming where the same behavior in a man would have been thought childish or bizarre. For instance, she seems never to have lost the habit or ability, which psychologists tell us is common in children but tends to die out in adulthood, of thinking in pictures—eidetic imagery. (She was intensely visual, as her ten years of lecturing and writing on art demonstrate.) Thus, once she became friendly with Murray she gave him two nicknames—Cheiron, from the kindly, sage centaur, and Ther, from Greek *therion*, "wild beast"—and in her letters never addressed him otherwise. In a letter to him from Algiers during Christmas 1902, she writes: "How absurd it is for this Polar Bear to be sent southward and a thin Kangaroo to be leaping about in the snow."[8] Translation: her theriomorph is the bear (she kept an old teddy bear as a prominent item of furniture in her rooms at Newnham, and was passionately fond of anything ursine), and his is the kangaroo because he was Australian by birth. Now this may be dismissed as embarrassing playfulness between friends, never intended for other eyes. But it does testify to something deeper: her natural intuitive feeling for what may be called (with all due reservations) "primitive" modes of thought. She even personified her books. She called *Prolegomena* "the fat and comely one," whereas the copy of Nauck's fragments of Euripides, a gift from Murray, became "the slim handsome one."[9] And in describing the Orphic tablets translated by Murray and printed as an appendix to *Themis*, she writes: "What a beautiful learned appendix and how Therish it is!"[10] Or she opens her review of J. C. Lawson's *Modern Greek Folklore and Ancient Greek Religion* by exclaiming, "Who loves not Cheiron?"[11]

But this playful and sentimental tendency toward the primitive and the "natural" tempered a profoundly intellectual nature. Jane Harrison was perhaps a sport among classical scholars of her time (or any time), but she was not there by sufferance. She was able to hold her own at the top of a male profession that at the time employed

perhaps the most rigorous scholarly criteria of all the various divi-
sions in the world of humane letters.[12] And it was the whole woman—
the whole person—whose work is here in question; the woman who
could write, acknowledging the role of sex in what seem to be purely
"intellectual" matters, "We watch the physical and emotional sides of
knowledge in our own minds: anyone who makes even a small mental discovery can note the sudden uprush of emotion, often a hot
blush, sometimes tears in the eyes. How can such a sensuous process
be insulated from a thing so interpenetrating as sex?"[13]

 After encountering such an insight from a maiden lady in her sixties, one is not surprised to learn that she was one of the earliest partisans—albeit an unwilling one, for her style of life had been formed
in a more inhibited time—of Freud in England. Her advocacy of his
work is only the best example of her amazing willingness to remain
open to new thoughts or, what is nearly as good, to recognize her
prejudices as such and compensate for them. In a delightful and
revealing essay called "Crabbed Age and Youth," she takes as her text
a remark much repeated in the 1960s but apparently uttered for the
first time by Rupert Brooke as an undergraduate: "No one over
thirty is worth speaking to." Her reaction is characteristic and worth
quoting:

> Now, when I had recovered from the blow to my personal van-
> ity—for, of course it was nothing else—I said to myself: "This is
> really very interesting and extraordinarily valuable. Here we
> have, not a reasoned conclusion, but a real live emotion, a
> good solid prejudice, a genuine attitude of gifted Youth to
> Crabbed Age. Give me an honest prejudice, and I am always
> ready to attend to it." The reasons by which people back up
> their prejudices are mostly negligible—not reason at all at bot-
> tom, but just instinctive self-justifications; but prejudice, rising
> as it does in emotion, has its roots in life and reality.[14]

The passage embodies the wit and the remarkable wholeness of
mind and heart that characterize her best work. It is playful paradox,
to be sure, but it goes deep. For all of Jane Harrison's mature schol-

arly thought was an attempt to get down behind and beneath rationalization to deeper-lying, and therefore more authentic, emotion. And thus her idea of religion, inspired by Émile Durkheim, another of the Continental thinkers whose work she helped to assimilate and popularize, is that it "is not the aspiration of the individual soul after a god, or after the unknown, or after the infinite; rather it is the expression, utterance, projection of the emotion, the desire of a group. . . . Religion, in its rise, is indistinguishable from social custom, embodying social emotion."[15] These ideas will be examined more closely later on; the point here is that the tone of this serious intellectual dismissal of theology and the emphasis on prerational social emotion is of a piece with the playful rhetoric of the more personal passage from "Crabbed Age and Youth" that likewise dismisses social rationalizations in favor of "emotion [that] has its roots in life and reality." In the latter essay she goes on to say that she has remained young by continuing to share one of youth's leading traits, a burning insistence on following the truth wherever it leads. One believes it to be true of her as of few others.

We have here a complex of behavior and belief in the life of one woman. We can say of her that she had a temperamental predilection toward the primitive and the emotional as more authentic than the developed and the reasoned, but invoking the word "temperament" is notoriously a way of excusing one's inability to proceed further in analysis. Or we can point to her fundamental understanding of the emotional basis of all human behavior, and her view of the interpenetration of what were conventionally distinguished as mental and physical, but these beliefs certainly do not "explain" her expressive style. We have come full circle: her emotional nature causing ideas that enhance feeling over reason to appear sound to her, and the ideas themselves being presented in a personal, passionate, "unscholarly" manner. We may fairly employ here the language of literary criticism: both the manner and matter of Jane Harrison's mature work form an integrated whole, both being the products of a unified vision of life. Thus, in an unpublished letter to Jessie Stewart, Hope Mirrlees, her closest friend during her last, "Russian" period and would-be biographer, wrote: " I am sure that you must realize the really great problems that we should have to deal with if a full life of Jane were written, as the intellectual and sentimental strands are inextricably interwoven."[16]

The passion with which she imbued her beliefs has another facet in her love for language. She tells us in her charming and all-too-brief memoir that if she had her life to live over again she would change but one thing: instead of devoting herself to primitive religion, she would become a student of language. Her purpose would not have been to become a polyglot; rather, in the best romantic spirit, she felt that truly learning a language is the best and indeed the only way to enter into the collective soul of its speakers. She says, in her little book on Russian aspects: "Twice in my life it happened to me to fall in love with a language. Once, long ago, with Greek. Again, only yesterday, with Russian. . . ."[17] Thus it was that her life, which had lost its *raison d'être* with the collapse of all scholarly work and loss of friends attendant upon the outbreak of war, regained its momentum in the study of Russian. And when in 1915, in an attempt to teach English to Russian émigrés, she began the language in earnest, she stopped all work on classics.[18] Her *Epilegomena to the Study of Greek Religion* (1921), though its title evokes the *Prolegomena to the Study of Greek Religion* of 1903, is not primarily about Greek religion at all but rather a deeply personal and mystical attempt to synthesize the ideas on philosophy, psychology, and religion that had grown out of her work.

2

Having run somewhat ahead of myself in telling the story, it is fitting to return to the beginning and narrate it in a more orderly fashion. Jane Harrison was passed over at graduation for a classical lectureship at Newnham because she was regarded as insufficiently "sound." Possessing an independent income, she was able to settle in London, and lived there for twenty years lecturing and studying at the British Museum. During these London years (the 1880s and 1890s) she became fluent in German (the language of classical scholarship) and took several trips abroad, visiting the great Continental museums, especially those of Germany. The valuable lessons she learned in Germany and in her work at the British Museum, especially in the interpretation of pottery and other artifacts, are everywhere to be seen in the abundant illustrations that are a mark of all her works. They are also evident in the way in which she consistently based her arguments primarily on things, not words. She was always basically an archaeologist rather than a textual scholar.

During these years she supported herself by writing and lecturing. And from Stewart and Peacock we know that it was also during these years (specifically the late eighties) that she passed through a profound crisis. The change this produced in her is readily revealed by a comparison of these early writings with the dramatically different later work.

Listen to her in the preface of *Introductory Studies in Greek Art,* first published in 1885.[19] She begins by asking why we should study Greek art.

> The answer is, I believe, found in a certain peculiar quality of Greek art which adapts itself to the consciousness of successive ages, which has within it no seed of possible death,—a certain largeness and universality which outlived the individual race and persists for all time. The meaning of this quality, which we call Ideality, it is the sole object of this little book to develop (vi).

The heart of the book is a critical examination of the sculpture of Phidias, about which she says, "Greek literature is the best and only comment on Greek art; what is expressed but undefined in Phidias is clearly articulate in Plato." And she concludes: "I shall be satisfied if, by the help of the wisdom of Plato, I can show any of the citizens of the state why, eschewing the dry bones of symbolism and still more warily shunning the rank, unwholesome pastures of modern realism, they may nurture their souls on the fair sights and pure visions of Ideal art" (vi).

This paragraph is as far as one can be from Jane Harrison after 1890. A reader of her later work would turn hundreds of pages in vain to see a mention of the word "Ideality" with a capital "I," for she is no longer interested in it. In fact, her mature work may be thought of as a countermovement to the idealizing tendency that so clam-

mily chills nearly every discussion of Greek art through the nineteenth century. Indeed, she never in any of her later work even gets
to Phidias and the fifth century; her entire focus shifts to the Archaic
age, and the statues that figure as illustrations are the early *korai* of
the seventh and sixth centuries. And as for Greek literature—and
Plato, no less!—being the best and only commentary on Greek art—
one can say only that just as her attention turns to Archaic art, so it
turns to preclassical literature. Plato will rarely be quoted; her most
frequent references will be to antiquarian writers and collectors of,
and commentators on, old myths and rituals. Literature will be ransacked to provide illustrations of rituals fallen into desuetude more
than read for its own sake. And as for the "rank, unwholesome pastures of modern realism," one can only grit one's teeth at the
Podsnappery and recall that the eighties featured the famous trials
in which Henry Vizetelly, Zola's translator and publisher in England,
was prosecuted by the National Vigilance Association and was con-
victed and imprisoned for selling obscene literature. The attitudes
suggested here are in fact completely uncharacteristic of the later
Jane Harrison, who is remarkably free of the prudery which one
might expect in a lady of good Victorian upbringing.[20]

The passage quoted above from *Introductory Studies in Greek Art*
presents the characteristic tone of the early Jane Harrison. But in
that work can also be found the elements typical of the mature work
of the next decades. For example, from the first chapter come these
words about the quest for origins:

> In bygone days of art-criticism originality was claimed for the
> Greeks as their especial, distinguishing gift. Original they were,
> but not in the narrow sense of borrowing nothing from their
> predecessors. The historic instinct is wide awake among us now.
> We seek with a new-won earnestness to know the genesis, the
> *origines* of whatever we study. . . . If critics in the past
> approached archaeology from the abstract and purely con-
> templative standpoint, critics of today incline to its historical,
> scientific aspect. Hence our first duty in speaking of Greek art
> is to show by the light of recent discoveries its relation to the
> art of Egypt, Assyria, and Phoenicia which preceded it.

This is the authentic nineteenth-century obsession with history that was a dynamic force in all of Harrison's work.

In another of her early works, *Myths of the Odyssey in Art and Literature* (1882), Harrison remarks in the preface:

> May I add one word to the end I hope to attain? I believe the educational value of a study of archaeology to consist far more in the discipline of taste and feeling it affords, than in the gift of definite information it has to offer. . . . the best gifts of archaeology,—the trained eye, quick instinct, pure taste, well-balanced emotion,—these we may be thankful if we gain in a lifetime (xii, xiii).

This passage, so evocative of Pater and the aesthetic movement, is illuminated by a few unpublished notes jotted down by Jessie Stewart in connection with a description of Harrison's early years. They are useful in providing a general context for this early work. They lack amplification but need none. Stewart wrote:

> love of brilliant generalisation
> rage for art in '80's
> Rossetti her favourite poet
> belief in beauty
> creation of beauty higher than research and
>   scholarship
> poetry must be Swinburnian
> the aesthetic movement made appreciation of
>   Greek vase painting possible
> Jane's urge aesthetic not scientific
> desired a pattern, not the truth
> regarded Dörpfeld and Ridgeway as materials
>   for pattern, i.e., her aesthetic sense
>   satisfied by conclusions elicited from
>   masses of data
> Verrall made Greek literature living—
> Jane made Greek religion living.[21]

Some of these jottings, like that about Harrison's favorite poet being Rossetti, are interesting without throwing any fresh light on her work; such a fact only "fits" the aesthetic milieu we know of from her undergraduate days, as recorded in the memories of fellow students: she was "the dominating figure in a group of friends; like a Rembrandt picture, with a highlight on her vital imposing figure, tall, willowy, the tight-fitting olive-green serge of the days of the aesthetic craze, her hair in a Greek coil . . . ,"[22] or "This was the Pre-Raphaelite period: we papered our rooms with Morris, bought Burne-Jones photographs and dressed accordingly."[23]

Others of these notes go much deeper, for example, "Jane's urge aesthetic not scientific," and "desired a pattern, not the truth." These remarks in fact point to attitudes that characterize all her work in both tone and content. For instance, to her the psychological fragmentation that resulted from the rationalistic view of religion as seen in Frazer must have been distinctly unsatisfactory from an aesthetic point of view. In this case, rationalism explains away, rather than explains, and leaves the phenomena unaccounted for. She must have seen Durkheim's view of religion as a projection of group needs and wishes as not only in tune with her own intuitions but unifying rather than atomizing and therefore more likely to be right: it was her "desire to see a pattern." (This of course does not mean that she did not believe Durkheim in fact to be correct, in an intellectual sense; only that she must have felt assured he was right because of the elegance with which so many kinds of phenomena were brought together and illuminated.) In the same vein we hear her writing to Murray about her colleague Arthur Pickard-Cambridge, who later composed the longest and most severe scholarly attack on the Cambridge group's case for ritual origins for tragedy: ". . . dear Mr. Pickard [-Cambridge], how like him to raise difficulties about the babe Bromios [i.e., Dionysus—see *Themis*, p. 92]—I am so weary of people whose minds are in bits—and for all his adorably kind gentle face one feels his mind is in rather small bits."[24] Many of us, perhaps all, make intellectual judgments in aesthetic terms; Jane Harrison is here only pleasantly explicit.

And finally, from Stewart's list, the "rage for art in '80's" and "the aesthetic movement made appreciation of Greek vase painting possible" suggest why Jane Harrison might have elected to popularize Greek art history in the eighties. The aesthetic movement, along with the efforts of those in the preceding generation, namely Ruskin and Morris, to generate a heightened aesthetic consciousness, made art and "culture" more of a mass commodity than ever before in Britain.[25] And we know that her lectures were very popular, both in the British Museum and with the other audiences, mostly schools, before whom she appeared.

I have already mentioned the personal and intellectual crisis through which Harrison passed around 1887. The facts are not as clear as they might be but enough exists to enable one to speak with some assurance. The cause, or at least one of the main causes, was the condemnation passed on her aesthetic standards and style of life, and especially on her method of lecturing, by her close friend D. S. MacColl. Apparently she was in the habit of delivering what she later called an "Epideiktikos Logos," a set or show oration, in which she would attempt to overwhelm her audience through her fervor and brilliance. MacColl regarded her lectures as performances of an overheated, sensationalistic, and superficial kind and related them to her desire to live her life as intensely and beautifully as possible. Her whole life seems to have toppled at this time, and she tells us that she went through a kind of "mystical" conversion. Such an experience, so typical of the nineteenth century, has as its characteristic rhythm "depression, loneliness, a sense of disaster bringing a 'conviction of sin,'" which leads without the conscious intervention of the will, to "exaltation, peace, and joy, a new focus, a sensation of oneness."[26] This dramatic and harrowing time came to an end when in 1888 in the company of MacColl and several other friends she paid her first visit to Greece.

One need not attempt to analyze this critical period further; it suffices to note it as the watershed after which everything is new and different. Not quite everything, to be sure—her penchant for origins, noted earlier in the study of Greek art, will remain but will now be exercised in the search for the roots of religion. But from this time on she eschewed sensationalism as a lecturer (although she was a very effective teacher at Newnham), and, more importantly, wholly changed her main interests. She remained an archaeologist, but no longer did she regard archaeology merely as an ancilla to literature, as she had in her book on the myths of the *Odyssey*. She still was committed to the search for beauty, but perhaps her crisis caused her to question her hitherto unexamined standards of the beautiful, and it is likely that her trip to Greece, scrambling around the ruins of Athens and learning of the latest findings from the director of the excavations, Wilhelm Dörpfeld, opened her eyes to a larger view of Greek art. But whatever it was, from then on she combined her interest in origins with her love of Greek art and used them to study the earliest Greek art, not its classical incarnation in the work of Phidias.

The "new birth" she experienced is displayed in the work she published in 1890, immediately after her return from Greece: a translation of Maxime Collignon's *Mythologie figurée de la Grèce*, entitled *Manual of Mythology in Relation to Greek Art*; and the long historical introduction to a translation of Book I of Pausanias, "Attica," by her friend Margaret Verrall, the translation and introduction published together as *Mythology and Monuments of Ancient Greece*. Even though the *Manual of Mythology* is a translation and not her own work, her preface sounds the new note that will typify all her future work.

> If we would know the truth about the origin of mythological types, it is to archaic art we must look,—to a time when the utterance of the artist, if sometimes rude and inarticulate, was always robust and sincere. Truth with the early artist comes even before beauty; as yet he works for a people whose faith is more developed than their senses.
>
> The study of mythography is in England yet in its infancy, but it may safely be prophesied that not many years will elapse before it becomes not only part of the advanced discipline of the classical scholar, but also an indispensable and attractive element in classical school teaching. M. Collignon's manual offers an admirable introduction to the study, and as no English handbook exists a translation was much needed.[27]

The profoundest result, however, of her personal upheaval was not these books, prophetic though they are of her later work. The

"new birth" through which she went was in fact a *rite de passage*, a
death and rebirth, which she would come to understand in *Themis*
as the paradigmatic Greek religious ritual. I am not claiming that she
wrote *Themis* as a result of the events of 1887–88. As we shall see, she
did not perceive the key role of initiation ritual until after 1905, a
long fifteen years after the events now being narrated. Nevertheless,
her scholarly work and her personal life were inextricably interwoven
in a way that is rare for most intellectuals. And I have no doubt that
she later embraced initiation and rebirth as enthusiastically as she
did because her own experience must have given her the subjective
feeling of "rightness" that she apparently needed before making an
idea completely her own.

3

Mythology and Monuments of Ancient Athens (1890) might be called
the first book of the Cambridge Ritualists, even though Jane
Harrison had at this time not even met Murray, Cornford, or Cook,
because it clearly indicates the general direction to be taken by the
group later. Its orientation, however, is still primarily archaeological, discussing the connection between the myths and the artifacts
that have been dug up; there is nothing yet about drama or any
other form of literature.

Here is Harrison in the preface, written, it should be recalled, in
the flush of enthusiasm attendant upon her return from Greece:

> I have tried everywhere to get at, where possible, the cult as the
> explanation of the legend. My belief is that in many, even in the
> large majority of cases, *ritual practice misunderstood* explains the
> elaboration of myth. . . . Some of the loveliest stories the
> Greeks have left us will be seen to have taken their rise, not in
> poetic imagination, but in primitive, often savage, and I think,
> always practical ritual. In this matter—in regarding the myth-
> making Greek as a practical savage rather than a poet or
> philosopher—I follow, *quam longo intervallo*, in the steps of
> Eusebius, Lobeck, Mannhardt, and Mr. Andrew Lang. The
> *nomina numina* method [i.e., Müllerian comparative mythol-

ogy] I have utterly discarded—first, because I am no philologist; and second, because whatever partial success may await it
in the future, a method so long overdriven may well lie by for a
time. That I have been unable, except for occasional illustra-
tion, to apply to my examination of cults the comparative
method is a matter of deep regret for me, and is due to lack of
time, not lack of conviction. I may perhaps be allowed to ask
that my present attempts be only taken as *prolegomena* to a more
systematic study.[28]

If myth arises from ritual misunderstood, to study myth we must fix
on what the primitives did, not what they (might have) thought.

At this point she is sure that a ritual misunderstood will fully
explain only a relatively small group of myths, even though she suspects that most myths should be so understood. And for all her
implied difference with Tylorian rationalism, she is still willing to
assume a "myth-making mind" inside which the investigator can
move. For instance, when later she considers a group of myths that
seem expiatory in tone but puzzling to us because it is not clear what
is being expiated, her conclusion is that the confusion exists only in
our minds—"To the myth-making mind that was simple enough."[29]

In her long introductory essay to this guidebook to the ruins of
Athens, Harrison reminds the reader of Otfried Müller in her careful dissection of the myths into their various components, except
that she has the inestimably great advantage of sixty-five additional
years of archaeology: she has, therefore, many more parallels at her
fingertips, and implicitly also a rather large body of evolutionary
ethnographic data and speculation as a theoretical framework. Her
emphasis on topography and vases implies that myths are not importantly (or at least primarily) to be thought of as verbal constructions
(which ultimately might be analyzed philologically) but as secondary developments of a cultic reality that was located in the physical
existence of Greece (not in the Greek imagination) and which
therefore had to be studied with that scene in mind.

As might be expected from the prolegomenon of a beginning
(albeit forty-year-old) scholar, the book is not of great theoretical

interest. As mentioned, she implicitly accepts an evolutionary development of both technology and psyche. And she makes clear her commitment to the comparative method in her expression of regret at not having been able to pursue this approach in what after all is really a handbook, intended for tourists clambering around the broken remnants of Athens.

Before passing to her later work it is appropriate here to note that *Mythology and Monuments* appeared in 1890, the same year as the first edition of *The Golden Bough*. The simple fact of contemporaneity seems conclusive evidence that any formulation such as that by Hyman, quoted in the introduction, which has ritualist criticism emerging from under the shade of *The Golden Bough* is mistaken. The important facts in this stage of Jane Harrison's life are not her reading of *The Golden Bough* but her archaeological training in general and her trip to Greece in particular. In Athens, Dr. Dörpfeld, the director of the excavations being conducted by the German Archaeological Institute, personally led her over the ruins of the ancient city, showing her how closely and strongly cultic reality stood behind mythic narrative (whether narrated in a story or depicted on a vase). And later she and MacColl had traveled to other important classical sites. Considering the idealistic tone of her earlier work, it can only have been the Greek experience, combined with a readiness to rethink her basic approach to the past, that led her to the theory of the precedence of ritual over myth. Nor was William Robertson Smith any more of a factor in influencing her thought, for we should surely have had some mention of her having attended the lectures that were printed as *The Religion of the Semites*, and no evidence to that effect exists. Add to this the fact that she was in Greece during part of the time that Smith was lecturing, and we may safely deny Smith any formative role in her ideas.[30]

All this notwithstanding, she read *The Golden Bough* soon after its appearance, for in the preface she contributed to the English translation in 1892 of a standard German manual on Greek mythology she briefly discusses the various approaches to mythology then available. After dismissing the philological viewpoint she turns to "the Folk-lore Method, of which Mr. Andrew Lang and Mr. J. G. Frazer

are, in England, the best known exponents."[31] She explains that this
method asks us to understand the origins of the Greek gods not in
light of the Vedas, "which is a relief, as so few of us can read them,"
but from what we have learned from the analogous practices of "the
contemporary Savage." She continues:

> The shock was severe at first, but we are settling down, and
> most of us now recognize the substantial soundness of the posi-
> tion. No less do we, and probably its original supporters, see
> clearly its inadequacy as applied to Greek mythology. It leaves
> us with the beginning of things, with certain primitive ele-
> mentary conceptions, and takes no heed of the complex struc-
> ture reared on the simple basis. The seductive simplicity of the
> "Corn-mother" and the "Tree-spirit," and, worst of all, the ever-
> impending "Totem," is almost as perilous as the Old Sun and
> Moon snare.[32]

So we see that Harrison has gone over and now numbers herself
as one of the folklorists. And we also see that she has moved so
recently that she still can offer criticisms of the new approach from
a relatively detached perspective; she is not yet the partisan she will
become. When she names Frazer she must be referring to *The Golden
Bough*, since he had published nothing of note between 1890 and
1892. Of its three editions this one, it should be recalled, was the
most ritualist. It was nevertheless not very strong theoretically, being
basically a series of what the nineteenth century called "disserta-
tions" on comparisons between the priestly kingship at Nemi and
analogous rites drawn from peasant or primitive practice. Thus what
she gained from Frazer was not the crucial connection between
myth and ritual, for she had that already in 1890 in *Mythology and
Monuments*, but the comparison between Greek religion and "savage" folklore. And here too *The Golden Bough* cannot have been more
than suggestive, because most of it is based on Mannhardt—that is,
Central Europe—and not on classical Greece at all. Nevertheless,
this quotation, drawn from her preface to a fairly obscure publication, clearly shows that by the early nineties Jane Harrison had been

persuaded of the basic worth of the anthropological approach; what she had now to do was to become enough of an anthropologist to employ it. This was to occupy her for the next decade.

Let us return to this noteworthy preface once more, for she goes on to outline what she deems to be the task of the student of Greek mythology, now that he has been given the key furnished by comparative anthropology. She says that even granting the basic analogy between "the stately ritual of the Greek temple" and "the sympathetic magic of the savage," this is but the beginning of the mythologist's work.

> He has the demons and spirits of primitive man at one pole, and the "gods of Olympos" at the other; while a link in this chain is wanting he knows no rest. It is not enough for him to hint airily that Dionysos may have been a bull or a tree. . . . what he must do, or fail, is to trace each Saga to its local home, to carry out the work that the great H. D. Müller [*sic*—K. O. Müller is meant] began before his time, to disentangle the "confederacy of local cults" from which the ultimate Olympian assembly was formed.[33]

The importance of the anthropological method to students of Greek mythology, which they are now beginning to realize, is that Greek religion must have evolved from more primitive forms and that therefore what passes as the fount of Greek religion—Homer—was in fact the end-product of a long religious development. But, she says, too little is yet known of pre-Homeric religion to warrant dropping hints to this effect, as some writers apparently were doing. "It may be possible ten years hence to write a manual on the historico-tribal method, but the time is not yet." So until that time comes the best thing to do is repeat the verities of the good Dr. Petiscus (whose original manual had appeared in 1863; this was a translation of the *twentieth* edition); at least he does not mislead or confuse the reader with cryptic hints about a new way of understanding the entire subject.

This last sentiment is remarkable as a rare example of Jane

Harrison favoring the prudent way over the speculative. Apparently, she had now become convinced that the folkloristic method offered so much promise, once it was worked out, that such premature and ill-considered guesswork must inevitably damage the real work at hand.

With the publication of *Mythology and Monuments* Harrison achieved a certain scholarly celebrity: she was invited to join the German Archaeological Society and was awarded honorary doctorates from Durham and Aberdeen universities. During the nineties, however, while she lived what seems to have been a rather unhappy existence writing and lecturing in London, she was groping toward the idea that there was a deeper, more primitive layer of gods underlying the Homeric stratum of Olympians. She published in the *Classical Review* a series of notes and reviews, some of considerable length, all on archaeological topics and some, interestingly enough, on the connections between artifact and literature: for example, in 1898 a twenty-page series of notes on the light shed on three odes of Bacchylides by the close inspection of certain vases.[34] Then in 1898 she was offered and accepted the first research fellowship at Newnham and returned to her old college for what would be a stay of nearly a quarter of a century.

The return to Newnham marked an epoch in her life. She had demonstrated her competence by achieving an international reputation as one of a handful of women in an ultra-conservative field of scholarship. By making the move she rejoined the academic world, in which she felt at ease.

During the twenty years that had ensued since she had gone down from Cambridge she had moved somewhat uneasily, searching for a subject matter. She began by attempting to elucidate the relations between Greek art and Greek literature, then shifted to the history of Greek art as seen from the viewpoint of archaeology, and finally had seen the light in sighting the darkness that underlay the lambent achievement of the classical period.

She was a Darwinian, like practically every intellectual of the time, but when she went back to the university she was not yet a competent anthropologist. Although she had embraced the comparative method she lacked as yet the materials with which to make wide-ranging comparisons. It is here probably that Frazer had his greatest influence—in putting at her disposal large bodies of comparative data illustrating certain recurrent motifs in primitive religion. During the five years following her return to Newnham, she threw herself into anthropology and paid less and less attention to literature; she made the acquaintance of the men who were to be her closest friends and co-workers; and she wrote the books that will assure her a place in the history of classical scholarship. It is to these years that I now turn.

Six

Jane Ellen Harrison and
the Cambridge Ritualists

At this point—Jane Harrison's return to Cambridge in 1898—we must broaden our focus for several reasons. First, the Cambridge Ritualists were not merely a group of Jane Harrison's friends; each member made unique and important contributions that are to be understood in terms of his own life as well as in relation to larger movements of ideas. Therefore it will be opportune to sketch the earlier (pre-1898) work of Murray, Cornford, and Cook so that we may proceed with the four of them together. It will then be possible to ascertain the changes in emphasis and direction that the work of the group made on each of its members. Second, the Ritualists were working within a larger social and intellectual context that requires a fuller treatment. Many scholars were working on primitive Greek religion, the origins of tragedy, and the relations between myth and ritual. Aside from noting the trends and marking the significant contributions within this body of scholarship as a whole, I shall concentrate on the study of classics in England and especially in Cambridge, for this was the immediate milieu that produced and received the Ritualists and their work.

Writing of classics at Cambridge ninety years later, one can only envy the intellectual situation of the Ritualists. Despite the fact that their work received severe, and sometimes even intemperate, criticism from their colleagues, they were part of an intellectual community that seems idyllic in some respects today. The university then was small; its members were all recruited from the same classes and shared the same goals; although classics no longer enjoyed the supremacy it had had a hundred years earlier, it still stood in high esteem. As a result the Ritualists were able to develop their ideas through conversations with and lectures to a large body of knowledgeable colleagues to an extent unimaginable today in the multiversity. From our standpoint it is only slightly fanciful to say that although there were only four Ritualists, the classicists and ancient historians and historians of religion of Cambridge and Oxford constituted an indispensable auxiliary, without whom the work of the Ritualists would have been impossible.

1

The history of Oxford and Cambridge universities in the nineteenth century is that of a power struggle: a group of conservative bodies (the colleges and the societies of fellows who ran them) intent on keeping their traditional powers and prerogatives were forced to accommodate themselves to a new order. Within this conservative context, classics, its pre-eminence as the keystone of liberal education challenged for the first time, represented by the end of the nineteenth century a bastion of diehardism. That is, from an intramural point of view, the Cambridge Ritualists represented a "new wave" in classics and therefore some of the opposition they faced was a result of a generalized academic conservatism that existed regardless of their ideas. This is not to dismiss their opponents but only to indicate that some of them were responding not only to their work but as well to the kind of change they were believed to represent. Another important fact: the academic pyramid was so steeply inclined and its top was so small that determined opposition from a single powerful individual such as William Ridgeway, the Disney Professor of Archaeology, could be exceedingly formidable in itself.[1]

In one sense, the struggle from about 1895 to 1915 over the value of the methods and findings of ethnography to the study of antiquity may be seen as a fiercer recapitulation of the battle waged in the preceding generation—the seventies and eighties—over the importance of archaeology in what had been up to that time a philological and literary discipline. The situation in the earlier period was described as follows by R. S. Conway, in his obituary of Ridgeway:

> Classical study . . . in the 'seventies and 'eighties, especially in England, was oppressed by an unintelligent orthodoxy [drawn] from the teaching of a few eminent Germans like Mommsen, Schliemann, and Karl Otfried Müller, whom it was the fashion to regard as infallible.[2]

After a struggle Ridgeway and his associates at Cambridge succeeded in making a place for archaeology. They enlarged the museums and their collections; they helped found the Society for the Promotion of Hellenic Studies in 1879, which began publishing its *Journal* in 1880; they helped establish the British School at Athens in 1886, which served to train generations of scholars in the methods of field archaeology, as well as carrying out important excavations.

Ridgeway, who had won his battle for archaeology by the nineties, was a brilliant man of independent mind but conservative temperament and Conservative politics; unfortunately he was as well of a bellicose disposition, dearly relishing a fight. And even his friends admitted that once he was engaged in a controversy he was not overly fastidious about using whatever came to hand as a weapon against his opponents.[3] A. B. Cook, who tangled with him many times, puts it this way in his gentlemanly fashion long after the dust had settled:

> Isolated and independent to a fault, he often ignored the work of foreign investigators. . . . This disdain for Teutonic *Litteratur* . . . served to draw the fire of indignant critics, and Cambridge has more than once witnessed the heartening spectacle of Ridgeway *contra mundum*.[4]

The Ritualists angered Ridgeway because he thought their ideas not merely nonsensical but pernicious as well, for in his mind Harrison and her friends represented everything that was wrong with modern life as well as being exemplars of shoddy thinking. They were, for instance, prominent among those who were trying to obtain par-

ity for the degrees awarded by the women's colleges, whereas
Ridgeway, predictably enough, was a chief mover in the antifeminist
forces. And we may assume that the Liberal and Fabian politics of
Murray and Cornford (Harrison in the early years was apolitical) did
not endear them to him either. Certainly Ridgeway was not above let-
ting his personal or political grudges fuel his scholarly vendettas, the
effect of which was to embitter the atmosphere considerably.[5]

Jessie Stewart has in general de-emphasized this element in her
biography, perhaps believing that the controversies were too evanes-
cent to interest the reader today; it really emerges, however, in the
unpublished letters of 1908 and thereafter, in which Harrison warns
Murray to be on his guard when he lectures at Cambridge because
Ridgeway and friends will be in the audience, or describing her
dread of an upcoming faculty meeting at which "the female question" would be discussed, and she could expect a personal attack
from Ridgeway.

But Ridgeway, despite his ferocity in polemic, was a first-rate
mind, and Jane Harrison especially owed much to him. Like her, he
was obsessed by origins, and he made their study his life work. In a
sense it did not matter what the phenomenon was—only its origins
interested him. Here is a brief list of some of his important publications: among articles, "The Origin of the Homeric 'Talent'"(1887),
"The Origin of the Stadion" (1897), "The Origin of Jewellery"
(1903), "The Origin of the Turkish Crescent" (1908), and "The
Origin of the Indian Drama" (1917); among books, *The Origin and
Influence of the Thoroughbred Horse* (1905), *The Origin of Metallic
Currency and Weight Standards* (1910), and last but not least *The Origin
of Tragedy* (1910). Thus even though on most questions Ridgeway
opposed Harrison and her friends to the death, they at least agreed
on the methods to be used in approaching them.

Cambridge was more archaeologically inclined than Oxford, for
two reasons. These, put briefly, were that Oxford did not have a
Ridgeway and it did have a Max Müller. Because of Müller the philological approach, particularly in the study of mythology, survived
long after it had been superseded at its sister university. Here is an
account by the ancient historian G. B. Grundy of his days as an
Oxford undergraduate reading classics, from 1888 to 1890:

The Greek History lectures of my time were of two kinds. Some I sampled were merely *précis* of Grote. Others were of a fashion which then prevailed at Oxford—and elsewhere—devoted to a destructive criticism of Greek authors, much of which seemed to me to be founded on evidence more slender than that of the authors themselves. The Minotaur tradition was a solar myth— whatever that might be; the Trojan War was legendary, and so forth. Nearly all this destructive criticism has proved to be false; but at that time it was regarded as showing great mental acumen on the part of the critics.[6]

To appreciate fully the remark about Grote, one should be aware that the first volume of the *History of Greece* appeared in 1846 and the last in 1856. And, as already noted, by 1888 Müller's solarism had been under attack for fifteen years by Andrew Lang and others.

Classics in both universities was textual study, narrowly conceived. For undergraduates the goal was to be able to construe a passage; that done, one had gone as far as possible. On a higher level, scholarship was still understood as textual criticism, with great ingenuity expended on establishing texts and explicating cruces. There was, with few exceptions, little or no attempt to use the text, once it had been ascertained, as a way of feeling oneself into what it might have been like to live in Athens—in other words, the old dream of philology had fallen away into textual study and antiquarianism.[7]

Here is Jane Harrison's own retrospect of the time, in her memoir, written in 1925:

Looking back over my own life, I see with what halting and stumbling steps I made my way to my own special subject [religion]. Greek literature as a specialism I early felt was barred to me. The only field of research that Cambridge of my day knew was textual criticism, and for fruitful work in that my scholarship was never adequate. We Hellenists were, in truth, at that time a "people who sat in darkness," but we were soon to see a great light, two great lights—archaeology, anthropology. Classics were turning in their long sleep. Old men began to see visions, young men to dream dreams. I had just left Cambridge

when Schliemann began to dig at Troy. Among my own contemporaries was J. G. Frazer, who was soon to light the dark
wood of savage superstition with a gleam from *The Golden
Bough.* The happy title of that book—Sir James Frazer has a ver-
itable genius for titles—made it arrest the attention of scholars.
They saw in comparative anthropology a serious subject actually capable of elucidating a Greek or Latin text. Tylor had written and spoken; Robertson Smith, exiled for heresy, had seen
the Star in the East; in vain; we classical deaf-adders stopped
our ears and closed our eyes; but at the mere sound of the
magical words "Golden Bough" the scales fell—we heard and
understood. Then Arthur Evans [excavator of Knossos] set sail
for his new Atlantis and telegraphed news of the Minotaur
from his own labyrinth; perforce we saw this was a serious matter, it affected the "Homeric question."[8]

Unfortunately, her eloquence cannot be taken at face value; she
has telescoped some events and omitted others. Note, however, the
remark about the relentless "lower criticism" of Greek texts as a
Cambridge specialty. But in fact there were men who represented a
new way in classics, even in textual study. One was A. W. Verrall, Jane
Harrison's most influential teacher and later very important as a colleague and friend. "Dr. Verrall, best beloved of Trinity tutors, was the
most inspiring . . . of classical scholars."[9] Although he never could be
persuaded that anthropology had anything to offer, he had, besides
his brilliance and daring in establishing and interpreting a text,

> a lively idea of the conditions of dramatic poetry. No English
> scholar before Verrall, and no earlier scholar save Otfried
> Müller. . . was possessed of a similar capacity of visualizing a
> Greek tragedy as a play to be performed upon a stage.
> Consequently, one vital aspect of this poetry was more ade-
> quately brought out in Verrall's commentaries than in those of
> his forerunners.[10]

Harrison says, in the introduction to *Prolegomena*, that her "debt
to Dr. Verrall is so great and constant that it is hard to formulate."[11]

But if we were to try to formulate the intellectual dimension of that debt by examining Verrall's work to get an idea of what the best contemporary scholarship on the tragedians was like, we must conclude that his principal importance to her must have been as an intellectual antagonist. For Verrall is the very model of the rationalist critic. His main thesis in *Euripides the Rationalist* (1895), which was already clearly implied in print as early as 1891,[12] is that Euripides can be understood only by supposing that most of the plays contain two levels of action and meaning. The surface action and thought, intended for the orthodox in the audience, observes the traditional pieties; the deeper stratum, embodying Euripides' true beliefs, undercuts them. Euripides is to be understood, then, as a nineteenth-century rationalist like Verrall, with his plays intended as a sustained critique of religion. Because Harrison and Murray based their arguments for the ritual genesis of drama primarily upon Euripides, such ideas as Verrall's, which were widely held, explain to some extent why the Ritualists were received with such hostility.

Verrall is thus important for two reasons: because of his influence on Jane Harrison and because the Ritualists (especially Murray) concentrated on Euripides in their work on drama. Verrall's originality often amounted to foolhardiness in his textual and dramatic criticism, and was in that sense unusual, but in his rationalism he was quite typical. He was a nineteenth-century gentleman and assumed that, *mutatis mutandis*, Euripides was one as well. His attitude was that of most (textual) scholars, who, because of their methods and assumptions, were concerned with the linguistic product of the writer's imagination rather than social and psychological elements that helped produce the work. I believe that Verrall, whose wife, Margaret, was a leader in psychic research, tended to think of Jane Harrison's work as resembling what his wife was doing—both were nonsense. "Though he was angelically kind," Harrison wrote, "I could see he thought it was a much ado about scarcely anything, and was puzzled why a sane person should write such stuff. . . . He could not and would not absorb 'stuffage' [the paraphernalia of archaeology] so he never found the real clue."[13] Occasionally he and Harrison, who was not shy either, would have heated arguments. For instance, in a partly unpublished letter to Murray (4 May 1907) Harrison writes:

You know don't you that AWV has discovered that the earth-
quake and fire in the *Bacchae* are all Hallucinations—I did not
realise how he hated the Bacchus whom I love so. He declares
he sympathises with Pentheus. "Any gentleman would be justly
annoyed if he found a wild bull in his stables," he said. We got
quite stormy over it.[14]

Ridgeway and Verrall were Cantabrigians; the situation at Oxford
in classical archaeology, mythology, and religion was not much different, personalities aside. L. R. Farnell may be taken as representative in the sense that he was open to new ideas; his work shows how
ethnography and evolution were assimilated by those who were not
intransigent like Ridgeway.[15] Farnell was a contemporary of Frazer
and Jane Harrison, both chronologically and ideologically, in that
he too accepted the basic validity of the evolutionary anthropological approach. He was extremely prolific, and his work on classical
archaeology and religion appeared from the early nineties until the
outbreak of the war. A man of great industry and erudition, but
rather unimaginative, he published the first volume of his magnum
opus, *The Cults of the Greek States*, in 1896. Its five large volumes, in
which all the religious forms and observances of all the Greek states
were catalogued and analyzed, took him twenty years to complete.
As it happened, the cult of Dionysus had been reserved for the fifth
and last volume, which appeared in 1909, so that it turned out to be
a timely contribution to the controversy then raging over the origins
of tragedy.

We shall return to his ideas on Dionysus and tragedy later; here
we might examine briefly his series of lectures called *The Evolution
of Religion*. They were given in 1904 and published the following year,
and thus are somewhat out of the chronology of this narrative;
nonetheless, Farnell's basic position remained constant so no violence is done by taking them up here.

Farnell is a Frazer with a less highly colored style and many fewer
ideas. He is a strict rationalistic evolutionist, who accepts the
Tylorian-Frazerian apparatus entire. Survivals are continually
invoked; magic precedes religion, which precedes science, etc. For
him the job of anthropology is to delve into and explain the inher-

itance from the immemorial past that every great religion has received and conserves within itself. "But many if not most of these facts [viz., religious survivals] may be regarded as functionally dead matter surviving in the more advanced system of belief, and as not belonging to its essential life."[16] Of course Farnell (like Tylor and Frazer) assumes that it is self-evident to all exactly what is dead and nonfunctional. Further, anthropology and comparative religion have shown us

> an extraordinary uniformity, in spite of much local variation, in ritual and mythology, a uniformity so striking as to suggest belief in an ultimately identical tradition, or, perhaps more reasonably, the psychological theory that the human brain-cell in different races at the same stage of development responds with the same religious speech or the same religious act to the same stimuli applied by the environment (9).

But, he says, although "anthropology's work is of wide vogue, its energy exuberant, and its influence in the future assured" (6), its practitioners seem to be losing the main thread. They (and here he must mean Harrison's *Prolegomena*) have been carried away by the results of the comparative method as applied to Greek religion and have overemphasized "the savage and primitive facts, missing the true perspective and misjudging the whole" (15).

Farnell also says that many scholars still confuse Greek religion with Greek mythology and traces this error back to St. Augustine. But, he claims, "myths are often irresponsible, capricious, volatile, and flit like a vapour round the solid structure of real belief and ritual" (26).

The pseudo-scientific rhetoric about the "human brain-cell" is typical and instructive. We have here the language of a proto-behaviorism, except that Farnell thinks of his metaphors as physiological facts. He sounds like an evolutionary biologist of the time discussing the way that a butterfly might have changed the colors of its wing spots in response to a change in the color of the foliage in its surroundings. The psychology implied is completely mechanist-materialist: the "environment" "applies stimuli" to the "brain-cells" of oth-

erwise passive humanity, which "responds." And all this about the
metaphoric and symbolically determined system that is religion.

It comes then as no surprise that the Ritualists regarded Farnell
as the type of the rationalism beyond which they were trying to
move. Probably because they did share many basic assumptions—
evolution, comparative method, folklore—he was a special enemy to
them. Indeed there must have been some personal animus opera-
tive as well, because every reference to Farnell made by Harrison or
Murray has a special barbed quality that seems unmerited by the
public record. Murray, in a letter to Jessie Stewart, cites Farnell's five
volumes (*The Cults of the Greek States*) as work that "now seem to
belong to the Dark Ages."[17] And in an unpublished letter to Murray
of 20 April 1907 Harrison speaks of having received for review
Farnell's "two large volumes [which] are simply *nil*." In another
unpublished letter to Murray written while convalescing from minor
surgery, she says (11 July 1908), "If you say Mr. Farnell is important I
shall send for my neolithic club [her fanciful name for a cane she
was then forced to use], he is essentially insignificant."

2

On the Continent the earliest and in some sense the most important
worker in this field was Nietzsche. His remarkable book *The Birth of
Tragedy from the Spirit of Music* was published in 1872, when most
German scholars were still hunting for the key to Greek mythology in
Müllerian solarism and when Mannhardt was still writing up his
ethnographic researches.[18] Nietzsche somehow sensed that the
famous "serenity" of the Greeks was only superficial, that there was
something wholly "other" beneath the surface, and that "the Greeks
will continue to remain totally obscure, unimaginable beings until we
have found an answer to the question, 'What is the meaning of the
Dionysiac spirit?'"[19] The answer is to be found in Nietzsche's celebrated distinction between Apollonian and Dionysian: the one exemplified in the dream, in plastic arts, in clarity, in separateness; the
other in intoxication, in music, in turbidity, in merging into the One.

For Nietzsche tragedy is the product of the Dionysian spirit: that
is, it is collective in origin, an image (and therefore Apollonian) that

emerges in the attempt of the Dionysian worshipers to break through the encapsulating ego and merge with the Power that animates the world. Tragedy, he says, is first and foremost a matter of the chorus.

> Thus we have come to interpret Greek tragedy as a Dionysiac chorus which again and again discharges itself in Apollonian images. Those choric portions with which the tragedy is interlaced constitute, as it were, the matrix of the *dialogue*, that is to say, of the entire stage-world of the actual drama. This substratum of tragedy irradiates, in several consecutive discharges, the vision of the drama—a vision on the one hand completely of the nature of Apollonian dream-illusion and therefore epic, but on the other hand, as the objectification of a Dionysiac condition, tending toward the shattering of the individual and his fusion with the original Oneness. Tragedy is an Apollonian embodiment of Dionysiac insights and powers, and for that reason separated by a tremendous gulf from the epic (56–7).

In the first stage, tragedy was the chorus and drama did not exist at all. There was no "audience" but only participating dancers. Only later when a separation had occurred between the active celebrants of Dionysus and those who looked on was it necessary to demonstrate the reality of the god to those who were not possessed by the god and thus experiencing him directly. Here is the beginning of drama, says Nietzsche: "It then became the task of the dithyrambic chorus so to excite the mood of the listeners that when the tragic hero appeared they would behold not the awkwardly masked man but a figure born of their own rapt vision" (58).

In a passage especially striking in its foreshadowing of the Cambridge thesis of ritual origins for the form of Greek tragedy, he writes:

> It is an unimpeachable tradition that in its earliest form Greek tragedy records only the sufferings of Dionysos, and that he was the only actor. But it may be claimed with equal justice that, up to Euripides, Dionysos *remains* the sole dramatic protagonist

and that all the famous characters of the Greek stage, Prometheus, Oedipus, etc., are only masks of the original hero (65–6).

It is then but a small step to Murray's "Excursus" in *Themis,* in which he is really documenting Nietzsche's assertion by showing how the stages in the life of the god underlie and give rise to the structure of the play.

Nietzsche understood that myth was a special symbolic language with insights of its own, expressed "partly in the secret celebrations of dramatic mysteries, but always under the old mythic veil." But it is the fate of myth to be degraded into history, "For it is the lot of every myth to creep gradually into the narrows of supposititious historical fact and to be treated by some later time as a unique event in history" (68).

In summary, Nietzsche, with neither comparative anthropology nor an evolutionary framework, and totally disregarding the historicism and facticity of nineteenth-century philology, intuitively anticipated the direction in which classical scholarship was going to move, and adumbrated thirty or forty years earlier many of the major achievements of the Ritualists. Historically *The Birth of Tragedy* is most noteworthy because it began a trend in classical studies toward searching for and emphasizing nonrational factors as determinants of human behavior. His book may be thought of as a check to the overintellectualization to which traditional scholarship was given. Nietzsche, however, lacked a sociology, so that he did not attempt to show how the creation of tragedy was related integrally to the rest of Greek social reality. It is here that Jane Harrison in *Themis* surpasses him—but nowhere else. The difficulty with *Themis,* as we shall see, is that like *The Birth of Tragedy* it too satisfies us by its imaginative design, but because it is not a suggestive essay on the psychology of the Greeks but, as its subtitle proclaims, "a study of the social origins of Greek religion," it is open to the historical criticism from which Nietzsche is largely immune. Nietzsche was able to "get away with" *The Birth of Tragedy* by not playing according to the rules of philological scholarship; Jane Harrison was trying to do something more difficult, if not more innovative—using the methods of historical scholarship, to show how Greek psychology and social structure and religion were inextricably interwoven.

As we might expect, the Ritualists valued *The Birth of Tragedy* highly. Harrison quotes it in *Prolegomena*, Cornford praises it in the preface to *From Religion to Philosophy*, and Jane Harrison, in an unpublished letter of December 1909, writes to Murray; "I have been re-reading *Die Geburt der Tragödie*. Have you read the book at all lately, it is real genius, and if you hate the German there is a French translation." (Her letters frequently refer to Murray's dislike of reading German.)

It is significant that she should have returned to Nietzsche in 1909, for she was then in the middle of writing *Themis*. But Nietzsche could not have been important to the Ritualists until and unless they had come to understand what he meant by the Dionysian spirit; he seems to have intuited it directly, but they came to it slowly, in reaction to the ubiquitous native rationalism, from a comparative study of primitive religion. Only then would he have really made sense to them, but for all that he indicated the direction they took, he cannot truly be said to have been their guide over the difficult terrain.

To sum up, we find British classics, conservative and embattled, generally resistant to anthropology. The resistance was due to an inbred conservatism as well as to theoretical problems within anthropology itself, which have been alluded to in the discussion of Frazer. So long as research into primitive religion was of a rationalistic empiricist cast and so long as a simple-minded Tylorian animism marked the deepest penetration of anthropology into religion, the new approach did not promise to shed much light on the classical world. Only when anthropology founded itself on a psychology that could deal with the unconscious was effective work possible.

This new psychological formulation, variously called animatism, pre-animatism, or the theory of *mana*, was associated especially with T. K. Preuss in Germany, R. R. Marett in England, and Lucien Lévy-Bruhl in France. Philip Wheelwright describes it as the idea

that the primary religious phenomenon, the primordial stage in religious evolution (if we choose to think chronologically), is something vaguer and more fluid than either gods or ances-

tral souls; that it is an undefined sense of presence, stirring awe
and perhaps dread in the beholder, capable on the one hand
of developing at length into an object of reverence, and on the
other of inviting attempts at magical control. Such is declared
to have been the primitive belief-matrix from which religion,
myth, and magic gradually, and sometimes divergently,
evolved.[20]

Wheelwright's statement is a good description of the reaction
against the old style of reductionist, intellectualist anthropology
practiced by Tylor and Frazer. But inexplicably he has omitted
the name of the leader of the new wave in anthropology, Émile
Durkheim. Just before the turn of the century Durkheim gathered
around him in Paris one of the most brilliant groups of scholars ever
to work in the field of sociology. Known as the *Année Sociologique*
school after the journal they founded in 1897, they pioneered what
would later be called the functionalist view of primitive religion.
Their main contribution was to show, in Marett's words, that religion, far from being the product of ratiocination, "stood for all the
socially approved . . . ways of dealing with supernormal powers as
conceived by a community."[21]
     The great influences on Durkheim were the French historian
Fustel de Coulanges and William Robertson Smith. Both men saw
that primitive religion was collective rather than individual in
nature, and that it was traditional and (in a closed society) obligatory. William Robertson Smith, as we have noted, offered a sociological analysis of religion, that is, that it arose from the nature and
structure of society. From Smith, Durkheim took several leading
ideas: that primitive religion was a clan cult and that the cult was
totemic, that the god was the clan itself divinized, and that totemism
was the most elementary or primitive, and in that sense original,
form of religion known to us.
     Durkheim undertook an analysis of religion as a symbolic system
and saw it as an integrated series of "collective representations,"
which seems to mean ideas shared by the whole of society. These representations are the concrete manifestations of a primitive people's
faith in the power that orders the world and maintains it as it ought

to be, which is to say the social order itself. Whatever ideas (theology) the primitives have are secondary to the rites that in fact create religious consciousness. For Durkheim, the individual, who normally sees few people through the year, is powerfully affected by coming together with his fellow clan members at special "sacred" times of the year. Transformed himself by the social energy thus liberated, "he transforms the environment which surrounds him." To account for the extraordinary way he feels at such times, he attributes extraordinary powers to otherwise mundane objects around him. "In a word, above the real world where his profane life passes he has placed another which, in one sense, does not exist except in thought, but to which he attributes a higher sort of dignity than to the first. Thus, from a double point of view, it is an ideal world."[22] These social gatherings are necessary, then, for the members of the society to reach the needed pitch of exaltation of feeling and thought, which in turn leads to ideal group conceptions. Religious ideas are thus produced by a synthesis of individual minds working together out of a prerational, or nonrational, effervescence of emotion.

This is an epitome of Durkheim's thought in its mature version, drawn from his great book *The Elementary Forms of the Religious Life*. But *Elementary Forms* appeared first in France in 1912, too late to be of use to the Ritualists, whose main work was done between 1908 and 1911. The book, however, embodies much earlier work that Durkheim had published during the preceding decade, and it is this material that was of primary importance for Harrison and the others.[23]

But although Durkheim was already enunciating in 1898 the views that would later be embraced with enthusiasm by Harrison, Murray, and Cornford (Cook seems never to have been convinced), none of them at the time knew his work.[24] However, even if they had known it, none of them (with the just-possible exception of Cook) yet had the necessary anthropological background and insight into primitive religion that would have permitted them to understand what Durkheim was getting at. For in 1898 Cornford was a recent graduate who had as yet published nothing; Cook was still a rationalist of the Tylor–Frazer sort, interested like them in amassing data on Greek religion of a folkloristic kind, and who had yet to stake out for himself his great subject—the worship of the sky-god Zeus;[25] and

Murray had just brought out his first important book, *A History of Ancient Greek Literature*, in 1897. At this time, before they knew one another, they each had happened upon anthropology but had little else in common.

3
—

Upon her return to Newnham, Jane Harrison joined the brilliant circle around her friends the Sidgwicks and the Verralls. Once again in a congenial atmosphere, she plunged into work, giving a series of lectures on Delphi in 1898–99 and on primitive Greek religion and mythology in 1899–1900.[26] And she was learning as well as teaching, for she attended Ridgeway's lectures on archaeology. Ridgeway had published an important article in 1896 called "What People Produced the Objects Called Mycenaean?" in which he had asserted, mainly on linguistic evidence, that the Mycenaeans, whose brilliant civilization in Crete and Greece dominated the Mediterranean for centuries, were the dark-haired people whom Herodotus called the Pelasgians, whereas Homer's bright-haired Achaeans were invaders from the north.[27] This distinction, which Ridgeway expanded at greater length in his important *Early Age of Greece* (1901), was the historical key Harrison needed to strip away the several layers of cult, as expressed in Greek myth and ritual, to get back to the earliest stages. "It threw a flood of light on the problems of myth and ritual that perplexed me," is her acknowledgement to Ridgeway in the preface to *Prolegomena*. Aside from Ridgeway's help, she also had the invaluable assistance of R. A. Neil, to whom she turned for advice on all sorts of philological problems. Indeed, her relationship with Neil was so close that they were engaged to be married when he died suddenly in 1901, a great blow to her. But by that time most of the work for *Prolegomena* was done, and, more importantly, she had met Gilbert Murray.

She had made Murray's acquaintance in 1900 at the home of his close friends the Verralls. Their friendship had started off slowly but burgeoned as they found much in common. In her first letter to him (24 August 1900), she says that she liked his *Ancient Greek Literature* so much that she had composed an effusive letter to him but burned it before she sent it. The postscript to the letter she did send is worth quoting: "I am so glad you thought Pandora convincing. I hope to send you soon Diasia with the Fleece of Cursing stolen by the impostor Zeus." The last phrase makes perfectly clear her attitudes to the Olympian gods, and especially to their chief, Zeus. As Jessie Stewart remarks, "Her lifelong antipathy to these too perfect, magnified humans became a standing joke [between herself and Murray and generally around Cambridge]. The superposing of the official cults on the primitive chthonic nature-cults was the theme of *Prolegomena*, and her sympathy was always with the superseded underdog."[28]

In 1900 Murray was among the most promising Hellenists in England. Of Australian birth, he had so distinguished himself at Oxford that, in competition with some of the leading scholars of the day, he was appointed professor of Greek at the University of Glasgow at the astonishing age of twenty-three. His predecessor, Sir Richard Jebb, had been as conservative as Murray was radical, and the latter created a sensation in Glasgow with his Fabian politics and his espousal of new and "immoral" writers like Ibsen. (He retired from Glasgow in the mid-nineties because of poor health.) He had married the eldest daughter of the duke of Carlisle, but "natural" class allegiances notwithstanding, his sympathy for his students, some of them desperately poor, made many wonder whether his highly promising career would not be ruined by his political heterodoxy. While at Glasgow, Murray began to specialize in the tragic poets, and especially Euripides. He had corresponded with the celebrated German scholar Ulrich von Wilamowitz-Moellendorff (1848–1931) about the possibilities of a Euripides lexicon. This led to a commission from Oxford University Press to prepare an edition in three volumes of Euripides (1901–03). After the publication of this edition Euripides continued to occupy Murray nearly uninterruptedly for another ten years, for he translated many of the plays and staged some of them as well, and finally in 1913 wrote an important critical book, *Euripides and His Age*.

The *History of Ancient Greek Literature* of 1897 that had so excited Jane Harrison's admiration was a survey of the subject that proved popular enough that a third edition was called for by 1907. When that edition appeared, Harrison wrote: "What a wonderful book. It has the germ of nearly everything in it. I see the Migrations, the Polis, the Traditional Book . . . and every time I read it it is fresh and means fresh things."[29]

A rather clearer idea of what she admired in Murray's work, however, may be gained from an unpublished letter she wrote to Murray in late 1902, just before the appearance of *Prolegomena*:

> Also do you mind my quoting you at the end [of *Prolegomena*]? Say frankly if I have borrowed too much [from *A History of Ancient Greek Literature*]. That sentence has been a sort of theological (mythological) Alpha and Omega to me and was long before I knew its inadequate author, in fact it first really stated the plot of my book [*Prolegomena*] four years ago.

Here is the "sentence"—in fact, three sentences—taken from the section on Euripides' *Bacchae*:

> Reason is great, but it is not everything. There are in the world things not of reason, but both below and above it; causes of emotion, which we cannot express, which we tend to worship, which we feel, perhaps, to be the precious elements in life. These things are Gods or forms of God: not fabulous immortal men, but "Things which Are," things utterly non-human and non-moral, which bring men bliss or tear his life to shreds without a break in their own serenity.[30]

As might be expected, Murray combined his attention to, and sympathy for, nonrational aspects of religion and literature with a conviction that the anthropological method offered the best hope of getting at what the Greeks really were like. Rejecting the romanticizing and the aestheticizing of the Greeks that had gone on earlier in the nineteenth century, he wrote:

> There is more flesh and blood in the Greek of the anthropologists, the foster-brother of Kaffirs and Hairy Ainos. He is at least human and simple and emotional, and free from irrelevant trappings. His fault, of course, is that he is not the man we

want, but only the raw material out of which that man was formed. . . ."[31]

Strongly impressed by Frazer, he wrote, in an article written to mark the centennial of Frazer's birth, "I remember the shock, the combined shock of interest and almost of horror, with which *The Golden Bough* burst upon classical scholars when it appeared in 1890."[32]1 The trouble with such a declaration is that it was written so long after the fact. While there is no doubt that Frazer had become the most famous anthropologist in the world by the time the third edition was published, he was totally unknown in 1890, and the first edition, though well received, cannot be called epoch-making.[33] And it may have been difficult for Murray, who had been of the anthropological persuasion for upwards of sixty years at the time he wrote this eulogy, to remember exactly what Frazer's reception had been at the very outset.

In any event he did have a strong community of interest with Jane Harrison, and on it they built a deep and intense friendship that lasted until she died (although it seems to have cooled somewhat after she left Cambridge in 1922). During the course of that friendship, Harrison would help Murray become a good anthropologist and archaeologist (of a literary kind), while he would be the unfailing source of answers to a myriad of her scholarly and especially philological queries. Further, his work on Euripides would provide a test case for their theories that the stages in the life of the Dionysian year-spirit stood behind the form of tragedy. The "Excursus on the Ritual Forms Preserved in Greek Tragedy" that Murray contributed to *Themis* was based mainly on Euripides, for Murray had lived with that dramatist for twenty years, as editor, translator, and theatrical adaptor, and knew his plays in a way that he did not know those of Aeschylus and Sophocles.

4

Although Jane Harrison, in the retrospective lines already quoted, asserts that her true subject was religion, it took her a long while to understand this. In the introduction to *Prolegomena to the Study of*

Greek Religion (1903), the product of her first years back at Cambridge, she says that

> literature is really my goal. I have tried to understand primitive
> rites, not in love of their archaism, nor yet wholly from a sin-
> gleminded devotion to science, but with the definite hope that
> I might come to a better understanding of some forms of
> Greek poetry. Religious convention compelled the tragic poets
> to draw their plots from traditional mythology, from stories
> whose religious content and motive were already in Homer's
> days obsolete. A knowledge of, a sympathy with, the *milieu* of
> this primitive material is one step to the realization of its final
> form in tragedy. It is then in the temple of literature, if but as a
> hewer of wood and drawer of water, that I still hope to serve.[34]

Why do we need such a bulky study (682 pages) of Greek religion as an ancilla to the study of Greek poetry? Its *raison d'être*, she says, is to correct the distortion produced by the exclusively literary approach to Greek mythology then prevalent in Britain. It was usual to regard Greek religion as entirely a matter of Greek mythology, and then to dismiss this mythology as merely a collection of enter-taining tales, meaning that Greek religion was either nonexistent or trivial. The problem arises especially in the accepted view of Homer. Scholars acknowledge that Homer stands at the fount of Greek lit-erature, yet his "religion" is not primitive at all. Instead, she says, the-ologically Homer represents the successful suppression of a great many "savage," "Pelasgian" practices and ideas that were to emerge and recur in the works of the tragedians. It is with this stratum, long overlaid and ignored, that she will deal.

   The paragraph quoted above further indicates that *Prolegomena* was still another blow struck in the battle between the philologists and the anthropologists. Harrison was really denying the sufficiency of the traditional literary (that is, linguistic) analysis of myth as prac-ticed by nearly all the philologically trained students of the subject. She was saying, as had William Robertson Smith, that the literary expressions of religious ideas in antiquity which we call myths are in fact secondary elaborations of something else, and to discuss these myths as literary texts of an autonomous kind without reference to that antecedent "something else" was fundamentally to mistake the nature of the material and thus to vitiate any conclusions.

The argument of the book is complex, and following it is difficult because it is studded with references to what are, even for many Hellenists, obscure texts. Fortunately, not all of it is relevant to the development of the Ritualist approach to literature, and so we shall here content ourselves with the sections that deal with the connections between ritual, myth, and literature.

Harrison begins (following Ridgeway) with the distinction made by the Greeks between the two forms of ritual called Olympian and chthonic. The former is the ritual of an invading people that has, in nearly every case, been overlaid on that of the conquered earlier inhabitants. However, when we examine the ceremonies of the important Greek holidays we are able to glimpse the lower, chthonic stratum, without an understanding of which many features of the festival rites are incomprehensible. Then comes the heart of the book—three long chapters, each analyzing the origin and meaning of a major festival. The main difference between the Olympian and chthonic rites is that the former are sunny and optimistic in tone whereas "the rites of the lower stratum are characterized by a deep and constant sense of evil to be removed and of the need of purification for its removal; that the means of purification adopted are primitive and mainly magical nowise affects this religious content."

Not very surprisingly to a reader of Smith and Frazer, she finds that these rites are sacrificial, and, following Frazer, that these sacrifices are intended to ensure fertility by magical means. After an examination of the spirits to whom these dark rites were performed—ghosts and devils—she concludes that "Man makes his demons in the image of his own savage passions." From here she traces the important step from "demonology to theology, from the sprite and ghost to the human and humane god." Here she shows that these human and humane gods approach the Olympian gods in their "simple, non-mystic humanity."

Because the book is a historical study of the development of Greek religion, at this point the author breaks away from the

indigenous festivals to discuss the two great Eastern religions that
then arrived in Greece: the Dionysian and the Orphic. Although
Dionysus will largely occupy Harrison in her later work, here
Orphism gets more attention. In the single chapter devoted to
Dionysus she points to his origins as a Thracian god of a cereal intox-
icant and later of the grape and of wine. And she suggests that the
word "tragedy," whose etymology was then in dispute, derives from
tragos, the grain spelt (from which a beer was fermented).[35] But of
the origin of the genre rather than the word, she has nothing to say.
Dionysus, she concludes, is "a primitive nature god laid hold of,
informed by a spirit of intoxication." More comprehensively, she says:

> With Dionysus, god of trees and plants as well as human life,
> there came a "return to nature," a breaking of the bonds and
> limitations and crystallizations, a desire for the life rather of
> the emotions than of the reason, a recrudescence it may be of
> animal passions. (436)

She lacks a theoretical way of relating her convincing demonstration of the Olympian overlay on the chthonic substratum to the rest
of Greek life. She concentrates on the evidence from antiquarians
(like Plutarch and Pausanias) and from artifacts that show the difficult stages in the "making of a god," but she has no social psychology adequate to the job of explaining why this might have happened
as it did.

The book is curiously disjointed because of the break between the
earlier account of pre-Olympian religion, mainly a study of festivals,
and the later chapters on Dionysus and Orpheus. The reason is that,
as she wrote the last chapters, she was coming into increasingly close
contact with Murray, who was working at the time on the religion of
Dionysus in connection with his translation of Euripides' *Bacchae*.
Thus she writes to him, on 10 September 1902, when most of
Prolegomena was complete:

> It's rather dreadful, the whole centre of gravity of the book has
> shifted. It began as a treatise on Keres [demons] with a sup-

plementary notice of Dionysus. It is ending as a screed on Dionysus with an introductory talk about Keres. Whose fault is that? *Never, never* again will I ask you to lecture when I am writing a book, a nice sound one too, it was, till last autumn.[36]

In the future, her collaboration with Murray would be complete from the start.

In the three years following the publication of *Prolegomena* (that is, 1904–06), Harrison led a very active life, lecturing at Newnham, writing two books, and traveling, mostly with Cornford, in Britain and abroad. During this time Murray's translation of *Hippolytus* was performed, and she supervised the archaeology for the production. There are a large number of letters to Murray, applauding his many translations of Euripides, several of which were performed. It is a time during which the Ritualists came together.

The writing she did was not enjoyable to her. One of her books was *Primitive Athens as Described by Thucydides* (1906), a difficult, detailed topographical study outlining the discoveries made by her old friend Dr. Dörpfeld in Athens. She did not want to write it but felt she could not refuse his request, for he felt his work had not been adequately understood in England. The other book, a "primer," *The Religion of Ancient Greece* (1905), was difficult too, because she had to skirt so many problems owing to its elementary format. The conclusion of that book is noteworthy, however. In speaking of the work yet to be done, she says: "the history of Greek religion is yet to be written. . . . [H]ow in its early stages did religion act on philosophy? Philosophy react on religion?. . . finally, a difficult and delicate task, what is the attitude of each literary author, his personal outlook and bias, how did each modify the material ready to his hand?"[37] The philosophical task was to be undertaken by Francis Cornford and the literary by Gilbert Murray.

It is unclear exactly how and when Cornford and Harrison met, but by September 1903 they were friendly enough for him to have been charged with proofreading *Prolegomena*. He had been a brilliant student of classics and philosophy, and although he did write one purely literary study—*The Origin of Attic Comedy* (1914)—he was always

more interested in the origins of philosophical thought than in
those of religion or drama. As W. K. C. Guthrie wrote, in his prefa-
tory memoir to Cornford's posthumous collection *The Unwritten
Philosophy and Other Essays*,[38] Cornford seemed to have been writing
one book his whole life long, from *Thucydides Mythistoricus* in 1907 to
his death in 1943. Its subject, "a basic truth about the nature of
human thought,"[39] was the following, taken from Cornford's inaugural lecture of 1931:

> If we look beneath the surface of philosophical discussion, we
> find that its course is largely governed by assumptions that are
> seldom, or never, mentioned. I mean that groundwork of cur-
> rent conceptions shared by all men of any given culture and
> never mentioned because it is taken for granted as obvious.[40]

Cornford's first book, *Thucydides Mythistoricus*, argues that
Thucydides never explains what we today would recognize as the
causes of the Peloponnesian War because his language lacked any
term for "causes." The reason for this is that he has no idea of cause
and effect or of natural law. Instead he employs a psychology that
derived from the older mythological stage of thought. Such thought
is coherent; it is based on a theory of the universe that sees events as
caused by autonomous "forces" or "spirits" that come from nowhere,
possess a man to act in a certain way, and then leave him and disap-
pear. Today we regard such forces as personifications, but Cornford
says they were no such thing to Thucydides, who thought of them as
mythical persons who acted when and as they pleased.

Certain characters and episodes in the *History* are completely
inappropriate from a realistic point of view; that they do not "fit"
their context had been noted and commented upon even in antiquity. They exist, Cornford says, to exemplify Thucydides' unconscious structuring of Athenian history so as to show Athens (the
tragic heroine) being inveigled, after initial success, into disastrous
adventures. That is, Thucydides' history is constructed on a tragic
pattern, and he is willing to forgo realism to emphasize it. The pattern is fundamentally that of Aeschylean tragedy, somewhat simpli-

fied. Its basic structural parts are a struggle that seems to be successful, followed by a dramatic reversal and then disaster.

This is a simpler pattern than that used by Murray in his analysis
of tragedy in *Themis*. One of the reasons for this is that Cornford,
unlike Murray, is not concerned with (Dionysian) ritual. He is really
conducting what might be called "second-order" myth criticism, in
that he is not analyzing tragedies according to any underlying seasonal ritual pattern, but rather proceeding from tragedy as a given
and showing how it in turn informs Thucydides' history. Therefore
he had no need to concern himself with ritual, which is relevant only
in deriving tragedy from religion.

Retrospectively, one sees *Thucydides Mythistoricus* as a dress
rehearsal for *From Religion to Philosophy* (1912), in that the early book
shows Cornford's preoccupation with the psychological and linguistic equipment of the Greeks as they attempted to found the very act
of thinking itself.

The book is dedicated to Jane Harrison, and she is quoted several
times; Cornford credits her with suggesting some corroborating evidence to be found depicted on a vase; likewise he quotes from an
unpublished lecture of Murray's. He employs the term *orenda* (the
Iroquois equivalent of *mana*), probably derived from Harrison,
along with a discussion of the Olympian gods as a superimposition
on the chthonic gods, a theory that is certainly due to her. But as yet
he does not know Durkheim—that is, he lacks a usable social psychology—so he contents himself with close textual analysis. In his
next book he will carry on this same investigation, but, armed with
Durkheim, will attempt to show *how* the Greeks moved "from religion to philosophy."

If Cornford settled down to begin explicating the connections
between religion and philosophy, Murray never got to carry out his
part of Harrison's plan concerning religion and literature. It seemed
for a time that he would, for he was asked to give the Gifford
Lectures on Natural Religion for 1908 at St. Andrews and had
announced "Ancient Religion and Modern Anthropology" as his
topic. But within six months he had accepted the Regius professorship at Oxford, and he had to withdraw from the project because of

poor health and the press of other work. He regretted the lost opportunity; Jane Harrison was devastated. In a letter to him of November 1908, she writes:

> What can I say? I had hoped the Professorship would give you more leisure for other work, not less. It is such a crushing disappointment that you should give up the Giffords that I cannot look at it with clear eyes. . . . [T]he gist of the disappointment is to me that I feel you will drift away from mythology and *origines.* You see there are only two people who are scholars and with literary minds who understand that these things are in back of everything—F. M. C. here for Cambridge and I hoped you for Oxford. The specialists don't count—they grub up the facts but don't see the relations—and it would have been so splendid that you as Professor should give those lectures. . . .[41]

Murray's other work at this time was of two kinds: translations (and theatrical productions) of Euripides, and his Lane Lectures at Harvard in 1907 on Homer, published as *The Rise of the Greek Epic.* Somewhat surprisingly, the Euripides translations, despite the fact that they are "popular" (meaning that they have only brief notes and introductions), contain nothing at all on ritual *origines.* The *Bacchae,* Euripides' most ostensibly Dionysian play, had been translated first (1904), when Murray had not yet arrived at the ritual theory, but he continued to bring out his versions one after the other and none of them has any more to say about ritual patterns than did the *Bacchae.*[42]

Although the connection between myth and anthropology to be explored in the Gifford Lectures went by the board, Murray tried to further the idea of the project in a small way when he became Regius Professor. In his inaugural lecture in 1908, called *The Interpretation of Ancient Greek Literature,*[43] he proposed several academic innovations that would broaden the scope of the students reading classics, such as exposing them to palaeography, anthropology, and other ancillary disciplines that they had previously never encountered. As it was then impossible for a student to take a degree in anthropology in either Oxford or Cambridge, this was the next best way of insinuating it into the course of study. The suggestion was received favorably, and its first fruit was the series of lectures called *Anthropology and the Classics*[44] given at Oxford that summer. The lecturers included Andrew Lang and Murray himself, but none of them is concerned with myth and ritual or the origin of tragedy.

<u>5</u>

Meanwhile, fresh discoveries were being made and new books were appearing that fundamentally influenced the work of the group. In 1906, for instance, the British archaeologist R. M. Dawkins, in Thrace to examine inscriptions, by chance happened to witness a springtime "mummers' play" that reproduced with remarkable fidelity many features of Dionysian worship as reported in ancient times. His report created a sensation because, unlike the many similar ancient and modern rites recounted by Mannhardt and Frazer, this one came from Thrace itself, the seat of Dionysian worship in antiquity.[45] It was hard not to make the evolutionary (or devolutionary) inference that this play was a survival in situ of a genuine, albeit by now degraded, rite of an ancient mystery religion: a "living fossil." The article was all the more impressive coming as it did from a scholar engaged in epigraphical research, that is, one not a partisan of the folkloristic method.

But more important was the reading that Harrison was doing. Henri Hubert and Marcel Mauss, Durkheim's principal co-workers, were publishing on magic and religion in *L' Année Sociologique* and elsewhere;[46] in philosophy Von Hügel's *Christian Mysticism* and J. A. Stewart's *Plato's Doctrine of Ideas* "impressed her deeply";[47] and in anthropology there was the Belgian Arnold Van Gennep's *Rites de Passage* (1909). But by far her most important intellectual find of those years was Henri Bergson.

Bergson has been so neglected today, at least in the English-speaking world, that it is difficult to imagine the magnitude of his reputation in the first quarter of this century. He represented the crest of the wave of vitalism that had been building over Europe throughout the latter half of the nineteenth century.[48] Jane Harrison in her memoir calls *L'Évolution Créatrice*, which she read upon its publica-

tion in 1907, one of the three epoch-making books in her intellectual life (the others being Aristotle's *Ethics* and Freud's *Totem and
Taboo*). About Bergson she says that she had gradually grown tired
of philosophy because it seemed to her

> a ceaseless shuffling of the cards, a juggling with the same glass
> balls, and then suddenly it seemed this new Moses had struck
> the rock and streams gushed forth in the desert. But I need not
> tell of an experience shared in those happy years by every
> thinking man in Europe.[49]

Bergson had a direct effect on *Themis*, for *L'Évolution Créatrice*
answered a question that had been troubling her for some time.[50] In
the introduction to *Themis* she explains that her discontent with the
Olympians finally began to come clear:

> I saw in a word that Dionysos, with every other mystery-god, was
> an instinctive attempt to express what Professor Bergson calls
> *durée*, that life which is one, indivisible and yet ceaselessly
> changing. I saw on the other hand that the Olympians . . . are
> not an intuitive expression, but a late and conscious represen-
> tation, a work of analysis, of reflection and intelligence.
> Primitive religion was not, as I had drifted into thinking, a tis-
> sue of errors leading to mistaken conduct: rather it is a web of
> practices emphasizing particular parts of life, issuing necessar-
> ily in representations and ultimately dying out in abstract con-
> ceptions.[51]

With Bergson the ingredients were all to hand for *Themis*.

Harrison had entitled her book *Prolegomena to the Study of Greek
Religion* advisedly; it was an introduction, a foray into uncharted territory. She had always had it in her mind to write a sequel of
Epilegomena, in which she would continue the work. As the months
passed after the appearance of "the fat and comely one," she grew
restive with it. She was increasingly aware of its shortcomings, and
her letters of 1905 and 1906 contain frequent references to revising
or rewriting the early book in the light of new data and new ideas.

Finally, on 7 October 1907, she wrote, in an unpublished letter to Murray, "I have today written [the first] five pages of *Epilegomena*." As it happened, *Epilegomena* would be reserved for the title of a later work, and the book she was then beginning would be called *Themis*. The four years it took her to complete *Themis* were a time of the greatest excitement and the closest collaboration among the members of the group; the climax came in 1912 when three of them produced major works: *Four Stages of Greek Religion, From Religion to Philosophy*, and *Themis*. Further, in the three years immediately following, Harrison wrote *Ancient Art and Ritual* (1913), Murray brought out *Euripides and His Age* (1913), Cornford published *The Origin of Attic Comedy* (1914), and Cook finally issued the first volume of his massive *Zeus* (1914).

The years 1912 to 1914, then, are the highwater mark of the group; within them they succeeded, by their lights, in clarifying the difficult problems that had been set for them by Harrison back in 1905 in the conclusion to *The Religion of Ancient Greece*. Harrison, Murray, and Cook had examined the nature and origins of Greek religion; Cornford and Murray had illuminated the origins of tragedy and comedy; Cornford had probed the difficult transition from religion to philosophy. The Cambridge Ritualists had accomplished their work.

Seven

Years of Achievement—1912-14

The Ritualists believed that in "collective thinking" they had a convincing explanation of the origins of Greek religion and culture, and their work attempts to illuminate the subject from several different points of view. These range from the literary-critical efforts by Murray and Cornford to argue that tragedy and comedy did indeed arise out of Dionysian ritual, to Cook's *Zeus,* in which the relations between myth-ritual and literature are analyzed from the historical, folkloristic, and linguistic perspectives. To discuss them all here, therefore, would be to lose the focus on literary criticism. So we must restrict the review to that important portion of their work from 1912 to 1914 that deals more or less directly with the origins of drama, for it is here that the "myth-and-ritual" approach was first worked out. The main documents are Jane Harrison's *Themis* (1912), with its "Excursus on the Ritual Forms Preserved in Greek Tragedy" by Murray; Cornford's *The Origin of Attic Comedy* (1914); Murray's essay "Hamlet and Orestes" (1914); and Harrison's *Ancient Art and Ritual* (1913).[1]

Since they will not be analyzed in detail, the other major works by the group dating from this period deserve at least brief notice. Cornford's *From Religion to Philosophy* (1912) explores the founding of philosophical thought by the pre-Socratics—his subject, to use Bruno Snell's title, is "The Discovery of the Mind." It is a study of the attempt on the part of these earliest thinkers to move beyond the traditional (that is, religious, myth-derived) intellectual categories, and it clearly announces the direction of Cornford's future work.

Cook's massive *Zeus*, the first volume of which appeared in 1914, is an encyclopedic account, in the compendious manner of Frazer, of *everything* pertaining to the Greek sky-god. It is, quite simply, an unreadable book. Cook has read everything (he and Frazer must have been the most erudite classicists in Cambridge), and thought freshly about everything, but he has lamentably failed in the basic task of imposing order on this material—even as much order as Frazer had managed. Like Frazer he too believed in facts for their own sakes, and Jane Harrison criticized him for not laboring hard enough to shape his material into a comprehensible whole. She makes the point clearly in a letter of 6 February 1921 to Murray, written when she was reading proof for the even more massive second part of *Zeus* that would appear ten years later; her comment applies equally to the earlier book.

> I am buried in A. B. C.'s proofs of *Zeus II.* It is teeming with brilliant discovery, far and away better than vol. I, and it will help me hugely in the plot of *Epilegomena.* . . . I send you A. B. C.'s letter because it explains though it nowise justifies his abominable neglect of plot. . . . Of course he [Cook] is utterly wrong about it being "the collection of facts that matters." The facts are dead unless they're interpreted. I wish you could persuade A. B. C. of that.[2]

"Plot" was Harrison's term for "imaginative design," and a would-be reader of *Zeus* soon understands what she is talking about. Reading *Zeus* is like listening to a brilliant though disorganized speaker. When Frazer reworked the loosely organized first edition of *The Golden Bough* into the much tighter second edition, he was helped by the relative thinness of his argument; Cook, on the other hand, was undone by the very fertility of his mind, with the result that the organizational confusion is nearly complete.

The other two major works, by Murray—*Four Stages of Greek Religion* (1912) and *Euripides and His Age* (1913)—have been excluded each for a different reason. *Four Stages* is a provisional historical reconstruction of the development of Greek religion, intended for a general audience. The early, pre-Olympian stage, in which ritual had not yet dissociated itself from myth, is covered in the first two chapters, which, Murray acknowledges in the preface, are little more than expansions of *Themis*. They are much more gracefully and clearly written than *Themis* but contain not much that is new.

One would think, however, that *Euripides and His Age* cries out for detailed treatment. A full-length study of Euripides, some of whose plays offer the best examples of ritually derived tragedy, by a critic who has studied, edited, and translated the playwright for over twenty years, and who has a radically new way of understanding the origin of tragedy: everything about the book seems to announce its importance. For all that, it is a disappointment. Perhaps because it was intended for a general audience, it does not go nearly so far as the "Excursus" in providing a closely reasoned basis for the Ritualist position; Murray instead contents himself with assertion rather than demonstration. He makes many allusions to Frazer and merely sketches (in about ten pages) his theory of the origin of tragedy from Dionysian ritual, which is entirely inadequate for so very novel an approach to tragedy in general and Euripides in particular.

Aside from the overall argumentative strategy, there are curious omissions in detail as well. For instance, Murray notes in his discussion of *The Suppliants* that the play opens with a scene of supplication before an altar. But that is all he says of the scene—he does not even remark, as he had in the "Excursus," that the scene has a ritual basis. And indeed the analysis of this play, as well as many others, contains nothing about ritual at all.

But odder still is the frequent and intrusive presence of a rationalistic tone that would suit Frazer but is surprising in Murray. One does not get in this book, as one does everywhere in Jane Harrison's work, a sense of the terror and darkness of the chthonic cultus; instead Murray speaks of the Athenians' "superstitions." An example: Murray has been (over-)emphasizing the importance of philosophy in the fifth century, and he says that despite the great intellectual and moral advances found in the work of the great thinkers of the time, most Greeks never stopped practicing "the silliest and cruelest old agricultural magic."[3] Such a culture-bound (and irrelevant) judgment calls into question the rest of his interpretation as well.

Finally, although one hesitates to doubt his fundamental understanding of the relation between ritual and literature, the analogy made to the *Bacchae* in the following passage misses the point completely.

> Let us imagine a great free-minded modern poet—say Swinburne or Morris or Victor Hugo, all of whom did great things—making from some local anniversary a rhymed play in the style of the Mysteries on some legend of a mediaeval saint. The saint, let us suppose, is very meek and is cruelly persecuted by a wicked emperor, whom he threatens with hell fire; and at the end let us have the emperor in the midst of that fire and the saint in glory saying, "What did I tell you?" And let us suppose that the play in its course gives splendid opportunities for solemn Latin hymns, such as Swinburne and Hugo delighted in. We should probably have a result something like the *Bacchae*.[4]

It seems to me that in such a case we should have nothing at all like the *Bacchae*, for one important reason: Euripides in his use of myth was unselfconscious in a way that modern writers can never be and never have been. This is true without getting into the difficult question of Euripides' own religious beliefs. For whatever his real position was—atheism or rationalism or severely qualified belief— Dionysian myth and ritual were in his bones in the way, say, that the belief in progress, whether consciously espoused or not, was in the bones of anyone born in the West in the latter half of the nineteenth century. It is difficult to think of an analogy that would be exactly right, but Euripides' use of myth is perhaps comparable to Cervantes' use of the literature of chivalry in *Don Quixote*; Dionysus was probably closer and more "available" to Euripides than chivalry was to Cervantes, but in both cases the relation between author and subject was complex; in neither case was there an effort at literary antiquarianism, as implied in Murray's example. Indeed, as we know today from the considerable number of twentieth-century writers who have attempted to use myths directly or indirectly, the aesthetic distance necessarily implied by literary archaeology seems to vitiate the power of the myth.

Having sketched these more or less peripheral works, let us turn to the books and essays that embody the heart of myth criticism. It is only fitting that we begin with the most important work of all: *Themis.*

1. *Themis*

In 1904 Cornford and Harrison traveled together to Athens to attend the Third International Congress of Religions. On the way back they stopped off in Crete, where they were shown some of the finds of the most recent campaign at Palaikastro by the British archaeologist R. C. Bosanquet. One of them was a stele containing the text of a ritual hymn to Zeus, dating from the second or third century A.D. (but the text was assumed to be much older), the so-called "hymn of the *kouretes*," discovered in what was probably a temple of Diktaean Zeus. The hymn had several puzzling features: it is addressed to Zeus as the greatest of the *kouretes* (young men), and he is described as having a band of *kouretes* with him, whereas Zeus is nearly always unaccompanied and is not usually pictured as a youth. The hymn describes what the singers, the *kouretes*, are doing: dancing for fertility and plenty and "for goodly Themis."[5] Harrison was struck by the strange text; the hymn stayed in her mind for the next three years, teasing her but not revealing its meaning. When she finally understood it, she wrote *Themis.* The dancing *kouretes* are to *Themis* as the "king of the wood" is to *The Golden Bough*; both books are ostensibly written to explain the meaning of curious rituals, and references to the rituals are important motifs in both texts.

Themis is a difficult book; its argument is complex and to a nonspecialist sometimes opaque. Moreover, it teems with ideas that make one sit back and ponder before reading on. Characteristically, *Themis* is not a neat book; one feels that much of it is a splendid improvisation, thrown off in the heat of inspiration.[6]

Fortunately, Harrison has done the job of analysis for us. Her introductions to the two editions (the second, issued in 1927, is virtually identical to the first) and the long analytical table of contents provide an admirable entrée to the "plot" and its author's intentions.

The introduction to the first edition begins in the typical Harrisonian manner: she approaches her book by way of its origins, explaining how it arose from *Prolegomena* and how it differs from that book. In 1907 Cambridge University Press asked her to prepare a new edition of *Prolegomena*. But by that time Murray had come out with *The Rise of the Greek Epic,* which had shown how Homer represented a smoothing out of the old rough divinities into a more "civilized"—in short, Olympian—form. Her sense of the superficiality of Homer's gods had by then become so deep, she says, that she no longer felt them to have any religious content at all, as opposed to the mystery cults of Dionysus and Orpheus, which seemed genuinely and deeply religious. "I was therefore compelled reluctantly to face the question, what meaning did I attach to the word religion?"[7]

In this connection here are her words from the introduction to the second edition. Having stated that the book is a study of group-thinking, she says: "Its object is the analysis of the Eniautos- or Year Daimon, who lies behind each and every primitive god; of the Eniautos- Daimon and his ritual. That the gods and rituals are examined are Greek are incidental to my own specialism" (vii). In other words, despite the fact that *Themis* is subtitled "A Study of the Social Origins of Greek Religion," its author is really proposing a general theory of the origins of religion. The book is thus analogous to Freud's *Totem and Taboo* (1913), in that both attempt to isolate and explain some universal mechanism—one sociological, the other psychological—that accounts for the origins of religion.[8]

In answering the question of the meaning of religion she acknowledges help from two sources in particular: Bergson and Durkheim. They enabled her to understand why Dionysus, the expression of *durée*, was always accompanied by a *thiasos*, a band of worshipers. She came to understand that this was not arbitrary iconographic convention but expressive of his deepest nature.

> The mystery-god arises out of these instincts, emotions, and desires, which attend and express life; but these emotions, desires, instincts, insofar as they are religious, are at the outset rather of a group than an individual consciousness. . . . [T]he

form taken by the divinity reflects the social structure of the group to which the divinity belongs. (xi)

Having now exposed these underlying assumptions concerning Dionysus, Harrison introduces her master idea as she proceeds to her argument proper. This is the notion of initiation, derived from Arnold Van Gennep's *Rites de passage* (1909). Zeus as the greatest *kouros* who is invoked in the Palaikastro hymn is *not* the Homeric father of the gods but (only) the projection of the group of dancing worshipers. (In other words, he is not yet a god at all but rather what she will call a group-daimon.) They are dancing a re-enactment of the initiation rite, or *dromenon* (the "thing done"), of the entrance into manhood. When the boy is initiated into the tribe, his "soul is congregationalized," to quote a phrase of Verrall's that she often repeats.[9] And this greatest *kouros* is the embodiment or personification or projection of the group life of the *thiasos*.

Next comes an analysis of the *dromenon* ceremony, because the religious idea of a *daimon* arises from the nature of a *dromenon*. "The *dromenon* in its sacral sense is, not merely a thing done, but a thing redone, or pre-done with magical intent. The magical dance of the *Kouretes* is a primitive form of *dromenon*, it commemorates or anticipates, in order magically to induce a New Birth." And now, importantly for literary criticism, "The Dithyramb, from which the drama arose, was also a *dromenon* of the New Birth. In the drama then we may expect to find survivals of a ritual akin to that of the *Kouretes*. Further, the *dromenon* is a thing which, like the drama, is collectively performed. Its basis . . . is a *thiasos* or *choros*" (xv).

A long analysis of the sacrificial rites performed at the leading Athenian festivals shows them all to be versions of the seasonal *dromenon*. "In Greece the chief seasonal *dromenon* seems to have been in spring; its object, the magical inducement of fresh life, for man, for other animals and for plants" (xvi). From these spring *dromena* arose two important Greek cultural institutions: athletic games, the most important of which were the Olympics; and the drama (whose name of course indicated its origins in *dromena*). This is the *raison d'être* for the chapter on the origin of the Olympic Games, by

Cornford, and the "Excursus on the Ritual Forms Preserved in Greek Drama," by Murray, showing how tragedy reveals its origins in spring *dromena*.

This spring *dromenon* is "conceived of as a conflict, a dramatic setting forth of the natural happening of the spring. This drama might with equal appropriateness be represented as Death followed by a Rebirth or as a contest followed by a victory" (xvi). She then introduces a new term, "*Eniautos-Daimon*," or Year-spirit. The Eniautos-Daimon is the group *daimon*, or spirit, who incarnates the "'luck' of the year." Although in ritual (or drama) he may bear the name of a particular hero, he is remembered as a "functionary [rather] than as [an] individual personality" (xvii). She explains that she has coined "Eniautos-Daimon" on the analogy of Mannhardt's and Frazer's "Corn-spirit" or "Vegetation-Spirit." Those terms are inadequate, however, because they are insufficiently comprehensive. The Eniautos-Daimon is the incarnation not only of vegetation "but [of] the whole world-process of decay, death, renewal."

Returning to drama and tragedy, one should say that Murray's "Excursus" was written not only to show the origins of tragedy in the spring *dromena*, but also to counter the views advanced by William Ridgeway in 1910 in *The Origin of Tragedy*. For just as *Themis* represented for Harrison the culmination of the work of many years, so *The Origin of Tragedy* did for Ridgeway. And as their ideas had diverged more and more, this question of tragic origins had become the principal intellectual contention between them, although, as noted, it was embittered by personal and political differences as well. From at least as early as 1904 Ridgeway had been lecturing on the subject. Thus we find Harrison writing, in an unpublished letter to Murray on 2 March 1904:

> It is most interesting, that [Euripides'] Hecuba "finds her prayer" when she turns to the dead. In Prof. Ridgeway's last lecture (he is to give it again at the Hellenic [Society] and you *must* come) he tries to show that drama arose from ritual and he instanced the end of the *Choephori*, and this [Hecuba] is a similar case.

That is, Harrison and Ridgeway agreed that drama arose from ritual—the question was *which* ritual. In 1904 she had not yet arrived at
the spring *dromenon* as the paradigm; Ridgeway was saying that it
arose from funerary ritual, primarily dances performed around the
tombs of heroes in the course of the ancestor cult.[10] As evidence he
adduced the passage from Herodotus (5:67–68) that tells how the
tyrant Cleisthenes, out of revenge,

> took away the sacrifices and festivals from Adrastus [the local
> hero of Sicyon] and gave them to Melanippus. Now the
> Sicyonians had been accustomed to honour Adrastus magnifi-
> cently. . . . The Sicyonians honoured Adrastus, not only in other
> respects, but with "tragic dances alluding to his sorrows," not
> honouring Dionysus, but rather Adrastus.[11]

This means, said Ridgeway, that the "tragic dances" were not
exclusively Dionysian in character—for the cult of Dionysus had not
yet been introduced into Sicyon—but honored a local hero instead.
Thus, arguing euhemeristically, Ridgeway claimed that tragedy (and
athletic contests as well) began in animistic ritual as attempts to placate the souls of dead men who had been famous in the locality.

It is unclear how thoroughly Ridgeway had developed his thesis
in these early lectures, but it is certain that his theory had been
funerary and euhemeristic from the start. So that when Harrison
and Murray began to develop their Dionysian and then Eniautos-
Daimon theories in 1908 and 1909, the issue was fairly and sharply
joined. The unpublished letters of 1908 and thereafter have as a
constant refrain the conflicts between Harrison and Ridgeway on
tragic ritual and women's equality. In a letter that can be dated (by
Jessie Stewart) no more precisely than 1909, she writes: "next week
I launch into a brand-new chapter [in *Themis*] on heroes—and daemons—it is all anti-animistic. I shall want you over it so dreadfully. I
have been goaded to it by Ridgeway's last utterances." And another
unpublished letter (26 May 1910): "I also think and hope that the
[discussion in *Themis* of the] Dithyramb will make hay of Ridgeway's
priority of the tomb-hero business, but on this point I want your
decision."

So there can be no doubt that *Themis* was intended as part of the polemic she and her friends were waging against Ridgeway, and by extension, all that he stood for: euhemerism, denial of women's rights, and closed-mindedness in general. In her gracious note in the introduction to the second edition, written just after Ridgeway had died, she calls him "the protantagonist of the Eniautos-Diamon, . . . who had gone where the noise of battle is for ever hushed" (viii). She and her friends must have thought of themselves as incarnations of the Eniautos-Daimon engaged in the recurrent and necessary battle with the forces of the past, the forces of death. Admittedly such thoughts must have been felt to be as fanciful as they in fact are, but it is impossible for persons as imaginative as Harrison and Murray not to have seen their own lives in these mythic terms.

Ridgeway did not deny the existence of the Dionysian element in tragedy but held it to be a secondary elaboration of what had originally been obsequies to a departed hero. As the testimony of Herodotus was undeniable, Harrison was obliged to analyze the meaning of the hero. Not surprisingly, for her the hero turns out to be none other than the Eniautos-Daimon, who is not a historical individual at all but a group manifestation or "functionary." The fact that Cleisthenes was able to transfer the "tragic dances alluding to his sorrows" from Adrastus to someone else shows that heroes, like Dionysus, are examples of the Year-Spirit. Further, it shows that "the ritual of the Eniautos-Daimon is substantially the same as the ceremony of death and resurrection enacted as a rite of tribal initiation" (xviii-xix). And true to the evolutionary doctrine of survivals, "This ritual with its attendant *mythos* lives on in the Mummers' Play and Carnival festivals still performed at spring time all over modern Europe."[12] In Athens uniquely the spring *dromena* was united with the epic stories to produce the tragic drama.

2. "Excursus on the Ritual Forms Preserved in Greek Tragedy"

Logically, then, we are led to Murray's "Excursus," which explains the relation between Homer, who supplied the tragedians with their plots, and the spring-*dromenon* of the Eniautos-Daimon, which determined the form of the tragedy. Because this is the first example of "myth-and-ritual" criticism, it seems reasonable to recapitulate Murray's arguments fully, both because of their intrinsic interest and because they provide a procedural model for later work.[13]

Murray begins by stating his assumptions concerning the origins and nature of tragedy. These, he says, are shared by most other anthropologically inclined scholars, like Farnell and Ridgeway. They are that tragedy originated as a "Ritual Dance, a Sacer Ludus, representing normally the Aition, or supposed historical cause, of some current ritual practice" (341). Further, in accordance with unanimous ancient tradition, this dance is Dionysian, performed in his cultus by his priests and worshipers. And further, that Dionysus is here to be thought of as the local Greek type of the Eniautos-Daimon, who is also exemplified in other deities like Attis, Osiris, and Adonis. And lastly, that comedy and tragedy are related in that they are different stages in the career of the daimon: "Comedy leads to his *komos* and *gamos*, Tragedy to his death and *threnos*" (341). This discussion is devoted solely to tragedy; the reader interested in the ritual derivation of comedy is directed to Cornford's *Origin of Attic Comedy.*

Murray notes that the eminent German scholars Hermann Usener and Albrecht Dieterich had argued recently that "a characteristic of the Sacer Ludus in the mysteries was a Peripeteia, or Reversal" (342). This turning point came when the darkness yielded to light and the doleful initiate discovered that the dead god was in fact resurrected. Such a peripeteia is thus in fact a kind of Anagnorisis, or discovery. Peripeteia is a normal constituent of any good story, but the reason it is associated by Aristotle with Anagnorisis (which is not a necessary ingredient of any story) as normal constituents of tragedy must be because of their ritual associations in the Sacer Ludus.

He then takes up Ridgeway's assertion that tragedy originated in local ancestor cult by turning to the passage in Herodotus in which the tragic choruses celebrating the god's sufferings were transferred to Adrastus. Murray asks what these sufferings were and answers that ancient testimony is silent on this matter because it was taboo to mention what really happened to the god. But through Herodotus' equation of Dionysus with Osiris, and then through his descriptions of Osiris' rites, we know that Dionysus was fated to undergo a *sparag-mos*—dismemberment—his body scattered over the fields, mourned for, and then recognized as come to life again.

Thus when we examine the generalized myth of the Eniautos-Daimon—that is, all the examples of the type, the evidence for which is conveniently brought together in Frazer—we find the following six stages:

1. An *Agon* or Contest, the Year against its enemy, Light against Darkness, Summer against Winter.
2. A *Pathos* of the Year-Daimon, generally a ritual or sacrificial death, in which Adonis or Attis is slain by the tabu animal, the Pharmakos stoned, Osiris, Dionysus, Pentheus, Orpheus, Hippolytus torn to pieces (*sparagmos*).
3. A *Messenger.* For this Pathos seems seldom or never to be actually performed before the audience. (The reason for this is not hard to suggest, and was actually necessary in the time when there was only one actor.) It is announced by a messenger. . . . This leads to
4. A *Threnos* or Lamentation. Specially characteristic, however, is a clash of contrary emotions, the death of the old being also the triumph of the new. . . .
5. and 6. An *Anagnorisis*—discovery or recognition—of the slain and mutilated Daimon, followed by his Resurrection or Apotheosis or, in some sense, his Epiphany in glory. This I shall call by the general name *Theophany.* It naturally goes with a Peripeteia or extreme change in feeling from grief to joy. (343–44)

Before going further, however, he must deal with one difficulty that threatens the whole inquiry: the Dionysian ritual ends in "a special final Peripeteia, from grief to joy, in connection with the Anagnorisis and Theophany" (344). But tragedies, though they may end "with a comforting Theophany," are sad. Murray's ingenious explanation lies in the well-known fact that tragedies were presented as trilogies, followed by an obligatory satyr-play. It was this fourth play that contained the happy ending. "The Satyr-play, coming at the end of the tetralogy, represented the joyous arrival of the Reliving Dionysus and his rout of attendant daimones at the end of the Sacer Ludus" (344).

But early in the development of the drama the satyr-play became differentiated from tragedy, and furthermore, the tragic trilogy began to be understood not as a unit but as three separate plays. This gave rise, says Murray, to two problems. The first was whether the tragic poet should finish his trilogy and depend on the increasingly irrelevant satyr-play to supply the theophany, or whether each tragedy should contain its own theophany. Murray answers that both types exist, but that the second kind is more prevalent. The second problem was "what is to happen to the Anagnorisis and Peripeteia?" Structurally they function as transition from the tragic threnos to the satyric theophany; "if anything, they go rather with the Satyrs." The result is that "these two elements are set loose. Quite often, even in the tragedies which have a full Theophany, they do not occur in their proper place just before the Theophany, yet they always continue to haunt the atmosphere. The poets find it hard to write without bringing in an Anagnorisis somewhere" (345).

These words of Murray's deserve comment, for it is just this kind of statement that attracted his opponents' sharpest attacks. Murray is saying that although tragedy derives from a Dionysian ritual, it doesn't really resemble the ritual as closely as it might—indeed, in some cases, not very closely at all. And he "explains" this variation from what is admittedly an inferred, hypothetical paradigm by imagining solutions to artistic problems that arise only when this pattern is postulated in the first place. Those who sympathize with this view see Murray's words as disarming criticism; those who regard the eniautos-daimon hypothesis as nonsense seize upon these "disarming" remarks and use them against Murray with what they conceive to be devastating effect. Thus Arthur Pickard-Cambridge, who composed the most detailed criticism of Murray and the Ritualists, spends many pages asking Murray why most tragedies do not conform to the agon-pathos-messenger-threnos-anagnorisis-peripeteia pattern. Murray's anticipation of these criticisms was to no avail.

In any event, Murray then turns to his three prize exhibits—three tragedies that display the pattern in its fully developed form, with all elements intact. Predictably, these plays are by Euripides—the *Bacchae*, the *Hippolytus*, and the *Andromache*. The *Bacchae*, perhaps because it is about Dionysus, is the clearest example of all. The only problem is that Pentheus, and not Dionysus, suffers the *sparagmos*, and is torn apart by the Bacchantes. But here, per the eniautos-daimon theory, "Pentheus is only another form of Dionysus himself" (346), so that this substitution is unimportant. Murray concludes: "The *Bacchae* is a most instructive instance of the formation of drama out of ritual. It shows us how slight a step [only the Pentheus-Dionysus substitution] was necessary for Thespis or another to turn the Year-Ritual into real drama" (346). This last statement is important for it implies that at least the early tragedians were *consciously* working with a ritual, not a theatrical, form.

The *Hippolytus* is "just one step further [than the *Bacchae*] from the original ritual." Hippolytus was of course another avatar of the year-spirit who suffers the fate of *sparagmos* and then resurrection. But here Hippolytus the hero is a mortal who dies at the end of the play, and the god who appears is not an eniautos-daimon but Artemis. To save the phenomena Murray must point to Hippolytus' resurrection in legend, and he hypothesizes an *ur-Hippolytus* in which the apotheosis was part of the dramatic action: "When we remember the resurrection of Hippolytus in legend, we shall suspect that in an earlier form of the Hippolytus-*dromenon* there may have been a resurrection or apotheosis of the hero himself together with his protectress Artemis. Drama has gained ground upon ritual" (340).

The *Andromache* departs even further from the pattern, in that "the persons are all varied: it is Peleus and Menelaus who have the contest; it is Neoptolemus who is slain and mourned; it is Thetis who appears as divine." Such thoroughgoing substitution, which "is certainly very curious," is explicable because the real death of Dionysus was unmentionable and, though it perforce had to be shown, could only be presented by indirection. "It may well be, for instance, that when Drama became public entertainment rather than religious celebration, objection was felt to an actual public mention or representation of the God's death."

The historian of literary criticism today, with the benefit of hindsight, finds in this kind of explanation a naive form of Northrop Frye's statements concerning the potential convertibility and equivalence in the realm of myth of literally everything. The important difference between Murray and Frye (who acknowledges his debt to the Ritualists) is that the former is still attempting to reconstruct a historical movement from myth to literature, whereas the latter does not fall into that "trap" but makes his argument formal, psychological, and ahistorical.[14]

Murray then proceeds to take up the several ritual components of the Sacer Ludus—agon, pathos, etc.—and examines each tragedy (and most of the fragments), noting whether and to what extent it embodies ritual form. If the *Bacchae*, *Hippolytus*, and *Andromache* depart from the ritual model, then *a fortiori* the other plays will show even more differences. Murray implies that we are to regard them in the light of variations upon a theme—that is, the similarities and not the deviations are to be understood as significant.

The theophany, "the most crucial" of the ritual structures, comes first. Murray finds that of Aeschylus' five extant tragedies, "two end with a final epiphany, one has a grand epiphany in each play [of the trilogy], one is uncertain but most likely had a grand final appearance of Zeus in state; one ends with a Threnos" (349). The Aeschylean fragments likewise reveal many other hints of epiphanies. He sums up the findings for Aeschylus:

> But it can hardly be disputed that in a surprising number of Aeschylus' tragedies we have found signs of either a definite epiphany of a god or the resurrection of a dead hero, or lastly the direct worship of a Year-Daimon. We cannot be certain, but we may surmise that some such epiphany of resurrection was quite as common in Aeschylus as in Euripides (351).

After examining all of Euripides' plays, Murray concludes "that the tragedies of Euripides usually end with a Theophany of a markedly formal and ritual character, closely suiting our conception of the Sacer Ludus of Dionysus as daimon of the Year-Cycle of death and rebirth. . . ." (353). Of interest in the discussion of Euripides is

Murray's statement, concerning those tragedies that do *not* end with the manifestation of a god:

> It is not part of my case to argue that all plays necessarily con-
> form to the same type. The sacer ludus of a Torch-race, like the
> Prometheia, or the sacer ludus of some particular Altar of
> Sanctuary like the various Suppliant Plays, has no particular
> reason for conforming to the scheme of the Dionysus-play,
> except the influence of custom and analogy. But we shall find
> even in these plays which have no obvious Theophanies some
> curious traces of the Theophany-form (352).

This is a remarkable admission, for if the Dionysian sacer ludus is only one member of a class of such sacred rituals, then the resemblances between distinctively *Dionysian* ritual and overall tragic form are merely fortuitous and imply no necessary connection between Dionysian cultus and tragic origins. This seems to undercut the basic argument, but Murray makes the statement casually and moves on immediately to other matters.

He turns to the first four ritual elements—agon, pathos, messenger scene, and threnos. First Euripides, the most formal of the tragedians in Murray's view, is canvassed, and most of his plays are shown to exemplify some or all of these ritual forms. Aeschylus is next, and his plays too yield their by now expected number of ritual resemblances.

But where has Sophocles been all this time? After discussing epiphanies in Aeschylus' fragments Murray purposely omits those of Sophocles: "the evidence would take very long to state" (351). It is not clear what this lengthy evidence is, nor what it is evidence for. But he does say that Sophocles, in regard to epiphanies as in everything else,

> is influenced more by the Ionian Epic and less by the Attic
> Sacer Ludus than the other two tragedians. It is just the same
> with the other forms. Sophocles deliberately blurs his outlines
> and breaks up his Agon and Messenger and Prologue into what
> we may almost call continuous dramatic conversation;

Euripides returns to an extreme clarity and articulateness and stiffness of form in all three (351).

And sure enough, when Murray does get to Sophocles' complete plays, they do not submit to the ritual pattern as readily as those of their illustrious peers.

Murray next takes up the prologue, which, in Aeschylus, grew first in the direction of drama, and then turned aside toward a definite religious form. He traces the history of the prologue from no exposition scene at all in the early plays to a simple prologue in the mouth of a single speaker to its completion as a dramatically realized expository scene involving two or more characters in the last tragedies of Aeschylus. Sophocles shows only the fully realized exposition, and seems to have been working toward a further development of the scene, which we see in Euripides. Noting the recurrence of women suppliants before an altar in Euripides' prologues, Murray finds that the prologue, having begun as a simple lead-in to the action to be presented (in Aeschylus), has become in Euripides "a solemn address spoken to the audience by a sacred or mysterious figure." The prologue is in Euripides completely integrated into the overall action, and it has "been markedly influenced by the speech of the god at the end" (362). The other ritual elements of the drama show the same course of development, with Sophocles marking a relaxation, a movement toward "naturalness" and away from the Aeschylean ritual stiffness, and Euripides marking a return to a more highly developed form of the underlying ritual structures.

Murray concludes the "Excursus" with the following paragraph:

An outer shape dominated by tough and undying tradition, an inner life fiery with sincerity and spiritual freedom; the vessels of a very ancient religion overfilled and broken by the new wine of reasoning and rebellious humanity, and still, in their rejection, shedding abroad the old aroma, as of eternal and mysterious things: these are the fundamental paradoxes presented to us by Greek Tragedy. The contrasts have their significance for other art also, perhaps for all great art. But aesthetic criticism is not the business of the present note (362–63).

So concludes Murray. What is the reader today to say? In making our comments we should bear in mind that this "Excursus," Cornford's analogous treatment of comedy which derives from it, and Murray's essay "Hamlet and Orestes," to be examined next, are the sole attempts at detailed demonstration made by the first generation of Ritualists. They constitute the theoretical and methodological foundation for all future criticism that seeks to expose mythic or ritual patterns underlying literature. It is to these essays that, for instance, Francis Fergusson refers when he writes, in *The Idea of a Theater*:

> They all [several leading twentieth-century critics], I think, assume that notion of drama which we owe to the Cambridge School of Classical Anthropologists. Cornford, Harrison, Murray, and others of this school have given us a new understanding of Greek tragedy by demonstrating its roots in myth and ritual, its implication for the whole culture of its time.[15]

Or Herbert Muller, in *The Spirit of Tragedy*:

> Aristotle informs us that tragedy grew out of the Dithyramb, sung in honor of the god Dionysus. Murray and other English scholars developed the thesis, by now widely accepted, that the rites of Dionysus in turn grew out of the prehistoric ritual of the Year-Daemon, who annually died and was reborn.[16]

Putting to one side the fact that the thesis was never "widely accepted," let us describe Murray's methods and conclusions. First of all, they are inferential, for the very good reason that there is little hard evidence on which to build a case. There is Aristotle's statement in the *Poetics* about tragedy arising out of the dithyramb, and a few other scattered notices in other authors—all writing centuries after tragedy began, in whatever fashion it did begin. Then there are the plays and fragments. So it was in Murray's day, and so it is today. Therefore, barring some miraculous find comparable to the Dead Sea Scrolls, any theory about dramatic origins must be largely guesswork.

Murray, however, is making a historical argument; he is trying to trace the development of tragedy from a real ritual that did exist in prehistoric Greece. That is, his argument would fall could it be shown that tragedy had some other origin—say, in a non-Dionysian ritual, or in no ritual at all. In this sense he is correct in stating that his essay is not aesthetic criticism. And yet his argument is not completely free of aesthetic judgments. For example, he seems to value Euripides at least partly because he reverted, with "extreme clarity and articulateness" (351), to Aeschylean forms, that is, to tragedy in which the contours of the underlying ritual are clearly visible. Conversely, Sophocles is to some extent devalued for representing precisely the opposite development from the Aeschylean model. This tendency is better illustrated in another piece of writing Murray did at about this time. Somewhat surprisingly he left off translating Euripides and turned to Sophocles; his version of *Oedipus the King* appeared in 1911. In the introduction to that edition he writes:

> It seems to me that Sophocles was feeling his way towards a technique which would have approached that of the New Comedy or even the Elizabethan stage, and would perhaps have done without a Chorus altogether. In Aeschylus Greek tragedy had been a thing of traditional forms and clear-cut divisions; the religious ritual showed through, and the visible gods and the disguised dancers were allowed their full value. And Euripides in the matter of outward formalism went back to the Aeschylean type and even beyond it: prologue, chorus, messenger, visible god, all the traditional forms were left clear-cut and undisguised and all developed to full effectiveness on separate and specific lines. But Sophocles worked by blurring his structural outlines just as he blurs the ends of his verses. In him the traditional divisions are all made less distinct, all worked over in the direction of greater naturalness, at any rate in externals. This was a very great gain, but of course some price had to be paid for it. Part of the price was that Sophocles could never attempt the tremendous choric effects which Euripides achieves in such plays as the *Bacchae* and the *Trojan Women*.[17]

Some of the literary-critical possibilities of arguing from mythic originals begin to appear in Murray's remark about the "price" Sophocles paid for moving away from ritual form. It should be admitted, however, that one's perceptions of the critical tendencies implicit in this "Excursus" are strongly influenced by hindsight, by our knowledge of the direction taken by myth-and-ritual criticism in the years that followed. More important here than this subtle bias in Murray's method of argument—and the bias is not at all subtle in other of his writings to be examined—is the larger question of the validity of historical arguments altogether. We are today much more sophisticated than were writers of Murray's day concerning critical method, and modern critics have paid a good deal of attention to the kind of genetic fallacy relevant here—the sort that confounds origins with essences. If Murray is right, then he has *at most* described the way tragedy arose, not what it is or became. Because tragedy may have begun in a fertility ritual, it does not follow that it is therefore "essentially" magical. Post-1945 myth critics especially have fallen into this error, seeing in ritual not only the origins but the "heart" of tragedy as well. And such modern writers have tended to value ritually based art precisely because of its ritual origins.[18]

3. *The Origin of Attic Comedy*

In the light of Murray's "Excursus," we may analyze Cornford's *The Origin of Attic Comedy* in less detail. This seems sensible for two reasons, despite the fact that the "Excursus" is a relatively brief essay whereas Cornford's study is a full-length book: (1) *The Origin of Attic Comedy* is a derivative work. More accurately, Cornford says in his preface that he had already begun a book on Aristophanic comedy but scrapped it in the light of Murray's "Excursus." Restudying the plays in that light, he says he was forced to conclude that the anomalous features of the Old Comedy could be explained only by postulating the paradox that comedy and tragedy have the same ritual source. He therefore completely rewrote the book to offer an argument for the origin of comedy correlative to that of Murray's for tragedy. (2) As might then be expected, the methods and findings of Cornford and Murray are generally similar. There is, however, a good deal of new material in Cornford—especially the last chapter, on the relations between comedy and tragedy—and we shall emphasize that.

Cornford begins by noting the strange form of Aristophanes' comedy, especially the way the choral *parabasis* acts to cut the play in two. In the first part he distinguishes several typical features: the prologue, the entrance of the chorus (*parodos*), and the *agon*, "the fierce 'contest' between the representatives of two parties or principles, which are in effect the hero and villain of the whole piece."[19] In the second part, which contemporary scholarship saw as a stringing together of bawdy and burlesque, Cornford finds several other features no less characteristic than those noted in the first part: "a festal procession (*Komos*) and a union which I shall call a 'Marriage'. . . ." Further, there are "two other standing incidents which fall between the Agon and the final Komos—a scene of Sacrifice and a Feast" (3). The paradigmatic plot, therefore, would be agon, sacrifice, feast, marriage komos. Cornford's hypothesis is that this "*canonical plot-formula preserves the stereotyped action of a ritual or folk drama, older than literary Comedy, and of a pattern well known to us from other sources*" (3; italics Cornford's).

The first part of the work concludes with a typology of motifs or themes in the old fertility ritual. These, familiar to readers of *The Golden Bough*, are (1) the carrying out and destruction of death, or evil; (2) the seasonal battle between summer and winter; (3) the analogous conflict between the young king and his old predecessor; (4) death and resurrection, as in the Dionysian ritual already adduced by Murray as the type of tragic ritual. Modern survivals— the mummers' plays, to be found all over Europe (at least until 1914), and the folk play in modern Greece that resembles Dionysian ritual—are invoked, as well as parallels from ancient Greece.

The ritual pattern having been established, in ideal form, from ethnography, Cornford then turns to Aristophanes. Each constituent element of the Old Comedy—the agon, the sacrifice and feast, the exodos, the chorus, the phallic songs—is taken up. And each is shown to exist, in a clear or attenuated form, in most or all of the comedies, and of course the general plot of each play is interpreted in a ritual light.

In addition, Cornford extends his inquiry beyond the analysis of plays as separate entities and attempts to establish a full character typology for comedy based on Aristotle's work in this area. It will be recalled[20] that Aristotle isolates three comic types: the buffoon (*bomolochos*), the ironist (*eiron*), and the impostor (*alazon*). Cornford shows that the *bomolochos* and the *eiron* are really two aspects of the same character, who is set over against the *alazon*. Thus there are, in his analysis, but two main comic character types: the impostor and the composite ironical buffoon, who is the hero. This impostor, in Aristophanes, has three essential characteristics: "(1) he interrupts the sacrifice or wedding-feast, and claims a share of the fruits of the Agonist's [i.e., the hero's] victory; (2) he has a vaunting, boastful, swaggering disposition; (3) he is regularly mocked, beaten, or otherwise mishandled, and driven away" (148). Given these traits, "we naturally look for further light to Dionysiac myth and ritual, where I believe, we shall find the figure we seek to identify" (148).

As Dionysian ritual had more than one form, Cornford selects the variant that best suits his purposes. This is the plot in which the god and his adversary are separate and distinct, but in which the antagonist is nevertheless a doublet of the god himself. The reason this version exists is that the rites were originally cannibalistic, climaxing in the eating of the dismembered god, who was first represented by a human being or a totemic animal. But "as civilisation gains over barbarism," the worshipers ask why the god must die. And they respond to this seemingly unnecessary death by splitting the god in two, with one of his aspects becoming a devil who kills the beneficent god. From this evolution of religious sensibility, we get the figure of the Enemy, or Devil, who comes to the same end as the dying god himself, as a result of the desire for vengeance on the part of the worshipers. This Enemy, or Antagonist, has all the features of the *alazon* or impostor noted earlier: "(1) He disturbs and outrages the rites which no profane eye should see. (2) He vaunts his insolent authority in boasts, whose vanity the power of the God will expose. (3) He is set at nought, beaten, blinded, torn to pieces, cast out, or like the Titans, blasted to ashes" (149).

The impostor now fits easily into the ritual scenario. In its serious form he is the interloper whose fate is a grim reminder of what happens to all those who approach the sacred mysteries in a profane spirit: Pentheus in the *Bacchae* is the best example. But "where the drama degenerated into a popular mummery, the incident [his scourging] would give an inviting opening for horseplay" (152). This figure and recurrent plot are seen as well in noncomic legends (for example, those concerning Perseus) and fairy tales. And the theme passed "from Tragedy to the New Comedy and thence into the long tradition of romance. . . ." (153).[21]

Thus far Cornford has more or less recapitulated, *mutatis mutandis*, Murray's argument in the "Excursus." He breaks new ground in his continuation of the analysis of character types by taking up the stock masks worn in comedy. He distinguishes the following types among those Aristophanic characters who bear the names of historical personages: the swashbuckler, or *miles gloriosus* (Lamachus, Aeschylus), the learned doctor (Socrates, Euripides), the cook or sausage-seller (Agoracritus), and the parasite (Cleon). In addition he discerns several other types based on age and sex: the old man and the young man, the old woman and the young woman. Cornford then asks how is this group of characters to be explained. The remarkableness of their stability as types and their recurrence in play after play is heightened when one notes that the mummers' plays and the modern Greek folk plays contain exactly the same *dramatis personae*. The answer is that "they are the set [of masks] required for the fertility drama of the marriage which is interrupted by the death and revival of the hero" (188).

Cornford explains that the young man and the old man are the New and Old Years. The swaggering soldier corresponds to the blusterer in the mummers' plays who kills the groom. The doctor brings him back to life, or else the cook rejuvenates him. The young woman is the bride in the marriage that follows his resuscitation. The old woman is a remnant of an old ritual scene, which dropped out of literary comedy—she is the Mother of the Divine Child. She survives as the amorous hag in Aristophanes. With the addition of the parasite, these ritual types constitute the stock masks for Aristophanes' historically based characters.

The most interesting section, both inherently and because it marks a real extension of Murray's argument, is the discussion of the relations between comedy and tragedy. Aristotle's well-known remarks about the origins of tragedy in the dithyramb and of comedy in the phallic songs of the countryside—how can these seemingly diverse origins be made consonant with the single Ritualist explanation? Cornford knows, of course, that his entire argument is inferential and speculative; as no solid historical evidence exists for his major contentions, all he can hope to show is that the myth-ritual pattern contained within itself the possibility for the dual development of tragedy and comedy.

He begins by recalling Aristotle's statement (*Poetics*, 6) that tragedy is the dramatic genre whose main concern is the embodying of an action, with character portrayal distinctly secondary; further, tragedy representing what we should call the organic working out of destiny in the affairs of men, the sense of internal structural necessity in the plot should be as strong as possible. Insofar as the tragedian attempts to render the rich idiosyncratic texture of his protagonist's life, he loses the sense of inevitability and universality that characterize the best tragedy. Comedy stands in marked contrast to all this. We want coherence in comedy, not inevitability. And, indeed, as the plot of a comedy attains the quality of inexorability, it tends to approximate tragedy so closely that the generic distinction is blurred. It was only the playwrights of the New Comedy who emphasized the tight plot, and they learned this from Euripides, not Aristophanes. For the Old Comedy is content to forgo the tragic sort of plot, in which everything issues necessarily from some given situation, and in which character is secondary to action, in favor of a looser arrangement of incidents in which the interaction among a group of characters is made the focus of interest.

Because the Old Comedy is relatively indifferent to plot architecture, it sticks closer to the old ritual pattern. For the tragic writer used the ritual pattern only to give an overall abstract shape to his play, but for its subject used traditional stories. Therefore, like all writers on historical subjects, he was constrained by the general direction of the action in his original and could not change it in any important sense, no matter how many minor innovations he might introduce. Comic subjects, however, were not taken from heroic legend, but, dealing as they did with the "meaner sort of people," were invented by the playwright from his observations of everyday life. The comedian does not depend upon his play having an inner rhythm that reflects the inevitability of the universe, and thus cannot contain any basic surprises, but instead depends on twists and turns in the plot to amaze and delight. For this reason, argues Cornford, the comic plot enjoys greater freedom than the tragic and therefore departs less from their common ritual basis.

Cornford quotes Murray, in *Four Stages*, to the effect that the rise and fall of the Eniautos-Daimon, as reflected in this ritual, "is a story of pride and punishment."[22] In the upward movement the new, ascendant year commits the sin of pride (*hubris*) and is slain as a consequence by his successor, who is the avenger of the sin. Thus the alternation of the seasons, which provided the original motive for the fertility drama, offers an analogue to the rhythm of tragedy.

"In Tragedy, the hero's enemy is his own *Hubris*; the conflict between this disastrous passion and its opposite, *Sophrosyne*, is fought out in his own breast. Thus, in the developed form of the tragic art, the two adversaries in the *Agon* are united in one person. . . ." (208). It will be recalled, however, that Cornford had already instanced the form of the sacer ludus in which the god and his adversary were split into separate dramatic personages—Dionysus and Pentheus. In such a case the hubris is no longer to be found within the hero but has been externalized in the antagonist. And it will also be recalled that Cornford had earlier argued that the intruder in the comedy is a doublet of the adversary in the agon. "The common note of all the Impostors was *Alazoneia*. What now becomes clear is that the *Alazoneia* is the comic counterpart of the tragic *Hubris*" (209).

The struggle between *hubris* and *sophrosyne* then takes place internally in tragedy, externally in comedy. A consequence of this difference is that tragedy, interested in eternal verities, finds stories in the body of legend or saga that illustrate this rising and falling rhythm reflective of heroic destiny. Comedy, having no such cosmic import, but content to illustrate the vagaries of human nature, conserves the variant of the ritual plot with the happy ending. "Comedy is bent on character, and fastens on those stock masks that Tragedy was bound to discard" (211).

As Cornford's argument is of the same general sort as Murray's, the overall critical comments made earlier apply here as well. But Cornford's work has come in for some specific criticism of its own. Even those scholars today who might be willing to grant that Greek comedy derives from a ritual original would not agree that Cornford's analysis of Aristophanes has been successful. That is, they reject the identifications he made of various incidents in the plays with their alleged ritual models. As Theodor H. Gaster, a sympathetic critic, has observed, "the principal over-all objection is, perhaps, that he did not distinguish sufficiently between those features of popular observance that serve (or once served) a *functional* purpose and those that spring from the quite autonomous but no less primitive element of sheer fun or high jinks."[23]

Furthermore, Cornford's specific interpretations of the plays have involved him in contradictions and inconsistencies. These have been pointed out in great, even painful, detail by Arthur Pickard-Cambridge, whose attacks on ritual origins in *Dithyramb, Tragedy and Comedy* (1927) were not confined to Murray alone. Thus he shows, for instance, that just as Murray had to wrench the plots of the tragedies to achieve the desired adherence to ritual, so Cornford too has done violence to the plays and to logic, the rigors of his scheme forcing him, for example, to identify the wrong characters as the New King and the ritual groom in several of the plays.

It would only be fair to Cornford for us to conclude by quoting these words from the end of his book, in which he anticipates the fierce attacks that would soon be leveled against him (and Murray) by historically minded scholars:

Many literary critics seem to think that an hypothesis about obscure and remote questions of history can be refuted by a simple demand for the production of more evidence than in fact exists. The demand is as easy to make as it is impossible to satisfy. But the true test of an hypothesis, if it cannot be shown to conflict with known truths, is the number of facts that it correlates and explains. The question left for the reader's consideration is whether, after following our argument, he understands better the form and features of this strange phenomenon, Aristophanic Comedy (220).

4. "Hamlet and Orestes"

The summary offered above of Murray's "Excursus" to *Themis* is incomplete in one respect. Whereas most of his essay offers a structural analysis of tragedy in terms of the ritual from which it was derived, there is a brief, suggestive discussion of the character of Orestes which is of a different sort. These remarks about Orestes were expanded to become part of the Shakespeare Lecture for 1914 that Murray gave to the British Academy. It is an example of a non-structural kind of ritual criticism—character typology. In his lecture, entitled "Hamlet and Orestes," Murray traced the connections, or at least the resemblances, between the most famous heroes of the two great ages of tragedy and speculated about why these parallels should exist and what they might mean.[24] Let us begin with Orestes in the "Excursus."

In examining the ritual forms preserved in Euripides' plays, Murray remarks that those plays in which Orestes appears display a peculiar formal "disturbance" (356). Orestes, he notes, is a hero who is reported dead, is mourned, and then returns in triumph. Murray suspects that the circumstances of his purported death and restoration more than accidentally parallel the life of the Eniautos-Daimon. That is, Orestes is a surrogate for Dionysus; but as the figure of Orestes becomes humanized, and as tragedy became less overtly religious and more consciously artistic, the supernatural aura surrounding this hero dissipated. Therefore, although Orestes' appearance in a play cannot be understood as a true theophany, Murray notes that it is likely to be associated with the messenger scene and the threnos—that is, with stages of the action where a theophany might have come in the ritual original.

There is more. Hermann Usener in 1904 had, on other grounds, concluded that Orestes was originally "a winter daimon and

'Doppelganger' to Dionysus, as Neoptolemus was to Apollo" (356).[25]
After surveying the scenes in which Orestes appears, Murray suggests
that he offers "some reminiscence of a daimon of the New Year who
in human form slays the Old Year in bull form" (356). But here it
ends, tentatively and inconclusively, as Murray returns to the basic
structural argument of the "Excursus." So we must turn to the lecture of two years later to see the further development of these ideas
about the morphology of dramatic character.

The subject of his lecture, Murray announces at the outset, "is the
study of two great tragic characters, Hamlet and Orestes, regarded
as traditional types" (205). Both characters are traditional: Orestes
occurs in many plays and poems, and Hamlet, besides the versions
of Shakespeare and Kyd, appears in a Scandinavian folk tale
(recorded by Saxo Grammaticus), the Icelandic *Ambales* saga, and
the *Prose Edda*. Murray will review the seven tragedies in which
Orestes occurs, and the several Norse and Elizabethan variants of
the Hamlet story.

The major points of comparison are as follows, in schematic form
(Murray of course amplifies each comparison with relevant citations).

1. In all versions—Greek and northern European—the hero is the
son of a king who has been murdered and whose throne has been
usurped by a younger relative. The murderer has married the dead
king's wife. The hero, impelled by supernatural commands, vows and
executes vengeance.

2. In all versions the mother is killed or nearly killed; but, as
Murray says, there is "some shyness" in the way this matter is treated.

3. The versions are unanimous in averring that the hero is mad or
thought to be mad, and that his madness is an essential constituent
of both his character and the dramatic action.

4. The hero is a fool. In the Scandinavian stories, Amlothi (as he
is called) adopts the guise of the mad fool until vengeance is his.
Hamlet is a "Fool transfigured" (213). That is, his language is often
that of the regular Shakespearean fool. He disguises himself, as does
Orestes; both heroes are distinguished by their dirty and disorderly
dress. Both are noted as well for their abusive language and their
cynical and bullying attitudes toward women.

5. In both traditions the hero has a friend and confidant who counsels him about revenge.

There are as well resemblances between the figures of the murdered king and his unworthy successor. The king in every case is idealized as a paragon of royal and manly virtue, being especially competent in the martial arts. Morally, the successor is, as might be expected, corrupt. Another important similarity is that "one of the greatest horrors about the father's death in both traditions is that he died without the due religious observances" (220). And lastly there is a curious ambiguity in most of the sources concerning the mother of the hero: although she has married the murderer of her husband, she is nevertheless portrayed in a sympathetic light.

These similarities resolve into two kinds: the first is of parallels in the general situation and action of the hero. The second, "much more remarkable," is that "when these sagas were worked up into tragedies, quite independently and on very different lines, by the great dramatists of Greece and England, not only do the old similarities remain, but a number of new similarities are developed" (224). No possible combination of historical connections can explain the fact that, for instance, the treatment of the story in the hands of the Greek and English playwrights is quite consonant in places where the Norse sources are at complete variance, for example, the handling of the madness.

If there is no historical connection—and everyone agrees there is none—between the dramatists and their sources, how then are these remarkable resemblances to be understood? Perhaps, suggests Murray, there is "some original connection between the myths, or the primitive religious rituals, on which the dramas are ultimately based" (226). If this is the case, then the similarities may be due to the handling by dramatic genius of the possibilites inherent in the original.

The original Orestes myth is of an old king supplanted by a younger man, who is helped by the queen—Agememnon, Aegisthus, Clytemnestra. The usurper is in due course dethroned and killed by the son of the old king, who is aided by a young queen—Orestes and Electra. In these stories, as in Hesiod's chronicle of the generations of the gods, the new king is the son of the old king and queen, so that while she aids him she does not marry him. The only exception to this general Greek pattern is the Oedipus story, which retains the old element of the mother-son marriage undisplaced.

"There is clearly a common element in all these stories, and the reader will doubtless have recognized it. It is the world-wide ritual story of what we may call the Golden-Bough Kings" (228). This of course is the sacer ludus celebrating and re-enacting the life of the Eniautos-Daimon. Assuming that the reader knows the work of Frazer and Jane Harrison, Murray contents himself with the briefest allusions to the key concepts involved. He also invokes Usener, whose work had been cited in the "Excursus" as well. Usener, it will be recalled, had concluded that Orestes was a winter spirit, the killer of the summer. Murray elaborates: "He is the man of the cold mountains who slays the Red Neoptolemus [the surrogate for Apollo, the summer] at Delphi; he is the ally of death and the dead; he comes suddenly in the dark; he is mad and raging. . . ." (229).

So much for the mythical provenance of Orestes. What of Hamlet-Amlothi? Without rehearsing all the evidence adduced, one may summarize as follows: Murray unsurprisingly finds that the Norse hero likewise is the king-slayer and "Bitter Fool" (231), and the queen-mother turns out to be none other than "our Mother Earth" (232), which explains why the mother is treated sympathetically despite her marriage to the usurping muderer. "One cannot apply moral disapproval to the annual re-marriages of Mother Earth with the new Spring-god. . . ." (232).

Murray now shifts from the myths and their heroes to the process by which the immemorial stories have been handed down. Here he engages in a bit of myth-making himself, of the sort we have seen in Tylor, Smith, and Frazer, conjuring up the mythopoeic savage as a human being different in every way from modern rational people. He draws a distinction between myth and history, in the latter of which, he says, the primitives were not interested. Instead these primitives were "too excited to observe, and afterwards too indifferent to record, and always too much beset by fixed forms of thought ever to take in concrete facts exactly" (236). The stories these people made up to accompany their rites grew and grew through the years with a life of their own.

The things that thrill and amaze us in *Hamlet* or the *Agememnon* are not any historical particulars about mediaeval Elsinore or pre-historic Mycenae, but things belonging to the old stories and the old magic rites, which stirred and thrilled our forefathers five and six thousand years ago; set them dancing all night on the hills, tearing beasts and men in pieces, and giving up their own bodies to a ghastly death, in hope thereby to keep the green world from dying and to be the saviours of their own people (236).

We have here arrived at Jung's collective unconscious: the whole human race vibrating at the same pitch, as the string of mythic memory is plucked. Or, as Murray puts it, there is "a great unconscious solidarity and continuity, lasting from age to age, among all the children of the poets, both the makers and the callers-forth, both the artists and the audiences" (237); in short, among the whole human race.

That certain primitive conceptions and certain primitive stories have an amazing durability has been demonstrated by the students of comparative religion, says Murray; why, then, are we surprised to see the same phenomenon in art? And "if this is so, it seems only natural that those subjects, or some of those subjects, which particularly stirred the interest of primitive men, should still have an appeal to certain very deep-rooted human instincts" (238).

Why should this be? Why should we feel, when we are moved by these old stories, that they are "particularly profound and poetical" (238)? Part of the effect comes from the original quality of the myth; part comes from the "emotional charm" that inheres in mere repetition:

I suspect that charm of that sort lies in these stories and situations, which are—I cannot quite keep clear of the metaphor— deeply implanted in the memory of the race, stamped, as it were, upon our physical organism. We have forgotten their faces and their voices; we say that they are strange to us. Yet there is that within us which leaps at the sight of them, a cry of the blood which tells us we have known them always (238–39).

Naturally, Murray hastens to add, the stories must be worked over by a writer of genius in order to realize the myth and make it live again; but aside from and beyond the gifts of the greatest dramatists there is,

> I suspect, a strange, unanalyzed vibration below the surface, an undercurrent of desires and fears and passions, long slumbering yet eternally familiar, which have for thousands of years lain near the root of our most intimate emotions and been wrought into the fabric of our most magical dreams. How far into past ages this stream may reach back, I dare not even surmise; but it seems as if the power of stirring it or moving with it were one of the last secrets of genius (239–40).

Before analyzing Murray's argument, one must say something of its rhetoric. It is startling, even amusing, to hear Gilbert Murray—than whom a more naturally ascetic, spiritual, and refined man can hardly be imagined—talking like D. H. Lawrence about "the cry of the blood." But this shock can occur only when we take our historical and critical categories too seriously. Lawrence and Murray, however different their temperaments, were after all contemporaries; it should not be surprising that Murray too could be touched by the powerful surge of irrationalism for which Lawrence is so eminently the spokesman.

Murray's overall use of such rhetoric is instructive as well. He tends to resort to it most often and most heavily when his arguments run out of historical steam. In a way this is natural; if Murray could have written more evidentially, he doubtless would have. But granting that, and granting also that some of what we might today call pejoratively "rhetoric" is the mark of a more ornate style then is current today, nonetheless Murray seems to become most overheated when the argument gets most exiguous.

Turning to more important matters, one sees that this essay is a prefiguration of the strongly Jungian tone of much later myth criticism. The argument starts out historical, like the "Excursus," but rapidly becomes psychological. The psychology being collective and unconscious, however, propositions based on it become difficult or impossible to test or use clearly. The questions one might put to Murray here are those that have been raised about archetypal criticism in general. When we are told that all humanity shares a common heritage of archetypal imagery, what do we know? Can a list of such archetypes be compiled? Is it possible to add an archetype—that is, is this collective memory a physiological mechanism, or is it amenable to cultural influence? Are we justified in assuming, without being able to establish a historical nexus, that everything in literature is connected inextricably with everything else? To be sure, such questions were especially important in the 1960s when Northrop Frye's Cambridge- and Bollingen-derived theories counted for more than they do today.

An analysis of Murray's assumptions is worthwhile in itself and as an indicator of the general theoretical position of myth criticism. In asking why and describing how we respond to tragedy, Murray assumes (1) that the class-name tragedy has an existence, a "life," of its own; (2) that "we" respond, that is, he assumes the existence of a common mind "out there" rather than a group of highly individualized minds; and (3) that we "respond," that is, that he can from his data make statements about the audience's reactions, which is a problem in aesthetics. Aesthetics is notoriously a study in which the data are, or should be, highly particularized, and in which historical variability is of great importance: different times and different places are distinguished by different kinds of responses. On this question, however, Murray is quite ahistorical.

If one were to question Murray about these assumptions, he might respond that the existence of archetypes collapses (2) and (3) in that the postulation of identical built-in mental "equipment" permits one to assume a homogeneous audience-mind and also controls the responses of that mind sufficiently so that one can formulate an aesthetics on that basis. So far as the reification of tragedy is concerned, he might reply that this is merely the sort of generalization necessary to make universally applicable statements.

After one reads this essay, one appreciates more fully Cornford's remark, in his obituary of Jane Harrison, that it was purely accidental that Durkheim's "collective representations" and not Jung's "collective unconscious" provided the Cambridge master key to primitive religion.[26] Indeed, both Cornford and Harrison were deeply interested in psychoanalysis, in both its Freudian and Jungian versions. Harrison levied on Jung and Freud in her personal philosophical synthesis, *Epilegomena to the Study of Greek Religion*; Cornford assumes Jung as a "given" in his long paper "Psychology and the Drama" (1922).[27]

Although the theoretical foundations of Jungian literary criticism are weak, its practical strengths should be noted as well.[28] Inasmuch as modern criticism in the English-speaking world, at least until the late 1970s, has gone in for close reading and *explications de texte*, the structural emphasis of archetypal criticism has acted as a complementary force to illuminate areas otherwise left dark.

5. *Ancient Art and Ritual*

The reader will have noted that the discussion of *Themis* gave way to Murray's "Excursus," and that no summation was attempted of that massive work as a whole. This was deliberate, because the year after *Themis* appeared Harrison brought out a sequel, *Ancient Art and Ritual*. As this work represents a simplification and clarification of the big book, it seems more appropriate to make it serve for both, particularly as it is more directly relevant to literature than is *Themis*.[29]

Ancient Art and Ritual was a volume in the nontechnical "Home University Library" series, and Harrison, freed from *Themis* which had weighed on her for four years, and as well from the constraints of scholarship, enjoyed writing it, as she makes clear in a letter to Murray of 14 September 1912:

> I have been reading some of *Art and Ritual* aloud to a sort of trial crew of Logan [Pearsall Smith] (no good of course) and Alys [Russell] and an old Miss Fry [sister of Roger Fry]—and they seemed to get tremendously excited over it and they say the plot is absolutely clear—so I am making it still clearer in places, and I hope when it is in proof it won't seem either obscure or irrelevant or even overstated. Coming back to it fresh, the main argument does convince me more than it ever

did as I wrote. Does this sound conceited? It isn't really. What
you put in your preface [to *Four Stages of Greek Religion*] about
me made me feel humble all over and so happy.
Yours,
K[er][30]

The object of the book is to show that art and ritual "have a common root, and that neither can be understood without the other. It
is at the outset one and the same impulse that sends a man to
church and to the theatre."[31] In other words, then, this is a study in
the social psychology and aesthetics of archaic Greece. To the considerable extent that the argument of the book simply repeats
Themis it will be compressed, and the new material will be emphasized in the discussion.

To investigate the connections between art and ritual Harrison
analyzes Plato's concept of mimesis, which she criticizes as wrong-
headed. Mimesis does not explain *why* men should wish to imitate
objects or actions. The phenomenon of imitation is more clearly
understood by studying primitive peoples. "Savages" *present* in their
art what they wish to happen—they "paint prayers" (25). "Ritual then
involves imitation but does not arise out of it. It desires to recreate
an emotion, not reproduce an object" (25-6).

The motive power of art (and this it shares with ritual) lies in an
apparently inborn human desire to express strongly felt emotion or
need by representing or doing something, usually the act in question. By examining primitive dance Harrison shows (using many
examples from Frazer) how dances represent ways of *enacting* what
is desired (for example, rain, success in the hunt). Art and ritual
require not only some emotional need but also a representation of
the object of that need. In Greek, a word for rite is *dromenon*, "the
thing done." *Dromena* are those things that are done collectively.
Savages, we are told again, have "thin and meagre personalities"
(37); as individuals they are ciphers—it is collectivity that sustains
them and makes them feel intensely.

Human beings are so constituted that they perceive something in
the environment, have an emotional response to it, and then act on
that emotion. Both religion and art arise in the second step of this

series—that of emotion. "Art and ritual, though perhaps not wholly ritual, spring from the incomplete cycle, from unsatisfied desire, from perception and emotion that have somehow not found immediate outlet in practical action" (41). Next, through repeating this representation, "a process of abstraction . . . helps the transition from ritual to art" (42). The particular stimulus that evoked the representation in the first place is forgotten, and "the representation casts itself loose . . . and becomes generalized. . . ." (42–43).

Ritual, then, is an imitation, but for practical ends: for example, the warrior dances the war dance to recapture the emotion felt in battle. She notes the several plays of Aristophanes in which men imitate animals, which she explains as a throwback to the prehistoric stage of totemism in which men thought of animals as brothers. Thus totemic dances are not mimetic but assertive of unity with the totem animal. Only later, when there is a distinction felt between men and animals, can one speak of imitation.

Chapter III concerns "Periodic Ceremonies." Such ceremonies are important in the movement from *dromena* to drama because they involve rites performed at fixed times. Primitive men were mainly interested in ensuring that their fields, animals, and women would be fertile, and these concerns are the springs of all art and all religion. Because seasons recur, rites to ensure fertility that are tied to seasonal rhythms easily become abstracted from the emotion that originally prompted them. "Ritual acts . . . which depend on the periodicity of the seasons are acts necessarily delayed [in their fulfillment]" (53). What a man waits and hopes for more and more easily becomes an idea, a source of value: "these periodic festivals are the stuff on which those faded, unaccomplished actions and desires which we call gods—Attis, Osiris, Dionysos—are made" (54). After noting a large number of such periodic festivals (drawn from Frazer), Harrison settles on the spring festival, that of Dionysus. From the recurrence of such festivals, with their May Kings and carryings-out of Death, "a conception, a kind of *daimon*, or spirit, is fashioned, who lives and dies again in a perpetual cycle. The periodic festival begets a kind of not immortal, but perennial, god" (72–73).

Turning now to the spring festival in Greece, she begins with

Aristotle's statement in the *Poetics* that tragedy and comedy originated in the dithyramb. The dithyramb was a spring song, a
"bull-driving" song—a fertility rite centering on the bull—sung at the
spring festival. The bull, emblem of power, was killed at the festival
called the Bouphonia, so that the people might share in his holiness
and *mana*. The bull is Dionysus: "Dionysos, the Bull-God, is but the
actual holy Bull himself, or rather the succession of annual holy
Bulls once perceived, then remembered, generalized, conceived"
(102–03). The movement is from *per*ception to *con*ception. Besides
being a spring song, and a bullsong, the dithyramb, as we saw in
Themis, was also the song of rebirth, or initiation. The god who grows
out of the all-important tribal rites of initiation is Dionysus, the
kouros, the "Divine Young Man" (113).

Chapter V focuses on the "Transition from Ritual to Art: The
Dromenon ("Thing Done") and the Drama." Recapitulating Murray,
she mentions the prologues, messengers, and chorus as ritual forms
embalmed and conserved in drama. Perhaps because Murray, for
reasons that are unclear, said little about the chorus, she concentrates on it. It is, in her view, obviously the remnant of the community of worshipers who sang the dithyramb. She hints at the archetypal *frisson* the audience even today experiences when the choral
songs, notoriously difficult to translate, are rendered into English
that approximates the beauty of the Greek: "then certainly there will
be some among the spectators who get a thrill from the chorus quite
unknown to any modern stage effect, a feeling of emotion heightened yet restrained, a sense of entering into higher places, filled
with a larger and purer air—a sense of beauty born clean out of conflict and disaster" (127). (We note once again the same rhetorical
urgency we saw in Murray when the argument gets cloudy.) She does
not say whence this special emotion comes, but it is fair by now to
supply the source: the *Anima Mundi*, or the collective unconscious.

Harrison points out that the word "orchestra," specifying the loca-
tion where the early tragedies were performed, meant "dancing
place" in Greek. That is, the chorus danced and sang the dithyramb
in the orchestra, and the spectators watched from the "theater." And
in the relation between the dancing-place and the watching-place,
which changed through time, we see the movement from ritual to

art, from "*dromenon* to drama." In the early time, most if not all those present participated actively, that is, they danced and sang, in the choric songs; later, most present were passive, that is, they watched. Ritual is an act in which one "believes" and in which one is immersed, in which there is no aesthetic distance between the doer and thing done. The festival of Dionysus changed from a "naive" performance of this kind to one in which there was a definite distinction between the doers and spectators, between "them" and "us"; "the *dromenon*, the thing actually done by yourself, has become a drama, a thing also done, but abstracted from doing" (127).

From this analysis, Harrison concludes that the main distinction between ritual and art is that, although both involve "a presentation or a pre-presentation . . . of life" (135), ritual always has a practical end whereas art does not. Art presents an imitation of life but does not issue in any immediate action. "The end of art is itself. Its value is not mediate but *immediate*. Thus ritual *makes, as it were, a bridge between real life and art*, a bridge over which in primitive times man must pass" (135; emphasis Harrison's). The "must pass" bespeaks her unshaken faith in evolution, albeit of a more sophisticated kind than that of Tylor and Frazer, and the sharp antithesis between life and art just as plainly roots her theory in the aesthetics of the eighties and nineties.

Having explained how the *dromenon* became the drama, and what that transformation meant, Harrison turns to the interesting question of *why* it happened as it did. The two main causes she sees for the development of drama were the "decay of religious faith . . . [and] the influx from abroad of a new culture and new dramatic material" (136).

The ritual forms in drama—chorus, agon, epiphany, etc.—subsisted because they had meaning in the old ritual. But as people grew sophisticated and doubted that *their own* dancing could induce the spring to return, their collective emotion cooled. At the same time, as a result of repeating the spring ritual over countless years, a daimon was created who was felt to be "personally" responsible for the continuity of the food supply. People began to feel that this spirit must be placated directly. Thus *dromena*, "things done," became worship; sacraments yielded to sacrifices. "Religion moves away from drama towards theology, but the ritual mould of the *dromenon* is left ready for a new content" (140).

The new wine for these old bottles was supplied by the innovation on the part of Peisistratos in the sixth century whereby plots were taken over from Homer. Another feature of Peisistratos' reforms was the institution of the Athenian Dionysia in the spring, the festival at which tragedy was always presented. These reforms, made for political reasons, were carried out from about 560 to 500 B.C. Aeschylus' first preserved play with a plot drawn from heroic story, *The Seven Against Thebes*, was presented in 467 B.C. "It all came very swiftly, the shift from Spring Song to the heroic drama was accomplished in something much under a century" (157).

Homer's poems were the result, and the summing up, of a heroic age, an age in which outstanding individuals distinguished themselves as opposed to the faceless collectivity of earlier times. It was a time of great migrations from the north, during which waves of invaders descended on Mycenaean Greece. Naturally, these upheavals disrupted local social arrangements, making it unlikely that older socio-religious forms would be transmitted intact. Luckily, however, Athens was nearly unique in being relatively unaffected by the invasions and migrations, so that its citizens were able to preserve the dithyramb and infuse it with new Homeric (that is, heroic) content.

Eight

Aftermath

We have completed the survey of the pioneering work in myth criticism; two tasks remain, however. First, for completeness' sake, the narrative of events and achievements of the founding generation, including a review of the critical reception, should be concluded. And second, a brief freehand account will be offered of the developments within literary criticism that directly issued from their work. This can be only a sketch because of the other influences (those, for example, of Jung and Cassirer) that soon made themselves felt. To explore all these currents fully would be to write a history of myth criticism, which is obviously beyond the scope of this essay.

1

In reviewing the critical reception afforded the work of the Ritualists, it is sensible to begin at the beginning, and not with the mature achievements of 1912, because the early reputations of the group's members obviously colored the reactions to their later efforts. In view of the number of publications involved, it is impossible to give more than an outline.

So far as Jane Harrison was concerned, her early work (from the eighties and nineties) was generally well received. It should be kept in mind that her books of this period were directed primarily to the large classically educated but nonscholarly audience. In her popularizations she was doing something new, interpreting Greek religion

and mythology first from the art-historical and then from the
archaeological-folkloristic points of view. Some at least of her more
scholarly early productions were reviewed in learned journals as well.
For instance, G. C. Richards wrote of *Mythology and Monuments of
Ancient Athens*: "It is no exaggeration to say that the book is the most
important archaeological publication that has appeared in England
for some time past," and he praised highly her "deep knowledge and
sound use of vases."[1]

Murray's career had started meteorically with the appointment to
the professorship at Glasgow in 1889, and his work on Euripides in
the nineties had established his scholarly reputation. But he attained
celebrity when his translations and then his stagings of Euripides
began to appear in the first decade of the century. When one adds
to this the popularity of his *History of Ancient Greek Literature*, which
went to three editions within ten years of its publication in 1897, and
as well his increasingly important political activity during this
decade, it is safe to say that Murray, while still a relatively young man,
had become one of Britain's best-known intellectuals. Although of
course he did continue to publish on Euripides, he also found time
to make himself an important exponent of the multiple-authorship
hypothesis in *The Rise of the Greek Epic*.[2] This foray into Homeric
scholarship took him into territory that had been a battleground for
over a century, and his book aroused the expectable opposition from
the unitarians. Among the new things in *The Rise of the Greek Epic* was
the analysis of Homer's deities according to the developmental
scheme first put forth in *Prolegomena*.[3]

It is not surprising that Murray always thought very highly of
Prolegomena, calling it "a work of genius," a book that "transformed
the whole approach to the study of Greek religion."[4] A more objective estimate of its acceptance lies in the fact that the work was immediately adopted as a set book for examinations, at least within her
own college. Harrison wrote to Murray in May term 1904, only six
months after the book's publication: "I blush for the [Newnham
College] examiners. Five questions are out of the Fat and Comely
One—I did give them tea but they didn't know before that I should.
Why it is a paper that *you* could answer."[5] And Jessie Stewart adds that

in the Classical Tripos (presumably for 1904) "the paper on Mythology and Religion included questions on the Cult of Dionysus, the *Anodos* of Gaia, Orphic hymns, and Attic festivals," which is to say that its acceptance was not limited to Newnham alone. Even today, however much its data and conclusions may have been superseded, *Prolegomena* is still acknowledged as an epoch-making book in the study of Greek religion.

Basically, then, with the exception of the running feud with Ridgeway, it was not until the appearance of the eniautos-daimon hypothesis that most scholarly criticism turned negative. To be sure, there were a few quick converts. J. A. K. Thomson in *The Greek Tradition* (1915) was one of the earliest adherents, completely accepting the year-spirit in his study of Euripides' *Alcestis*.[6] A more influential (that is, more established) scholar than Thomson to write favorably of the *dromenon* hypothesis was Walter Leaf, in *Homer and History* (1915). But the work of 1912 and 1914 was generally not well received, mainly because it was, in its sociological-anthropological orientation, radically out of sympathy with the dominant textual-mindedness of classical scholarship. Some examples: J. T. Sheppard praised Murray's lucidity and grace in *Four Stages of Greek Religion* but saw its main hypotheses as inadequately proved and in any case themselves based tenuously on still more hypotheses. He compared the thinness of the argument in *Four Stages* with the richness of *Themis*, all the while granting that evidence cannot be adduced in a public lecture as it can in a scholarly monograph. For Sheppard the utility of the anthropological approach was still to be proved, and was therefore too new to make it fit for popular exposition: "But at present, it seems to me, criticism ought to be the work, not popularisation."[7]

Not all of Murray's critics were so gentle as Sheppard, however. For instance, Murray contributed an essay called "Greek and English Tragedy: A Contrast" to a volume entitled *English Literature and the Classics* (1912). Reviewing the book, the American scholar Paul Shorey, always much given to invective, singled out Murray's piece for special attention: "The recent fashion of romantic and sentimental anthropology seems to have made a complete conquest of

Professor Murray, and while the mood is on him he can see in Greek literature nothing but origins and survivals."[8]

The review of *Themis* in the *Classical Review* was sympathetic in its tone but critical in its conclusions. Its author, W. M. L. Hutchinson, began delightfully:

> Miss Harrison is the Scholar Gypsy of Hellenic studies. In this book we find her ranging "still untired" the accustomed fields and, to our regret plunging into the dark and devious coverts of savage anthropology: while from her generous self-revelation we learn with what undiminished ardour "a fugitive and gracious light she seeks." If that light be still "shy to illumine," if what she hails as the true gleam be no more than philosophical *feu follet*; that does not affect the real value of her achievement. For the road to Truth is paved with good heresies; and if indeed *Themis* embodies one, it is of the very best kind—at once brilliantly suggestive and a direct incitement to controversy.[9]

After giving a fair summary of the book's main conclusions, Hutchinson argued first that Cornford's chapter on the origin of the Olympic Games was completely in error, and then that Harrison likewise had erred in her reading of the Palaikastro stele as a tribal initiation text. He pointed to the fact that whereas initiation in preliterate peoples takes place at puberty, the myths she sees as initiation stories deal with Zeus as an infant. He continues, quoting Harrison:

> "When the Greeks lost touch with the tribal customs which involved the rite of adolescence, *we may suspect that they invented* or at least emphasised Infant Initiation" (p. 20, italics mine). That sentence is typical of the book. The charm, and it must reluctantly be added, the weakness of *Themis* lies in its uncontrolled subjectivity. We catch the author's enthusiasm; we sympathise with her frank "delight and amazement" whenever a fresh piece of evidence fits into her theory; but we cannot help seeing how frequently that theory depends on assuming that a

thing is true because you "suspect"—and wish—it to be true. It is all magnificent—but how much of it is science?[10]

That the First World War meant "goodbye to all that" is obvious. One gets a clear sense of the disruption of scholarship it caused from these words of Harrison's, written in April 1912. From a review of Baudissin's book *Adonis und Esmun*, they give a sense of exhilaration at being on the crest of a wave:

> The attention, then, of scholars all over Europe is now fully focussed on the year-gods who die and live again; who are, in fact, but the utterance and emphasis of cyclic change, of life and growth. This focus of attention is but one phase, we think, of a wider movement—that known in popular parlance as "vitalism," the most brilliant scientific exponent of which is Professor Henri Bergson. The eternal and immutable gods such as the Olympians in their "brazen" heaven have stood for a now somewhat discredited conceptualism. Their supremacy —it may be only for a time—seems threatened. It is, however, an open secret that we may expect shortly, from the pen of our most learned Greek mythologist [A. B. Cook], a monograph on the Father of Gods and Men, the Olympian Zeus himself. We shall look forward eagerly to see whether behind the figure of even Zeus is found to lurk the shifting shape of a year-*daimon*, a god who does not "live at ease," but dies each year that he and his worshippers may live anew.[11]

With September 1914 it was all over. No longer was there "a focus of attention" of scholarly eyes all over Europe; the "wider movement" of vitalism was likewise an early casualty of war. Scholarly work of all kinds came to a halt. In Cambridge, Cornford astonished everyone by becoming a marksmanship instructor to recruits; none of his colleagues had known he was a crack shot. When he returned to Cambridge after the war, it was to continue his study of philosophy, first the pre-Socratics and then Plato. At the very end of his life, however, he returned to his old subject—the pre-philosophical origins of philosophy. His last book, *Principium Sapientiae*, left incomplete at his death in 1943, resumes the inquiry of thirty years earlier in the light of new findings from the Semitic Near East. And one of the last essays he completed, in 1941, is an attempt to explicate "A Ritual Basis for Hesiod's *Theogony*."[12]

A. B. Cook likewise entered government service in the war, returning to Cambridge in 1919. Immediately he set about readying the second volume of *Zeus* for the press; after a great deal of trouble it finally appeared in 1924. But Cook, apparently the most modest and unprepossessing of men, completely lacking in what Harrison called in a letter to Murray "*l'art de se faire valoir*,"[13] was passed over for academic preferment several times until, in 1931, he was appointed to the newly created Laurence chair of archaeology.

As this narrative has not had much to say about Cook, a few words about him might be appropriate here. For two main reasons Cook was not, and is not, known outside the scholarly world. First, he wrote only two important books—the two huge volumes of *Zeus*—and most of his early work was presented exclusively to his colleagues in the form of articles and monographs. Nor did he, unlike Harrison or Murray, do much reviewing for general magazines. But more important was the fact that, unlike Murray, Cornford, and Harrison, Cook was not a good writer. I have already remarked his devotion to, and belief in, fact for its own sake, as well as the overall unreadability of his books (to a nonspecialist). Since he had no particularly literary interests, and did not publish on literary subjects, Cook's role in the work of the group has perhaps not been made clear. He seems to have functioned as Harrison's ultimate authority on matters ethnological and philological. Jessie Stewart calls him "perhaps the most erudite and fertile of her helpers."[14] He was always willing, no matter how busy, to break off from his own work and answer her queries, and his conversation must have been of great help and comfort to both Harrison and Cornford. Because (except Murray) they all lived in Cambridge and saw one another often, they had no reason to write to one another, so that there are, unfortunately, few letters extant among them.[15]

Perhaps the most noteworthy of Cook's contributions to *Themis* is known, however. Harrison, knowing that her work would come under searching review from her less speculative colleagues, took pains to buttress her argument wherever possible by textual and philological evidence. One of the most troublesome points to her was the derivation of "dithyramb." She had, in the brief discussion in *Prolegomena* of Dionysus, canvassed the possible derivations of the word and had found them all impossible.[16] Many scholars had attempted etymologies, but none was persuasive. Then, in January 1911 she wrote to Murray (in an unpublished letter):

> I must tell you that amazing A. B. C. has derived dithyramb:
> Δι--θυρ--αμβοσ
> Δι--θορ--αμβοσ
> Zeus—leap dance—song
> Mr. [Peter] Giles [Master of Emmanuel College] says that the philology is unimpeachable—the song, as it were, that sets Zeus leaping.
>
> It seems that in Thessalian and a lot of North dialects *u* regularly stands for *o* in unaccented syllables (Hoffman).
>
> Still more amazing, he was cherishing this as an obscure curiosity arrived at through dialects, and he never saw that it was the *megistos kouros thore*-ing till I sprang at him yelling for joy as it confirms my whole theory that the dithyramb is the new birth in spring—the kouros attains maturity and then leaps in the dithyramb for the spring. . . . Please keep the dithyramb secret as it is A. B. C.'s *thunder* and tabu from mere Oxford.

Cook was definitely more conservative than Harrison, Murray, or Cornford, at least insofar as the eniautos-daimon was concerned. His reservations are expressed in two unpublished letters dating from this time. One from Cook to Murray of 23 August 1913 voices the writer's disapproval of "Eniautos-Daimon" as a phrase: "but I daresay it is all a question of words. I hate 'daemons' of all sorts, and 'year-daemons' worse than any."[17] Good friends reluctantly but pointedly disagree here, and one of them is courteously mitigating the sharpness of their differences by downplaying it all as "a question of words." In any event, one cannot imagine any of the other three in the group making such a statement.

The other letter, written by Harrison to Cook about two years earlier (8 September 1911), is obviously meant to counter Cook's objections to the eniautos-daimon hypothesis, which he must have expressed after reading *Themis* in manuscript. Note that Cook clearly at this time does not know of Murray's "Excursus," which implies that the decision to include it was made at (more or less) the last minute. She writes:

> The point at which we are really at issue lies deeper. I do not believe that the drama took its form from the cult of Dionysos except in so far as he was one of the thousand-year daimons. The Mummers and May Day plays are not survivals of the cult of Dionysos but of a thing far more widespread. . . . I am greatly pleased that the analysis of drama in general commends itself to you—it will I think be immensely strengthened by Prof. Murray's excursus which is to follow chapter VIII and which will I think interest you; it teems with facts. To conclude, and it is time! I am intensely conscious that my theories (and the book will be a tissue of theories) need a much broader basis both of psychology and probably ethnography, and it is probably rash to publish it as it stands, and I stand to lose such reputation as I have. I write really not to instruct but because I cannot begin to think until I have discharged all the theories that welter inside me and put everything out of focus, but the bits you accept I have confidence in.[18]

The first three sentences imply that Cook balked at making the speculative leap from the historical deity Dionysus to the generalized class of eniautos-daimones, particularly as that leap was based on a very new and unfamiliar psychology and sociology. He wished to try to derive the mummers' plays historically from the cult of Dionysus, rather than plunge into what must then have seemed a philosophical and psychological void. I have no doubt that Cook's reluctance to go the whole of the long way with the others arose from the fact that he was the only one of them to remain a recognizable Christian. No doubt he saw how easily not only Zeus and Dionysus could emerge from a froth of primitive emotion, but Jesus as well.

As for Harrison (as already noted), with the outbreak of war she became enamored of the Russian language and its literature, and moved away first from classical studies and then from Cambridge itself in 1922, spending her last years in Paris and Spain. During that time she brought out *Epilegomena to the Study of Greek Religion,* a personal synthesis of her work on primitive religion, along with elements of Bergson, Freud, and Jung. She returned to England shortly before her death, in 1928.

Of the foursome, Murray had always been the most politically aware and active, and when the war started he dropped his scholarly work and immediately became a leading apologist for the Allied side within intellectual circles and even more importantly for the cause of postwar international cooperation. He was one of the first and best proponents of the League of Nations in Britain, and after the war maintained his political interests and activities upon his return to Oxford. Although often in poor health, he continued to lead an amazingly productive scholarly career until his death at ninety-one in 1957.

He never wavered in his faith in the eniautos-daimon hypothesis, and after the war conducted an active campaign on its behalf. Thus, in 1920 he contributed an introduction to a widely used edition of Bywater's translation of Aristotle's *Poetics.* In it he explained that Aristotle was mistaken about tragic plots (that is, in saying nothing about ritual origins for tragic plots) because in his day New Comedy playwrights invented their plots.[19] Aristotle therefore used the word "mythos" (plot) in its fourth-century and not its earlier meaning. Murray says that characters in tragedy retained the names of historical personages for aesthetic reasons; the underlying reason for this practice, however, was that "the drama and the myth were simply two different expressions of the same religious kernel."[20] Likewise Aristotle was mistaken about theophanies, especially in Euripides, because, "having lost the living tradition, he sees neither the ritual origin nor the dramatic value of these divine epiphanies" (13).

But Aristotle was not completely in the dark about tragedy; Murray is willing to admit that some of what he says is correct. For instance, he was right in his remark that all tragedies must contain an *anagnorisis* and a *peripeteia.* "The clue to [why this should be so] lies, it can scarcely be doubted, in the historical origin of tragedy" (14). That is, they are the last two steps in the sufferings of Dionysus, transformed into and enacted as a dramatic ritual. Here and elsewhere Murray's tone is one of complete self-assurance. Never in this introduction, or anywhere else, does he indicate that most of his colleagues utterly rejected the hypothesis.

The fundamental difference between the Ritualists and their opponents was clearly exposed in Murray's response to Arthur Pickard-Cambridge, who had savaged the *dromenon* theory in *Dithyramb, Tragedy and Comedy* (1927). In the same year Pickard-Cambridge used the appearance of the second edition of *Themis* to renew, in brief compass, the attack he had made in his book. The editors of the *Classical Review*, in which Pickard-Cambridge's review appeared, asked Murray to respond by having him review *Dithyramb, Tragedy and Comedy*.[21]

Murray begins with a generous acknowledgment of the merits of Pickard-Cambridge's book, thanking him for his corrections on several small points. But he responds to Pickard-Cambridge's main charge—that it is impossible to apply the eniautos-daimon hypothesis in detail to Greek tragedies—by pointing to the major shortcomings of *Dithyramb, Tragedy and Comedy* and by extension, of the historical criticism it embodies. First, he says, Pickard-Cambridge refuses to countenance any conclusion that has been reached by reasoning by analogy. Murray instances Lobeck's *Aglaophamus*, that massive compendium of mid-nineteenth-century knowledge about Greek religion, and says that because Lobeck knew nothing of modern anthropology—in particular "savage initiation ceremonies"—all his erudition was wasted. And of course the comparative method as used in anthropology is tacitly based on a fundamental analogy among all human cultures in its assumptions that comparison is possible and that items of culture are in some sense commensurable.

Pickard-Cambridge refuses to have anything to do with analogy, but insists on textual or archaeological evidence before he will grant anything—well and good. But why, Murray asks, must he also deny the evidence of Herodotus, who says that the rites of Dionysus were nearly identical with those of Osiris? Or of Plato, who says that the subject of the dithyramb was the birth of Dionysus, which Pickard-

Cambridge dismisses as a "joke." The reason, Murray asserts, is that Pickard-Cambridge has "an instinctive repugnance to the whole idea of 'origins' or development" (222). Rather, Pickard-Cambridge's "own theory is that Dithyramb is Dithyramb, and Tragedy is Tragedy, and Satyr Play Satyr Play, and that nothing ever turned into anything else."

But an even greater obstacle to Pickard-Cambridge's understanding of what the eniautos-daimon hypothesis really means comes from a semantic difficulty. Although Pickard-Cambridge knows that the meaning of words is determined by their cultural context, and that therefore any translation—especially one from an ancient to a modern culture—must be informed by historical understanding, he refuses to face the consequences of this idea. "He argued," says Murray, "that if something belongs to Dionysus it cannot be connected with a tomb ritual . . . if with wine, not with funerals. . . ." (222). But to argue like this is to miss the point that in ancient Greece all these seemingly disparate items were closely associated with one another. Murray says that "it is through analysis of Greek words and ideas that the problem of Tragedy will . . . eventually be solved" (223). The difficulties involved in solving the problem have been formidable, but they have yielded to a series of inspired workers who have applied the findings of anthropology: the first great insight was Ridgeway's, in insisting on the importance of tomb ritual; the next was that of the Ritualists (although he modestly chooses not to name them) in understanding that Dionysus is not simply the fat Bacchus but rather a Year-God who dies so that his people may live; and the third great advance has been the identification of the widespread mummers' play as the direct descendant of Dionysian ritual, which has permitted us to see that comedy is the marriage of the revived god and tragedy is his death. "But it seems rather sad that Mr. Pickard-Cambridge has learnt so little from the work of his fellow students" (223).

Murray was really saying that no matter how many difficulties or discrepancies may exist in the detailed application of the eniautos-daimon hypothesis, historical criticism is perverse in refusing to appreciate what the hypothesis does supply—a coherent explanation of otherwise disorderly data. Pickard-Cambridge and others of his persuasion—that is, most classicists—would argue that the theory is worth maintaining only if it indeed explains the facts *as they exist* in the plays. In their view the theory only "works" if it is used with an excessive willingness to shut one's eyes to its defects and compensate for them with quantities of imaginative sympathy, which makes it no theory at all. It seems to come down to a temperamental difference: some people value coherence so highly that they are willing to tolerate more disparity between fact and hypothesis than others, for whom such discrepancies loom so large that they cannot share the pleasure that such an "explanation" might afford.

But Murray's most significant response to Pickard-Cambridge was not in this review but in the long discussion of "Greek Drama: Origin" he wrote as part of the article on "Drama" in the fourteenth edition of the *Encyclopaedia Britannica* (1929). So far as publicizing his position was concerned—and Murray was always adept at popularization—this was a master stroke. Probably more than anything else it assured the wide dissemination of the theory, and perhaps explains why, relatively speaking, so many of the general public know of it, whereas only classicists know of Pickard-Cambridge. And of course, not only are nonclassicists unaware of the overwhelmingly negative scholarly appraisal of the Ritualists' work, but they would be unable to appreciate the severity of that appraisal in any event. It is safe to say, however, that for most classicists the final word was Pickard-Cambridge's, and they seem surprised when they encounter the Year-spirit in literary criticism or elsewhere.[22]

Murray had not yet had his last word. In 1943, he reversed his previous position, expressed thirty years earlier in the "Excursus," that New Comedy marked a turning away from the ritual pattern. It will be recalled that Cornford, although devoting himself mainly to Old Comedy, had indicated that later comedy had not completely eliminated the ritual plot. In "Ritual Elements in the New Comedy," Murray attempted to demonstrate that Cornford was right and that ritual elements are to be discerned in all forms of Greek drama.[23]

He begins by noting five stock elements in Euripidean tragedy that connect it with New Comedy: (1) a girl is raped, (2) which results in a child who is exposed to die, (3) and a mother who then undergoes many troubles, (4) followed by a recognition or revelation scene, and (5) a reversal. These five elements recur again and again because we are really in the presence of a ritual myth. The five stages translate as follows into ritual terms: (1) the Earth is impregnated by a sky god, (2) the Spring-child is born but is not visible, (3) the Earth is without vegetation and starves, (4) the new vegetation appears, (5) *peripeteia* and celebratory *komos.*

This explains "the curious monotony of theme" in the New Comedy and also what otherwise must have been an "incredible immorality of society," were we to assume that the plays give a realistic portrayal of the times. (Here Murray's own puritanical bent is all too evident.)

Murray postulates the following stages in the history of tragedy on the basis of what he regards as a conservative desire on the part of the Greeks to hew to the ritual of Dionysus even when there was a general revulsion from the phallic crudities of Aristophanes. (1) First all subjects are Dionysiac, (2) then other myths that are amenable to dramatic treatment are gradually introduced, (3) and finally, after a reaction against this freedom, an attempt is made to return to subjects deemed more appropriate to the Year-God.

> In the "Excursus" which I contributed to Jane Harrison's *Themis* I showed that certain plays contained all the features of the Osiris ritual: a Contest, a Sparagmos or similar ritual death, always related by a Messenger; a *threnos*, or lamentation; a Recognition and Theophany. I was wrong, as Mr. Pickard-Cambridge pointed out, in attributing too exclusive and original an importance to this type of play, but its existence is clear, and is best explained, I think, as an attempt to get back to Dionysus when he seemed to be neglected (52).

Thus Murray, although belatedly giving ground to Pickard-Cambridge, reverts to the Frazerian practice of inferring motives from behavior. In this case, it seems fair to say that if Murray is right he has demonstrated the existence of a certain overall rhythm and shape to Greek drama; his explanation of why the Greek dramatists wrote as they did, however, totally lacks support. It should also be noted that Murray seems here to have changed his mind on another important point: whether or not the playwrights were aware that they were conforming to a pre-existent ritual pattern. In the "Excursus" he had implied that at least Thespis and Aeschylus were consciously adapting a dramatic ritual into a ritual drama. In "Hamlet and Orestes" Murray invoked "a great *unconscious* solidarity and continuity, lasting from age to age, among all the children of the poets" (emphasis added). Here he implies that Aeschylus and Euripides, at least, knew that they were embodying a ritual pattern.

In 1951 Murray returned to the subject for a last time, offering still another version of the ritual myth of the Year-God, which in turn appears in tragedy.[24] Following his earlier prescription, expressed in the review of Pickard-Cambridge, that the problems of Greek tragedy would be resolved through exploring the meanings of the key Greek terms involved, Murray begins with *eniautos*, Harrison's word for the Year-Spirit. The word means something like "recurrent vital day" (implying periodicity), or the day that marks the coming again of an important time. "The arrival of each *Eniautos* is the beginning of a new Aion or Age" (120). Dionysus, whose name means "Young Zeus, or Zeus the Son, the New King," is the *eniautos* because his advent marks the passing of the old. He is the new age, the flowering of all that is green.

Hesiod, who gives the myth in its oldest form, tells of the supersession of one generation of gods by the next, until we come to Zeus and Dionysus. There seem to be two variants of the relations between these deities: in the Olympian story Zeus is the eternal father, "but to another, and apparently more original conception, the series has no conclusion, since the Old Zeus gives way to a New Zeus, and he at the end of the year will pass it on to another new Zeus" (122).

Examining the figures in this sequence—the Old King, the Earth Mother, and the Young King—we find (in the oldest version) that the Old King is an enemy to his children. He is also a *pharmakos* (scapegoat) who is expelled. The Mother, who abides as king follows king, always is on the side of the young against the old. And the Young King, or Son, is likewise clearly defined as good, as opposed to his father, who is bad. He is the redeemer of all who, like his Mother, have suffered under the iniquities and pollutions of the past generation.

The passing of the old and his replacement by the new supplies one of the recurrent plots in tragedy. The reason for its use in tragedy is, of course, that "it expressed in parable that birth of the *Dios Nusos*, or Young Zeus, which was the central myth of the Festival. The story might not be dramatically sympathetic, but ritually it was a necessity. It had to come in somewhere" (124).

Murray argues that the idea of the eniautos-spirit who redeems the world from the pollution of the past *aion* and relieves his suffering mother, the earth, from her anguish

> is a widespread and profound element in Greek religious tradition. And I cannot help noticing that it goes further, and plays a great part in that intense flowering of religious and mystical aspiration which resulted from the meeting of Greek, Hebrew, Egyptian, and primitive Anatolian thought in the age which is called Hellenistic, and which has had such a lasting influence on the world (126).

He goes so far as to find the influence of this ritual story in the general tendency of Hellenistic and later Mediterranean religion (including Christianity) to yearn for a savior whose advent will inaugurate a new age. He traces certain avatars of this figure in the myth and ritual of the eastern Mediterranean and concludes:

> It cannot but strike any student of these ideas how many of them seem to occur, either independently or by imitation, in many different Mediterranean myths and how many have lived on in certain forms of Christianity. They seem to have in them, as I have suggested, much of what Dr. Jung calls Primordial Images; the metaphors or symbols which recur constantly in the human mind, as instruments to express or satisfy certain deep-seated emotions for which there is no scientific terminology (127).

The longing for purification takes two forms. Generally it expresses itself in the need for personal repentance and reconciliation. This tendency appears in the drama as well, in the words of forgiveness voiced by the god at the end of many Euripidean tragedies as well as in many plays of the New Comedy. The other form is the longing for the purification not so much of oneself as of the whole world—the general destruction and rebirth associated with biblical apocalyptic. This tendency manifests itself in revolutionary strivings everywhere. "Primordial Images shall we call them, dreams of mankind which 'never happened but always are'? Often we cannot but wish that they would stop and leave us in peace; but I doubt if we could live without them" (128).

2

In his reply to Pickard-Cambridge, Murray had distinguished three great advances in the understanding of tragedy through the use of anthropology. The third of these was the realization that the mummers' plays, found throughout Europe in rural communities down to 1914, were in fact related to the worship of the year-spirit that prevailed in ancient times. R. M. Dawkins in 1906 had happened upon a folk play in Greece that reproduced in all essential particulars the Dionysian ritual. His report had generated new interest in Britain in what had hitherto generally been a subject for discussion in county antiquarian societies. New examples were reported from all over Britain and Europe, and it was inevitable that someone would attempt an overall treatment. This was done by Roger Tiddy, a talented young Oxford lecturer who was killed in the war. Although his book was published in 1923, he had completed his work before the war, so that it properly belongs at this point in the discussion.[25]

Tiddy justifies his inquiry into "folk literature" on the same basis that one might use in studying the eighteenth-century background in order more fully to understand the literature of that period. To him the creator of folk literature is a clearly defined group called "the folk." "In the main most people will probably agree that it is worth while looking into the origins of some of the simpler and more popular kinds of literary art, if only on the chance that they may throw some light on their more complex offspring" (61). Tiddy recognizes that the evidence is slim and does not claim to have an ironclad case; rather, it is "the accumulation of small indications" which must convince (61).

In this would-be reconstruction of the history of folk literature, the Renaissance is the villain, for until then society was basically homogeneous and all classes enjoyed whatever amusements there were. After the Renaissance, however, with the introduction of classical subject matter, a split between the classes developed. The older culture survived among the peasantry, but now peasants are dying out and so is their traditional literature.

> As a preliminary to any study of folk literature it is important to consider his [the peasant's] temperament and his idiom. But to do this is, of course, to make an assumption which may perhaps not be justifiable in fact. It is to assume that the modern survival of the peasantry is a fair representative of the folk that made traditional poetry and drama and dance. Of course he cannot be the same. He is, for one thing, merely a survival, not part of a really living community. He is probably rather a degenerate survival: for he has suffered, through some generations at least, by the decay of his industry, by comparative neglect and isolation, and perhaps from worse things than that. But despite this I am inclined to think that English country life, underneath its lethargy and inertia, does still preserve something on the basis of which we can reconstruct the life of the folk in the past centuries. In this faith, for it can be no more, I take the peasants whom I know as evidence of the folk who made folk literature (65).

This passage once again illustrates the tendency to mythopoeia that writing about myth brings out: read "savages" for "peasants" and "mythology" for "folk literature" and this paragraph might serve as a theoretical foundation for any of the investigations of myth that took place until Malinowski in the 1920s.[26] This *de haut en bas* tendency seems to be built into all such discussions, since they can only take place when the writer is less naive (or innocent) than those he is writing about (the peasants or savages who are still living in the

stage of mythic consciousness). We should not wonder then at the
hardiness of degenerationism, which is a version of the myth of the
golden age; in this case, current mythology is seen as the wreckage
of the true wisdom of ancient times. The echoes of the myth of
"merrie Englande" (we are reminded too of Hardy's reflections on
the death of the peasantry in *Tess of the d'Urbervilles*) are English variants on this mythic structure. I remarked earlier that the growth in
interest in savages in Britain grew in direct proportion to the spread
of empire. It seems reasonable to extend the colonial analogy to the
domestic scene: the lower classes in England, and particularly the
agricultural workers, were exploited as few colonial populations
were. Tiddy's words, written in 1914, give witness to the fact that the
rural masses were still felt to be so significantly "other" that a
detached "scientific" attitude was appropriate in studying them.

In any case the folk are conceived to be, in the best romantic style,
closer to the nerve of life; their talk ("for [them] all poetry is talk"—
65) is more passionate and convincing than ours, more enriched by
natural imagery because they are, quite simply, closer to nature than
we are. Likewise the folk are humorous, although like their imagery
their humor is simple—wit is unknown, and anything "different"
makes the peasant laugh. But Tiddy warns us not to idealize the folk,
as Wordsworth did (and as did Yeats and the "Celtic Twilight"). This
idealization,

> which naturally arises in any even moderately sympathetic
> mind . . . cannot possibly help . . . colouring one's appreciation
> of the thoughts and words of poor people. . . . In any attempt
> to define or to explore folk literature, the pathos which we are
> apt to find in poverty or helplessness must simply be dismissed
> (68, 69).

This well-taken caution does, however, serve to warn us that the
interest in things folklike that swept parts of the English upper
classes at the end of the nineteenth century was strongly literary and
sentimental-humanitarian (much like a good deal of the interest on
the part of white American intellectuals in black music during the
latter part of the twentieth century); "the folk" tells us more about

the minds that constructed the concept than about the folk themselves. The same caveat must be entered concerning the savage, obviously a blood relation.

In his second lecture, Tiddy asserts his thesis: that the mummers'
play, although without a clear history and today possessing very little of the dramatic at all, "bears distinct traces of a ritual origin, and
thus enables us to draw certain conclusions as to the taste of the
peasantry in drama" (70).

> At a very early period English literature, like all literature, was
> entirely of the folk and entirely communal. Like the literature
> of the Greeks, it originated in religious ceremonies. In the
> Norse mythology vegetation gods can clearly be descried
> behind the splendid panoply of heroism with which a later and
> nobler imagination has invested them, and the agricultural
> religion of England was no doubt a primitive form of the Norse
> mythology. In the ceremony of primitive religion various
> means were used to secure the fertility of earth and flocks and
> tribe; and in England at least two separate means of attaining
> this end were practiced (70).

The first of these is by mimetic magic: specifically, by putting a
representative of the new year through an ordeal at the hands of the
old year so rigorous as to prove fatal, only to have him revive. This
rite, become communal, survives in the decapitating movement so
prominent in the sword dance. The other main magical technique
for achieving fertility is to eat some incarnation of the spirit of
growth, thereby gaining his power by ingestion. Likewise, this notion
is (dimly) to be discerned in the hunting imitated in some of the
Morris dances.

Both the mummers' play and the sword dance retain their ritual
origins, in that they both present "a combat, a death, and a revival"
(72); therefore they should be seen as descendants of a common
original. Tiddy then lists other characteristics of the plays that attest
to ritual origins: for example, "occasional indications of the idea that
the victim is the son of the conqueror" (74); the importance and
universality of the doctor (that is, the witch doctor or medicine

man). He asserts that the influence of the original ritual drama is also to be seen in the medieval mystery plays insofar as character types are concerned [for example, "The Garcio may be a ritual survival connected with the cheeky boy of the Ritual Play, or, with equal probability, he may both in the Ritual and in the Miracle Play be purely a dramatic invention" (96)]. From the need of the priests to enliven their morality plays they took the crowd-pleasing types from the miracles, and thus from the ritual plays, especially in the character types of "the Ruffler [that is, the boisterous soldier] and the Mischief-maker" (109).

Tiddy concludes that the parallels he has adduced between folk and literary drama "are due for the most part, though perhaps not entirely, to the influence of folk drama upon the professional dramatists whose trade obliged them to neglect no means of satisfying the less educated sections of their audience" (132).[27]

"The influence of the folk drama upon professional dramatists" is the subject as well of another application of the eniautos-theory developed at about the same time as Tiddy's: Janet Spens's *An Essay on Shakespeare's Relation to Tradition* (Oxford, 1916). This brief essay, hard to find today, is an effort to understand in a new way the implications of the fact that Shakespeare in some sense emerged from, and was nourished by, a particularly flourishing folk tradition in Elizabethan England. It is little more than a sketch, and its importance lies in its limitations, which are more important than its achievements.

Briefly, Spens is trying to broaden greatly any future consideration of Shakespeare's relation to folk tradition. By 1914 it was a commonplace that Shakespeare was indebted to folklore, and antiquarians had for more than a century amply documented that indebtedness. Spens, a student of Murray and armed with the eniautos-theory that she had derived from Frazer and Harrison, was suggesting that "tradition" in Shakespeare had to be understood in a deeper and more complex way than had hitherto been suspected.

One has only to heft her book and those of Harrison, or even that of Tiddy, to see that Spens is not interested in piling up masses of evidence, as the other Ritualists had done. Instead, she proceeds basically by intuition, hypothesizing lost folk plays as the links connecting what we know of Elizabethan folklore with Shakespeare's plays. To do this, she assumes that the structural components and motifs of the plays are at least analytically separable and thus, for example, is willing to isolate Antonio as a "scapegoat" in *The Merchant of Venice* and "derive" this "figure" from undoubted scapegoat rituals in primitive times.

The book as published seems to have grown out of an essay she wrote as a member of Murray's advanced seminar. E. R. Dodds told me, in 1969, that in 1913-14 he was one of a small group of students who were supposed to study Euripides with Murray. Instead the sessions of the group developed into rather rarefied colloquies between Murray and Spens, who had already done some work on the ritual origins of drama and had views of her own on the subject, particularly on the importance of the scapegoat in tragedy.

Although some of the book was probably student work, it had real effects on Murray, Harrison, and especially Cornford, as witnessed by several letters.[28] Murray sent the book, or at least a draft of it, to Harrison in November 1913; she read it and was impressed. Here is her (unpublished) reaction to Murray:

> The Scapegoat is splendid. The most exciting thing I have read for years. She has put her finger on the very spot, the real essence of tragedy, and tho I am not sure if she knows this on the essential difference between Comedy and Tragedy— Comedy is all the Renouveau (ending with a marriage—and old men turned young men), Tragedy Renouveau plus Scapegoat, and—what we have all been fumbling for—it was the perception of the Scapegoat element in epic saga by that genius Aeschylus that created Tragedy—that lifted it out of the Mummers' Ritual. I was spellbound the moment she compared Ophelia to Cassandra—because those two always give me the same almost unbearable excitement and release and she explains too why no one is any good till they are mad and melancholy. F. M. C. and I have been breaking our heads as to what was the real essence of Tragedy as contrasted with Comedy—both being based on the Mummers' plays and here it is in a moment—I cld be jealous if I weren't so glad, and how happy you must be who started it all,

and what fools are they who say you can understand English literature without Greek. . . .

Spens's essay came just in time to be used by Cornford in his book on comedy. Here is an extract from a letter from Cornford to Murray of 1 April 1914, just after *The Origin of Attic Comedy* had appeared:

> I did hear from JEH something of Miss Spens's Pharmakos, which struck me as original and important. Indeed I shoved in a good deal more about the Pharmakos in consequence. We have neglected the apotropaic side in emphasising the fertility aspect; though both are so marked in Comedy—apotropaic and fertility in the sex element. I suppose Death is a riddance and atonement, not a mere prelude to resurrection—more than we allowed for.

From the same time—spring 1914—two letters from Murray to Spens herself are of interest. On 17 April 1914 he remarks:

> By the way, I have just been re-shaping a syllabus on the Religious Background of the Bacchae and found that the argument did not go satisfactorily. On working it over I found that it was—I think—because I had left out the Pharmakos from my scheme of tragedy. Just your point. I will think over Orestes as an outcast.

And on 28 March, some three weeks earlier, Murray writes:

> I am sending you a copy of Cornford's new book on Comedy. I think in general it strengthens your case considerably, as showing the influence of the Mummers' Plays on literary drama. . . . The Pharmakos turns up in Comedy as an Alazon, or Boaster apparently, at any rate as an unwelcome intruder, and has to be driven out.

Spens's work had other effects as well. Murray writes to her on 29 March 1914:

I have just been invited by the British Academy to give its annual Shakespeare lecture this summer. . . . It occurred to me that I might lecture on your sort of line, calling attention to your book. I would chiefly run the Orestes-Hamlet business, and the effect of the Year Ritual on Drama as well as Religion.

In preparing his lecture, however, Murray had some second thoughts on the central importance Spens had assigned to the pharmakos. He writes to her on 25 June 1914, just after the lecture:

By the way I think the difference between Tragedy and Comedy is probably merely this: that Tragedy comes from a regular Trauerspiel, a Ritual Lamentation like the Adonis rite, and Comedy from almost anything else. The other things tend to be made comic or at least cheerful. And, I incline to think, even your Pharmakos can be made into a joke, if people want to do so. Like the kicking out of the Alazon in Cornford; or even the Guy Fawkes procession or the sawing in two of Judas.—What do you think? I should be sorry to upset your nice apple-cart, but it looks to me as if the Pharmakos was not in itself the special cause of Tragedy.

This seems to have been the end of the matter. In 1921 Murray asked Harrison to insert a footnote reference to Spens's *Essay* in her *Epilegomena*, but she never did.[29] Spens, for her part, went on to become a well-known Renaissance scholar; her later works on Spenser bear no trace of her venture into myth and ritual.

3

In 1920 came the first application of ritualism to nondramatic, non-classical literature: Jessie Weston's *From Ritual to Romance*.[30] In this book Weston attempts to show that the Grail legend is derived from, and is in fact an account of, fertility rituals dating from pagan times that persisted into Christian Europe. Her debt to Frazer and the Ritualists is clearly and explicitly acknowledged. She draws especially upon *The Golden Bough, Themis,* and Murray's "Excursus" for her discussions of the evolution of deity and of the enduring ritual forms in the mystery religions that shaped later literature.[31]

Weston's scholarly career, spanning as it did the quarter century from 1890 to the First World War, recapitulated the general movements within the fields of mythology, folklore, and comparative religion already noted. She began in the nineties as a romantic Wagnerian, translating Von Eschenbach's *Parzival* in order to get a better sense of the great composer's use of sources.[32] After more popularizations of Wagnerian material, she entered Arthurian studies proper, translating several of the more important romances. Around the turn of the century she became interested in tracking down and identifying folkloristic sources and analogues, especially Celtic ones, for the Arthurian heroes. Then, shortly after it appeared in 1900, she read the second edition of *The Golden Bough* and was "struck by the resemblance existing between certain features of the Grail story, and characteristic details of the Nature Cults described" (3). As she thought about it more, she began to wonder whether in the Grail cycle "we might not have the confused record of a ritual, once popular, later surviving under conditions of strict secrecy" (4).

By 1909 she had worked out the main lines of the theory offered in *From Ritual to Romance*. Moreover, she had been for some years active in occult circles, and her endeavors in that direction had convinced her that her ideas were correct.[33] But she was as yet unwilling to publish because she knew she lacked sufficient objective, historical evidence. Then she came across the so-called Naassene Document, a ritual text from a Gnostic Christian sect in the Near East that dates from about the second century A.D. This document, containing as it does striking resemblances to incidents and phrases from the various Grail stories, was the missing link in the chain of evidence she needed.

As important as the Naassene Document to her work was the fact that at this time she became acquainted with the work of the Ritualists:

> The perusal of Miss J. E. Harrison's *Themis* opened my eyes to the extended importance of these Vegetation rites. In view of the evidence there adduced I asked myself whether beliefs

which had found expression not only in social institution, and popular custom, but, as set forth in Sir [*sic*] G. Murray's study on Greek Dramatic Origins, attached to the work, also in Drama and Literature, might not reasonably—even inevitably— be expected to have left their mark on Romance? The one seemed to me a necessary corollary of the other, and I felt that I had gained, as the result of Miss Harrison's work, a wider, and more assured basis for my own researches (viii).[34]

Postulating that the Grail romances were the *disjecta membra* of an ancient pre-Christian cultus that celebrated the death and resurrection of an eniautos-daimon, Weston offers a detailed explanation of their complicated action and interrelationships, as well as a guess concerning their authorship. As one might expect, her arguments, *mutatis mutandis*, resemble those of the Ritualists—comparative, ethnographic, and structural—that have been examined at length, and for that reason we shall pass over them in silence. Suffice it to say that the book, clearly and persuasively written, was greeted with enthusiasm at first, by both the public and the scholarly community.[35] Hyman quotes statements of approbation from such well-known anthropologists and folklorists as R. R. Marett and Sidney Hartland, as well as from the Ritualists themselves.[36] One notable scholar who registered general support (albeit with some reservations concerning the sketchiness of her evidence) for Weston's reading of the Grail cycles was Roger Sherman Loomis in his *Celtic Myth and Arthurian Romance* (1927). Soon afterwards, however, he underwent a complete change of mind and decided that her thesis was worthless; in succeeding books over the next forty years he took pains to deride her ideas as so much fine-spun moonshine, completely without redeeming qualities (see, for example, the comments in his 1963 work *The Grail*).

Weston was not the only one to see the relevance of the eniautos-daimon pattern to nonclassical materials. In the same year, 1920, in which *From Ritual to Romance* appeared, Bertha Phillpotts published *The Elder Edda and Ancient Scandinavian Drama*. Predictably, this was an effort to explicate Old Norse literature from the point of view of the fertility religion of pre-Christian ancient Scandinavia. Phillpotts suffered the same fate as Weston: her book made a brief sensation, only to be attacked and then dismissed by historically minded scholars on the basis of lack of evidence.

In 1921 Margaret Murray brought out *The Witch-Cult in Western Europe*, which argued that the practices suppressed as witchcraft in the Middle Ages were in fact the tag end of the old fertility religion that had continued to exist in odd corners of Europe right through a millennium and more of Christianity. Once again the same story was played out: Murray's evidence—the records of witchcraft trials in the fifteenth and sixteenth centuries in England and France—was said to be "too late," too sketchy, and of questionable value.

4

As we have seen, over the past half century the Ritualists and their work have been first cried up and then decried. Today the consensus among classicists and ancient historians is emphatically negative. A representative example is Gerald F. Else, the most recent surveyor of the question of the origins of tragedy, who, after disparaging Murray's ritual hypothesis, continues:

> Murray's alleged ritual sequence and the misreadings and misinterpretations that have flowed from it are a particular instance of a much broader, more pervasive phenomenon: the determination at all costs to find the origin of tragedy in religion, and therefore in ritual. (I say "and therefore in ritual" because in a culture like that of Greece, where there are no true sacred books, the nerve center of religion is necessarily found in cult, that is, in ritual.) It is curious that our secularized, "scientific" age should follow this bent so persistently.[37]

He offers no other examples of this "bent" aside from that of Murray, and is unwilling to speculate about why this should be so (finding it merely "curious"). Even if we assume that Pickard-Cambridge and, after him, Else are right and that Murray et al. were wrong, Else's rejection invites comment, nonetheless. His intention is to dismiss ritualism as an epiphenomenon of the Zeitgeist—

because moderns hunger for religion, their scholars serve it up to them in an oblique and sophisticated form.

The argument is tempting—as it explains ritualism it also explains it away—but on two counts it will not stand up. First, there are biographical and chronological problems. It is basically an academic version of Philip Rahv's free-swinging 1953 attack on mythography in general, in which he asserted that the postwar interest in myth was best understood as a reflex of a modern "failure of nerve" and that writing on myth was really a flight from the iron lessons of history and an attempt to smuggle religion in through the back door, having ejected it through the front. That may have been an accurate piece of cultural diagnosis for the 1950s, but it does not describe Britain in the decades before the First World War. As I indicated in Chapter Two, it is incorrect to see the "rise of anthropology" as a direct response to the publication of *The Origin of Species*. Obviously Darwin and evolutionary social thought in general did at least exacerbate (if not create) a spiritual crisis for thoughtful people, but by the 1890s such people, especially in the agnostic Oxbridge milieu, had long habituated themselves to their melancholy situation.

Likewise, the parallel between the Ritualists and the post-1945 generation of mythographers is unpersuasive in that, unlike the latter, the former were not reeling from the shock of world cataclysm. Rather, Harrison, Murray, and Cornford are best understood as the last representatives of nineteenth-century rationalism, albeit a rationalism *in extremis* as its assumptions were tested in the First World War and found wanting. (It is worth noting that Else does not label their contemporaries Frazer and Farnell as bootleggers of religion.) It seems facile to write them off as having allowed their spiritual needs to co-opt their scholarship fatally.

The evidence for this is amply supplied in the Moncure Conway Lecture Harrison gave, with Murray in the chair, to the Free Thought Association in March 1919. In the address, entitled *Rationalism and Religious Reaction*, she eloquently puts the case for the immanentist and subjectivist view of God and religion then gaining ground in postwar Britain. Jane Harrison was remarkable for her capacity to remain receptive to new ideas, and one can see this lecture as an early version of the position she took three years later in

Epilegomena to the Study of Greek Religion. The point here, however, is the way she and Murray, in his introductory remarks, both clearly align themselves with the older generation of rationalists. To be sure they were rationalists with a difference (Murray tells of hearing Harrison speaking "disrespectfullly of an imagined being whom she called 'Old Rat'—'rat,' I regret to say, being merely short for Rationalist"), especially when compared with men like Frazer and Farnell. But Murray might well have been speaking for Harrison as well as himself when he said

> for my own part, dully and perhaps blindly, I can only cling to my faith in Rationalism, as I understand it, meaning not an exclusively Rationalist treatment of problems, but a belief in the sovereign power and need of thinking clearly, and setting truth always first and not second or third. If thought has led us astray, we can only trust that more thought will lead us right again.[38]

Thus on the level of biography and chronology—Else seems to have retrojected the postwar spiritual climate of "The Waste Land" and the "lost generation" back before the First World War—the argument will not stand.

Biography aside, however, there is another and larger issue. Again stipulating that Harrison, Murray, and Cornford were essentially mistaken about the facts, and that the theoretical foundations of the ritualist approach are thus fatally undermined (at least so far as ancient Greece is concerned), it is not clear what consequences may be said to flow from this. Else views the fact that literary critics have yet to hear the news proclaimed by Pickard-Cambridge as a "discouraging . . . manifestation of intellectual lag between one field and another," implying that were the word to get around, then Ritualists would simply (have to) go silent.[39] But this is not obvious, at least from the point of view of literary criticism. One may acknowledge that theater historians should be aware of the criticism of the Cambridge position, and thus adopt it at their own peril when writing about the origins of drama. That said, however, such criticism does not vitiate ritualism when it is recognized *not* as a historical description of what took place in the development of Greek culture but as a literary-critical paradigm. In other words, Else may well be right in terms of history, but it is an unnecessary simplification to assume that history is the only relevant criterion; there are matters here to which his censure does not apply.[40]

The analogies of psychoanalysis and Marxism immediately come to mind. Since their promulgation, both systems have been repeatedly attacked as unscientific, as based upon untenable or untestable assumptions, and as insufficiently rigorous methodologically. To acknowledge the force of such revisionist criticism does not detract from the power of the systems, seen as great metaphors or (in Joseph Campbell's phrase) as "myths to live by." Likewise with ritualism: one need not accept Northrop Frye *in toto* to appreciate that ritualism in his hands has been combined with archetypal psychology to provide what even his adversaries concede are often brilliant insights into literature. The same is true in the case of Kenneth Burke, at least as erudite and eclectic as Frye, for whom ritualism is but one ingredient in an intellectual stew that includes larger portions of Marx, Freud, and Aristotle.

In the nineteenth century literature was understood largely in historical and biographical terms. In our time the trend has been away from historical criticism to formalism and the analysis of literary language. Seen in these terms, it seems to me that there is a place for a yet-to-be-developed ahistorical version of ritualism as well, and therefore that the Cambridge Ritualists may not have labored entirely in vain.

5

When one attempts to carry the survey of the effects of the Cambridge Ritualists forward from the 1920s, three tendencies stand out clearly. First is that the disciplines most affected by the Ritualists have been those with more speculative and impressionistic methodologies—pre-eminently literary criticism, of course, but also philosophy to some extent. Those to whom ritualism seemed congenial in more "*wissenschaftlich*" studies, like classics, anthropology, or history (especially biblical and Near East studies) have been scholars of a more speculative turn of mind—those able to tolerate the rather large uncertainty factor in ritualist formulations in return for what seems a satisfyingly comprehensive explanation. The same comment might be made concerning the effects of psychoanalysis, in both its Freudian and other branches, on other disciplines—these days the most diehard Freudians tend to be teaching literature, not treating clients.

Second, it seems worth noting that in those more "scientific" fields mentioned above, the reason the Ritualists have fallen into disfavor (not that the Cambridge tide at its height ever reached flood stage) is not that their assertions have been controverted by new information. The Ritualists' work is synthetic; they were not fieldworkers but rather were attempting to bring to the classics in general and the question of the origins of the drama in particular methods and approaches developed elsewhere. Ritualism has been swept away not by an access of new facts but of new theories. Quite plainly, Durkheim, Freud, Bergson, and Smith—from whom Frazer, Jane Harrison, and the others largely derive—are no longer the last word, or even the next-to-last word. Thus when Durkheim lost his pre-eminence as a sociologist of religion, so did his Cambridge followers in classics—except that, to a remarkable degree, this news never reached the followers of the followers.

Third, even in the case of those few scholars today who do acknowledge their indebtedness to the Ritualists (as mediated by Northrop Frye), that influence has been substantially diluted by infusions of a more sophisticated psychology and anthropology than existed at the turn of the century. Thus one might say that the Ritualists constitute one intellectual grandparent, and in the current generation of scholarly offspring one sees here and there a cluster of traits that puts one in mind of the older generation. But everyone, scholars included, has four grandparents, so that while characteristics may be said to "skip" a generation, with the result that the child resembles no one in the family so much as a grandparent, such cases tend to be uncommon: the Cambridge influence is only one gene on the intellectual chromosome today. To drop the metaphor, Frazer and the others are no longer a real intellectual presence, as they certainly were through the first half of the century.

In the last fifty years Freudian and Jungian psychology and structuralist anthropology have become the property of literary intellectuals, and much of the "myth" criticism produced since the Second World War has been inclined in these and other non-Cambridge directions.

Finally, even most of those who find the Cambridge position useful have had to modify it importantly in order to keep it viable. Post-1945 literary criticism no longer believes in origins. Here is Northrop Frye, writing in 1957: "To the literary critic, ritual is the *content* of dramatic action, not the source or origin of it";[41] he is echoed by Theodor H. Gaster, the eminent Near East scholar, who generalized the relation of ritual to literature as follows: "In other words, what is really at stake is not the dependence of a particular composition upon an actual performance, but rather the paralellism between a pattern of narrative and a pattern of ritual, or—to put it in broad terms—the ultimate relation of a genre of literature to a genre of ceremony."[42] The effects of this drastic and important change will be examined below.

Before getting to literary criticism, and because the Cambridge influence has been generally diffused at the same time as it has been diluted, it seems worthwhile offering a brief sketch of some of the effects of the Ritualist position on nonliterary scholarship. Among classicists, the Ritualists have never fared well. Since Pickard-Cambridge's onslaught in *Dithyramb, Tragedy and Comedy* in 1927 it has not been easy to find a good word for their work among Hellenists. Two notable exceptions have been, in their quite different fashions, George Thomson and T. B. L. Webster. For the former the work of Jane Harrison, along with that of the pioneering American sociologist L. H. Morgan and of course and pre-eminently Marx and Engels, has remained alive and meaningful. In *Aeschylus and Athens* (1941) and the two volumes of his *Studies in Ancient Greek Society* (1949), Thomson has pursued precisely the path blazed by Harrison in *Themis*—namely, the study of initiation rituals in ancient society, ritual, and (dramatic) literature. Thomson, mainly because of his Marxism, was entirely a loner in classical studies—there was no "Birmingham group" and his brilliant work has become the exclusive property of the Left by default. As in Jane Harrison's day, only a few ancient historians (like M. I. Finley and Ronald Syme) have been equipped or inclined to analyze the social and economic structure of ancient society.[43]

An equally eminent if more orthodox scholar is T. B. L. Webster; for that reason his relatively kind words on behalf of the *eniautos* theory deserve mention. It is mildly ironic that the vehicle for his qualified rehabilitation of the Ritualists was his 1962 revision of *Dithyramb, Tragedy and Comedy*.[44] In reworking and updating that standard work, Webster dropped altogether the polemic against Murray and Cornford. In its place he offered a reassessment of the *eniautos* theory fifty years after *Themis*: "Put briefly it is this: rituals of the *eniautos daimon* type in the Mycenaean age very early (and certainly before Homer) gave rise to myths which were dramatized very early and so established a rhythm which was so satisfying that other stories from other mythological cycles were approximated to it."[45] Nevertheless, this sentence does not mean that Webster can be counted as a latter-day Ritualist. Despite his greater willingness (greater than Pickard-Cambridge, at any rate) to accept ritual explanations and connections, he also writes: "The only conclusion which seems legitimate from the literary evidence is that, on the one hand there *may* have once been an undifferentiated performance involving both serious and grotesque elements out of which high tragedy and comedy could be evolved . . . but that, on the other hand, there is no sufficient proof of it. . . ."[46] Webster pointedly bases his statement on "literary evidence" only, explicitly ignoring ethnographic parallels. (Murray and especially Cornford also acknowledged that the Greek evidence was largely wanting, which was why they were using comparative data in the first place.) But of course this is neither an accidental nor a trivial qualification, for modern classical scholars like Webster, with greater anthropological sophistication than their predecessors, are no longer interested in making such comparisons.[47] Webster's remarks may be the harbinger of wider, albeit qualified, acceptance of the work of the Ritualists by their professional descendants.[48]

In anthropology the trends that led to the "dethronement" of Frazer and the comparative method have already been noted; here it is enough to offer a respected judgment on the Ritualists by the eminent British ethnographer E. E. Evans-Pritchard. In his 1962 Evans Lectures, published in 1965 as *Theories of Primitive Religion,* he pursued his long-running argument with the Durkheimians by counting the Cambridge group as among those beguiled by the French siren song into venturing out of their depth; needless to say, like most such overly ambitious swimmers, they drowned. Like Freud in psychology, Durkheim in sociology receives the reverence due the founder but his views in general—and especially those on (primitive) religion—have been harshly criticized by succeeding generations of anglophone sociologists and anthropologists; few today would call themselves "Durkheimians."

In the allied field of folklore, which like classics and anthropology treats myths and rituals as primary data, the myth-ritual position has not fared any better. Folklore studies, immensely important at the turn of the century in Britain, experienced a sharp downturn after the First World War, mainly as a result of the turn toward functionalism that fatally undermined their evolutionary theoretical basis. In the United States the last twenty-five years have seen a dramatic reversal in the decline of folklore, at least as an academic pursuit, but its intellectual impulse has remained basically taxonomic, as witness the magnum opus of its acknowledged doyen, Stith Thompson's massive *Motif-Index of Folk Literature* (1936–50). Over and above the massive empiricism of Thompson's work, the major theoretical developments have been the work of the Russian formalists like Vladimir Propp, so important to Lévi-Strauss.[49] In any case the general attitude of folklore has been decidedly inimical to ritualism.[50]

Another nonliterary area in which myth-ritualism has had an impact has been in comparative religion and especially biblical and Near East Studies. S. H. Hooke, long identified with the Ritualist position, edited two collections of essays, *Myth and Ritual* (1933) and *The Labyrinth* (1935). In them the contributors argued that Near Eastern sacred literature, iconography, and architecture had roots deep in the myth-and-ritual pattern established at the dawn of the Western tradition. This largely comparative approach was carried on by several Scandinavian scholars in the 1940s: Ivan Engnell, *Studies in the Divine Kingship in the Ancient Near East* (1943); Tor Irstam, *The King of Ganda* (1944); and Sigmund Mowinckel, *The Psalms in Israel's Worship* (1962; original edition 1951). The Scandinavians argued that, contrary to what had always been supposed, the Hebrews like their neighbors *did* assimilate the notion of a divine king, except that in their case the king was Yahweh: the result, they said, is that some scriptural texts, and especially several psalms, are best understood as libretti composed as accompaniments for enthronement rituals for Yahweh in the Temple. The controversy such views stirred up has long since died down. It is generally agreed that their work was helpful in forcing a review of received ideas, but it has attracted few supporters.[51]

This trend in biblical studies continued into the 1950s with the publication of a third symposium edited by the long-lived Hooke called *Myth, Ritual and Kingship* (1958), which contains a notably temperate re-evaluation by S. G. F. Brandon called "The Myth and Ritual Position Critically Considered." In it he concluded that a good many of the high hopes of the thirties have had to be discarded in the light of new archaeological data, and others can be maintained only in a much more qualified form than had been previously enunciated.

The other publication that ought to be mentioned in this survey is T. H. Gaster's *Thespis* (1950; substantially revised, 1961), in which he argues for a common dramatic seasonal ritual pattern underlying most Near Eastern sacred literature. This pattern, although analyzed somewhat differently from Murray's ritual schema in the "Excursus" in *Themis*, is in fact a variant of it. As Gaster says in his revised version:

> The Seasonal Pattern survived not only in formal myth but also—albeit in severely attenuated guise—in the hymns and chants associated with the liturgy. It may be recognized in the structure of several Biblical Psalms, while sophisticated literary developments of it may be detected in the same way in the choral odes of the *Bacchae* of Euripides, in the Homeric *Hymn to Demeter*, and even in some of the hymns of the medieval Church.[52]

It is not easy to square the explicitly genetic claims of this statement with that from his "updating" of *The Golden Bough* (1959) quoted above at the beginning of this discussion, in which he argues that effects of the seasonal pattern are to be discerned only in generic structure, not in specific texts.

In comparative religion, a field that in the United States is today best represented by the school of Mircea Eliade, Frazer still lives. He is frequently cited in works of Eliade's like *Patterns of Comparative Religion* (1965) or, in a different vein, *The Sacred and the Profane* (1957), and many of Eliade's books share the encyclopedic qualities of their Cambridge predecessor. But Eliade, of course, far from being an anticlerical rationalist, was a Catholic and a Jungian; nor could he, with his knowledge of the East as well as the West, be so easily faulted for ethnocentrism as Frazer. Indeed, the last true-believing Frazerian was probably the late E. O. James, who continued to bring out massive Frazerian compendia right through the 1930s.

In philosophy the Cambridge impress is fainter, although perceptible for all that.[53] Obviously it is not to be found in the work of ordinary-language philosophers but rather in that group interested in the philosophy of culture, language, and thought, in man as a symbol-creating and -using being, and in phenomenology. The most distinguished representative of that school in the twentieth century was Ernst Cassirer, and the second volume, *Mythical Thought* (1925; English translation, 1955), of his *Philosophy of Symbolic Forms* is devoted to a study of myth as one of the major (autonomous) symbolic forms—on a par with language—that humans have evolved to express and give intelligible form to their lives. Cassirer, then, is not investigating mythology in detail; he assumes the ethnological data and inquires into the needs that myth (presumably) satisfies and the dynamics by which it operates. He is implicitly claiming a social as well as epistemological function for myth, and in that sense draws upon the line of thinkers like Durkheim who were so important for the Cambridge group. (Frazer, Tylor, and the other rationalists, because of their strictly intellectualist notion of the function of myth, are not important for Cassirer.) Much of *Mythical Thought*, indeed, is an effort to reconstruct the relationship that might have

prevailed between primitive men and their environment that led
them to create myth in ancient times, the times that produced the
religions and finally the philosophies of the ancient world.

6

Frazer and the Ritualists were not literary critics; literature was never
their primary interest. Rather, they were historians of ancient religion who more or less casually, as a byproduct of their main concerns, developed a new way of thinking about literature. Their
method was genetic and historical, seeking origins and derivations.
And in that sense it was the direct outgrowth of the historicism of
classical philology, which in turn shared the overall romantic interest in (primitive) origins.

The materials they worked with—myths and rituals—had been subjects of inquiry ever since Homer and Hesiod, but myth could not
begin to be studied in a systematic, scientific way until the absolutist
claims of its main vehicle—religion—were felt to be superseded and
until adequate means existed for collecting and classifying myths.
The first condition had been satisfied by the critique of religion carried out by the philosophers from Hume to Comte; the second, not
until anthropologists like Tylor, Smith, and Lang created the conceptual framework necessary for classification and analysis, and until
enough data on primitive life had been gathered from the burgeoning colonial empires of the late nineteenth century.

All this has been discussed or alluded to earlier in this essay. It
might be fruitful here, in conclusion, to attempt a general comparison between myth criticism and other types of anglophone literary
criticism current until the advent of deconstruction. Such a comparison may illuminate the extent to which myth criticism has been
assimilated into the critical "mainstream."

Myth criticism is essentially, and not only chronologically, a twentieth-century phenomenon. It bears little relation to the three critical tendencies dominant in turn-of-the-century Britain and
America: what one might call the rationalist positivist school, which
emphasized a "scientific" vocabulary, *à la* Taine; the aesthetic formalists, the best-known of whom was Walter Pater; and the cosmo-

politan moralists like Matthew Arnold and Leslie Stephen. However much these groups disagreed with one another, none of them was irrationalist; none was looking for, or prepared to accept, psychological mechanisms (such as archetypes) as formative agents in the process of literary creation. Some of them emphasized the writer's intention, some the intellectual and moral milieu in which the writer lived and on which he drew. But none had the transhistorical view of myth criticism. To be sure, there was a strong psychological tendency in English romantic criticism, but the associationist faculty psychology of the nineteenth century was unable to deal usefully with the unconscious. Thus myth criticism, in its irrationalism and its emphasis on collective phenomena like primitive religious ceremonies, is fundamentally of our time.

In another sense we can understand ritualism as part of the broad revaluation of Christianity that took place in Protestant Europe around the turn of the century. Here I refer to the fundamental repudiation of the nineteenth-century liberal view that religion was primarily a matter of ethics, and in that sense was analyzable and comprehensible. This was the "reasonable" theology, so bitterly attacked by Kierkegaard, Nietzsche, and Dostoyevsky, that had conceived of God as "the Friend behind Phenomena." To take one influential contemporary work as an example, Albert Schweitzer's *The Quest of the Historical Jesus* (1906) had emphasized, in what was then a revolutionary way, the apocalyptic element in Christianity and the eschatological aspect of Jesus' message. Another landmark was Karl Barth's *Commentary on the Epistle to the Romans* (1917), which insisted on human sinfulness and God's remoteness—a theology relevant to the crisis of the war but probably incomprehensible to those nineteenth-century writers who had conceived of Jesus as basically a gentleman like themselves. And finally, we have the development of "form criticism" by Rudolf Bultmann and his school, which proceeded to analyze the text of the New Testament with the same rigor that had been applied to the text of the Old Testament in order to isolate the authentic sayings of Jesus and also to "demythologize" the text—to find and then discard everything in the Gospels that assumed the mythological world-view of two thousand years ago and replace it by an interpretation of the remaining core relevant to our times.

Myth criticism, from a philosophical point of view, is the child of the modern analysis of symbolic systems, just as from the literary point of view the study of myth is the child of the symbolist movement. As cultural anthropology discovered that myth and ritual lay at the heart of every religion and every society, so the symbolists found myth, and its analogue the dream, at the heart of what they judged to be authentic literature. Jung has argued that modern people, at home by day in a world of technological miracles, by night in their dreams enter into the same mythic consciousness as their rude ancestors and employ as part of the inbuilt universal symbolic language the same primordial symbols in their dreams as are found undisplaced in ancient myths. Jung has analyzed dreams as if they were literary texts, and seemed to believe that dreams have "cognitive" value in the sense that they teach us about ourselves.

Northrop Frye has written:

> In looking at a picture, we may stand close to it and analyze the details of brush work and palette knife. This corresponds roughly to the rhetorical analyses of the new critics in literature. At a little distance back, the design comes into clearer view, and we study rather the content represented: this is the best distance for realistic Dutch pictures, for example, when we are in a sense reading the picture. The further back we go, the more conscious we are of the organizing design. At a great distance from, say, a Madonna, we can see nothing but the archetype of the Madonna, a large centripetal blue mass with a contrasting point of interest at its center. In the criticism of literature, too, we often have to "stand back" from the poem to see its archetypal organization.[54]

This metaphorical description of the critic's activity in relation to the work of art indicates myth criticism's major role: to act as a salutary corrective and complement to the intense, close-up lexical analysis that dominated literary criticism in the English-speaking world from about 1930 to 1970. But it also points to one of the major shortcomings of myth criticism: its neglect of considerations of value. Myth criticism is genetic and structural in approach and, as implied in Frye's words, essentially descriptive. But if we accept that all tragedies are derived from the cult of Dionysus, do we know anything about why certain plays are more effective and affecting than others? Murray's argument from archetypes in "Hamlet and Orestes" is inadequate because even if we all—playwright and audience alike—are interconnected by a subtle bond of inherited images and sympathies, we are no nearer to knowing why one play is better than another. The myth critics, eighty years ago and today, have generally got around this problem by analyzing works that are universally acknowledged to be good. But the method does not seem to have within itself any means of developing standards of evaluative judgment. To extend Frye's image, archetypal criticism not only lets us see the major constituent forms of the work, but also gives us a view of the Form (in the Platonic sense) underlying those forms. This Form does not figure in the finished picture, which is, after all, the object of criticism. Disclosure of the Form is interesting so far as an idealist aesthetics is concerned, but it is of no great help in apprehending the picture as in itself it truly is.

Appendix: The Golden Bough *and* The Mediaeval Stage

Although the work of Frazer and the Cambridge Ritualists engendered much literary criticism that attempted to uncover ritual origins for various genres and works of literature, the first effort of such an anthropological kind appeared before any distinctively "Cambridge" point of view developed—E. K. Chambers' *The Mediaeval Stage* (2 volumes, 1903), still cited even now. The clearly acknowledged debt to Frazer is greatest, naturally enough, in those sections of his work in which Chambers offers a speculative reconstruction of the origins of medieval drama.

To understand why Chambers found Frazer so congenial, one must be aware of the two rival explanations of the beginnings of drama in medieval Europe. The first sees the rebirth of drama as arising from the practice of representing or acting out brief liturgical tropes such as the well-known "Quem Quaeritis?" as part of the service at certain solemn festivals in the church year; the second understands drama as originating in humanity's "mimetic instinct" that had earlier expressed itself in the many and various pagan rituals that the Church repeatedly and unsuccessfully tried to suppress right through the Middle Ages. This second theory, then, denied that "drama" as such required or depended upon the existence of either a secular institution like the Roman theater, which in any case was eclipsed with the downfall of the Empire and had never been firmly established in northern Europe, or the Church. Instead, the "rise" of medieval drama is no creation *de novo* but in fact a natural outgrowth of the round of seasonal rituals (so copiously documented by Frazer and Mannhardt) that gave birth, quite independently, to Greek drama a millennium and a half earlier.

Chambers, who subscribed to this second theory, found in *The Golden Bough* and its author exactly what he wanted at exactly the right moment. (Chambers began writing in 1895; therefore *The Golden Bough* for him was the two-volume first edition of 1890, which gave more importance to ritual origins than did its two successors.) Frazer was an anticlerical rationalist like Chambers, and there must have been an instant meeting of the minds; the result is that *The Mediaeval Stage* is packed with references to *The Golden Bough*. [1] Not surprisingly, both Chambers and Frazer had encyclopedic tendencies and both were passionate collectors of facts for their own sake. [2] Chambers' "List of Authorities" illustrates this sort of rampant empiricism, consisting as it does entirely of works of historical scholarship, without a single theoretical or critical work. [3] All these tendencies, as indicated in the discussion of Frazer, were part of the larger effort then being made by scholars in the humane and social sciences to raise the status of their fields by assimilating their methodologies to those of the natural sciences.

Notes

Preface

1. Chase mentions them exactly twice, in footnotes only: the second reference is worth quoting to give his attitude: "Mrs. [Susanne K.] Langer often depends on Gilbert Murray and Jane Harrison for opinions on primitive thought. But why these . . . old Edwardians when the American anthropologists are full of glad tidings?" *Quest for Myth* (Baton Rouge, LA 1949) 147 n. 5.

2. "Cultural Anthropology and Contemporary Literary Criticism," *Journal of Aesthetics and Art Criticism* 11 (1952) 46-54. The same is true of Wallace Douglas, "The Meaning of 'Myth' in Modern Criticism," *Modern Philology* 50 (1953) 232-42. For a somewhat more up-to-date survey, see Robert Ackerman, "The Fortunes of Cambridge: Myth and Ritual in Anglo-American Criticism," *Social Science Information* (Paris) 15/6 (1976) 919-28.

3. Hyman, "The Ritual View of Myth and the Mythic," in *Myth: A Symposium*, ed. Thomas A. Sebeok (Bloomington, IN 1958) 137-52; Rahv, "The Myth and the Powerhouse," *Partisan Review* 20 (1953) 635-48. Both have been reprinted, along with many other pieces (including those of Douglas and Block cited above) in a useful anthology edited by John B. Vickery, *Myth and Literature* (Lincoln, NE 1966).

4. Hyman, never one for moderation when his blood was up, believes that "the ritual view has illuminated almost the whole of Greek culture, including religion, philosophy, art, many of the forms of literature, and much else. It has done the same for the games, songs, and rhymes of children; the Old and New Testaments; epic and romance, edda and saga, folk drama and dance, folktale and legend, Near East religion, modern drama and literature, even problems in history, law, and science." Hyman 149.

5. Good examples of such temperate writing are to be found in the introductory chapter of W. K. C. Guthrie's *The Greeks and Their Gods* (London 1950), and in Herbert Weisinger's moderate and reasonable reply to both Hyman and his antagonist Stith Thompson. Thompson, the eminent folklorist, attempted to rebut Hyman in the symposium already cited, and Weisinger's response came in his neatly titled "Between Bennington and Bloomington," in *The Agony and the Triumph* (East Lansing, MI 1964) 172-79.

6. For a taste of the language used about Frazer and his followers (inter alia) by some anthropologists, see the apoplectic introduction, by John Greenaway, to *The Anthropologist Looks at Myth*, eds. Melville Jacobs and John Greenaway (Austin, TX 1966) xiii. An example of the classicists' wrath, somewhat more calmly expressed, is Joseph Fontenrose's polemic monograph, "The Ritual Theory of Myth," *Folklore Studies* 18 (Berkeley and Los Angeles, CA 1966).

7. (New York 1962) 439.

Chapter One

1. *The Eighteenth Century Confronts the Gods* (Cambridge, MA 1959) 132.
2. Manuel 133.
3. H. F. van der Meer, "Euhemerus van Messene" (diss., Amsterdam 1949).
4. Manuel 26.
5. In many ways Bayle's life offers remarkable parallels with Frazer's. Both were anticlerical polymaths, true "athletes of the study," to use R. R. Marett's eulogistic description of Frazer. Both were unimpressive theoretically, but the works of both were powerful through the sheer bulk of the material presented. Both were distinctive stylists, much given to irony. Both expressed their antagonism toward religion by devoting their lives to reading and digesting mountains of data concerning it. The missing term in the Bayle-Frazer anticlerical connection is Ernest Renan, who was Frazer's model as an intellectual enlisted in the struggle to *écraser l'infâme.* For Frazer and Renan, see Robert Ackerman, *J. G. Frazer: His Life and Work* (Cambridge 1987) 93-94.
6. As for instance between Germany and Persia, on the basis of the accidental coincidence in meaning of several homophones. Holger Pedersen says that this supposed special relationship between German and Persian bedeviled philological study in the nineteenth century. *The Discovery of Language: Linguistic Science in the Nineteenth Century,* trans. J. W. Spargo (Cambridge, MA 1931) 7.
7. Max Fisch, intro. to *The Autobiography of Giambattista Vico,* trans. Max Fisch and Thomas Bergin (Ithaca, NY 1944) 46, 47.
8. Emery Neff quotes Gibbon, writing fifty years *after* Vico, to the effect that "wars, and the administration of public affairs, are the principal subjects of history." *The Poetry of History* (New York 1947) 82.
9. Giambattista Vico, *The New Science,* 3 ed., trans., abr., and rev. by Thomas Bergin and Max Fisch (Garden City, NY 1961) para. 385.
10. Throughout, Vico speaks only of gentile society and its institutions; a devout Catholic, he accepted the Church's doctrine that the Hebrew branch of the Semitic line had a special dispensation. This did not, however, prevent his book from being placed on the Index.
11. Manuel 161.
12. Chase 17.
13. In the year of Montesquieu's *Spirit of the Laws,* 1748, David Hume wrote in his *Enquiry Concerning Human Understanding:* "Would you know the sentiments, inclinations, course of life of the Greeks and the Romans? Study well the temper and actions of the French and English: you cannot be much mistaken in transferring to the former most of the observations you have made in regard to the latter. Mankind are much the same, in all times and places, that history informs us of nothing new or strange in this particular." Quoted by Neff, 230 n. 13.

14. The idea goes all the way back to Hippocrates (*On Airs, Waters, and Places*); cf. Herodotus ad fin. For this and several other classical references I wish to thank Prof. W. M. Calder III.
15. Quoted in Chase 36.
16. Chase 36.

Chapter Two

1. Hans Meyerhoff in his introduction to the source book he edited, *The Philosophy of History in Our Time* (Garden City, NY 1959) 10.
2. Emery Neff (*The Poetry of History* 23) translates the advice to the reader from Herder's first book, *Still Another Philosophy of History for the Culture of Humanity* (1765), as follows: "sympathize with the nation, go into the era, into the geography, into the entire history, feel yourself into it."
3. G. F. Gooch, *History and Historians in the Nineteenth Century* (Boston, MA 1959) 18.
4. Pedersen 79.
5. See G. N. Knauer, *Die Aeneis und Homer* (Göttingen 1964) 91ff (esp. 91 n. 2). F. A. Wolf was Heyne's student.
6. Mr. Casaubon in *Middlemarch* (set in 1830-1) is of course involved in the lifelong task of writing *A Key to All Mythologies*. George Eliot makes several references to his pamphlets on the Greek and Egyptian mysteries. Making Casaubon an adherent of this school of mythography, by 1830 completely outdated, is yet another way for Eliot to indicate the fustiness of his mind.
7. *Aglaophamus* is still cited today.
8. Gooch 38.
9. K. O. Müller, *Introduction to a Scientific Study of Mythology*, trans. J. Leitch (London 1844) 240.
10. Pedersen 248.
11. As noted earlier, Sir William Jones had first called attention (in 1786) to the relationship between Sanskrit and Greek and Latin, but Rask did not know Jones' work.
12. Jakob and Wilhelm Grimm are of course the exemplars of the combination of nationalistic folklorism (*Kinder- und Hausmärchen*) and philology.
13. The essay appears in Müller's collection called *Chips from a German Workshop* (II, 1-142), often reprinted. I use the second American edition (New York 1869).
14. Müller II, 77.
15. Müller II, 63-64.
16. Other comparative mythologists in Europe and America agreed with Müller's general philological method, but concluded that mythology really referred to fire, or clouds, or other zoological or meteorological phenomena. Andrew Lang, Müller's arch antagonist, had a field day exposing the disgreements among the various schools of comparative mythologists.

Seemingly the only datum upon which they could all agree was the equivalence Jupiter = Zeus Pater = Dyaus Pitr.

17. Andrew Lang, *Modern Mythology* (London 1898) 1.

Chapter Three

1. *Darwinism and Modern Science*, ed. A. C. Seward (Cambridge 1909) 494–511; rpt. in *Alpha and Omega* (Cambridge 1915).

2. *Evolution and Society* (Cambridge 1966) 114.

3. J. H. Buckley, *The Triumph of Time* (Cambridge, MA 1966) 15.

4. Glyn Daniel notes the great changes that had been wrought in the time sense by the end of the third quarter of the century: "In 1875 Schliemann came to London and read a paper to the Society of Antiquaries of London on his remarkable discoveries. The discussion was opened by W. E. Gladstone, who had himself published, in 1858, a book entitled *Studies on Homer and the Homeric Age*. In this book there was no mention of prehistoric archaeology or indeed of any possibility that anything other than literary criticism could illuminate the problem of Homer. Yet by the time, less than twenty years later, when he is speaking to the Society of Antiquaries, the existence and relevance of prehistory were very much in his mind.

> When many of us who are among the elders in this room were growing up, the whole of the prehistoric times lay before our eyes like a silver cloud covering the whole of the lands that, at different periods of history, had become so illustrious and interesting; but as to their details we knew nothing. . . . Now we are beginning to see through this dense mist and the cloud is becoming transparent, and the figures of real places, real men, real facts, are slowly beginning to reveal to us their outlines.

Daniel comments that these shapes looming through the haze were of three kinds: more knowledge about the great historical civilizations of antiquity; knowledge of societies (like the Hittites) about whom nothing had been known; and finally, "facts about the development of man's culture before the historic civilizations or in areas alongside the historical civilizations." Glyn Daniel, *The Idea of Prehistory* (Baltimore, MD 1964) 54–55.

5. In his long, hostile critique of James Mill's *Essay on Government* in the *Edinburgh Review* of 1829, Macaulay said that the pleasure principle was either trivial or it was false, depending upon whether it were taken as merely true by definition or else descriptive of human behavior. In his *Autobiography* J. S. Mill stated what he had learned at dire personal cost: that any theory that stopped short of explaining *why* people attached pleasure or pain to things they want or do was useless.

6. Burrow 98.
7. For a survey that makes clear the air of genial unconcern in the writing of the time in Britain about myth, see James Kissane, "Victorian Mythology," *Victorian Studies* 6 (1962) 5–28.
8. D. D., "Mythology," *Encyclopaedia Britannica*, 8 ed., 15: 759–68; A[ndrew] L[ang], "Mythology," *Encyclopaedia Britannica*, 9 ed., 17: 135–58.
9. *Modern Mythology* 4.
10. Richard M. Dorson has traced with admirable clarity the complicated history of this long controversy in "The Eclipse of Solar Mythology," and I am indebted to his essay for many details. It appears in *Myth: A Symposium* 25–63. It is worth noting that Lang was not the first critic of solar mythology. John William Donalson, the author of the article on "Philology" in the eighth edition (1853–60) of the *Encyclopaedia Britannica*, a staunch comparativist himself, had strong reservations: "Mythology cannot always be treated according to the laws of language. When we recognise a community of religious fable among a number of different nations, this may be the result of contacts subsequent even to a comparatively historical period, or it may arise from something common to the human mind, and suggested by circumstances which may occur in any country, and at any epoch. . . . Comparative philology, as it appears to us, is only valuable, when viewed in connection with ethnography, and when a due regard is paid to the antiquity of the myths and to the circumstances under which they originated" (17: 357). Lang's war with the solarists may fairly be thought of as a development of the position adumbrated by Donalson decades earlier.
11. It is perhaps not a coincidence that the occult movement, which is based on the recovery of this ancient wisdom, experienced a great resurgence just as solarism, which had lent scientific cachet to the theory of degeneration, was being supplanted by progressive and evolutionary hypotheses. For the continued strength of degenerationism in the nineteenth century, see George W. Stocking, Jr., *Victorian Anthropology* (New York 1987).
12. Although Lang was careful to point out that when he first met Tylor at Oxford in 1872 he had read none of his books, having become interested in anthropology through the works of his fellow Scot McLennan on totemism (Burrow 237). He had been interested in folklore since childhood.
13. For a fuller account of Lang's remarkable intellectual migration from full-blown evolutionist to Christian degenerationist, see Ackerman, *J. G. Frazer* 150–53.
14. These criticisms are dealt with in detail in the discussion of Frazer in Chapter Four.
15. Dorson 26.
16. His early exposure to the Aztec ruins in Mexico, however, did bolster his

faith in evolution, for the Aztecs had clearly created an advanced civilization without foreign assistance.

17. Appropriately enough, for Tylor frequently refers to savagery as "the childhood of the race."

18. E. B. Tylor, *Primitive Culture*, 2 vols. (London 1871); I quote from the sixth edition of 1920, I, 285.

19. Tylor, *Anthropology*, rev. ed. (London 1924) 387.

20. For Tylor's views on myth, see Robert A. Segal, "In Defense of Mythology: The History of Modern Theories of Myth," *Annals of Scholarship* 1 (Winter 1980) 3–49.

21. In a long, eulogistic article, the French historian of classical religion Salomon Reinach wrote in 1911 that Smith's many achievements could be summed up in the epitaph "genuit Frazerum." ["The Growth of Mythological Study," *Quarterly Review* 215 (1911) 423–41.] In fact, however, Smith was Frazer's intellectual "father" for only a short time. They must have agreed almost immediately that their friendship would continue despite profound intellectual differences. See Ackerman, *J. G. Frazer* 70–72.

22. For a survey, see John W. Rogerson, *Old Testament Criticism in the Nineteenth Century* (Philadelphia, PA 1985).

23. *The Religion of the Semites* is all that remains of the three series of Burnett Lectures that Smith gave from October 1888 to October 1891 on the topic "The primitive religions of the Semitic peoples, viewed in relation to other ancient religions, and to the spiritual religion of the Old Testament and of Christianity." Smith's failing health prevented him from preparing for publication any but the first series, which he brought out in 1889. Smith then revised them, and the second edition was seen through the press by his friend and biographer, John Sutherland Black, and by Frazer, in 1894. A third edition, with much valuable material added by Smith's student S. A. Cook, appeared as late as 1927. Meridian Books published a photographic reprint of the second edition in 1956, from which I shall quote.

24. This was recognized by Bishop Samuel Wilberforce in his attack on the contributors to the notorious collection of *Essays and Reviews* (1860) when he said that no one who "'with Niebuhr had tasted blood in the slaughter of Livy can be prevailed upon to abstain from falling next upon the Bible.'" Quoted by Basil Willey, *More Nineteenth Century Studies* (London 1956) 143.

25. Smith, *Religion of the Semites* 16.

26. J. G. Frazer, "William Robertson Smith," in *The Gorgon's Head and Other Literary Pieces* (London 1927) 281. This eulogy originally appeared in the *Fortnightly Review* for May 1894.

27. Frazer, "Preface to the First Edition," *The Golden Bough*, 3 ed. (New York 1935) I, xiv.

28. Smith 17–18.

29. Smith 18.

30. Here myth becomes a Tylorian survival, just as it does for Müller. It is appropriate to add that the absolute precedence of ritual over myth remained an article of faith only for hard-line ritualists like Hyman and Lord Raglan (*The Hero*); to my knowledge, no one now writing on the subject is willing to be so doctrinaire.

Chapter Four

1. For the last fifty years one has been able to number defenders of Frazer on the fingers of one hand and still have several fingers left over. The foremost of them today is the Popperian historian of science I. C. Jarvie, who has been carrying on a sporadic polemic with Edmund Leach and others because he believes that they have made the study of social structure paramount at the expense of cognition. Even he, however, praises Frazer less for being right than for being bold. See Jarvie's *The Revolution in Anthropology* (London 1964); "Academic Fashions and Grandfather Killing—In Defense of Frazer," *Encounter* 26 (April 1966) 53-55; "The Problem of the Rationality of Magic," *British Journal of Sociology* 18 (March 1967) 55-74. William J. Goode, *Religion Among the Primitives* (Glencoe, IL 1951) 240-58, thinks highly of the Cambridge Ritualists, but the highest praise he can muster for Frazer is as "a masterly, energetic compiler" (241). Bronislaw Malinowski ["Sir James George Frazer: A Biographical Appreciation," in *A Scientific Theory of Culture and Other Essays* (Chapel Hill, NC 1944) 179-221], in an essay redolent with filial piety and ambivalence, admits that Frazer will not go down as one who has advanced our understanding of religion, ancient or modern. On the other side, modern negative appraisals abound; the morbidly curious need consult only the entries in the Bibliography by Chase, Evans-Pritchard, Harris, or Leach. Many of their points were made in Frazer's own time by Lang (*Magic and Religion*) and A. A. Goldenweiser, *Totemism: An Analytic Study* (New York 1910).
2. For example, E. E. Evans-Pritchard, *Theories of Primitive Religion* (Oxford 1965) 1; M. J. C. Hodgart, "In the Shade of *The Golden Bough*," *Twentieth Century* 167 (1955) 111-19.
3. See, for instance, Northrop Frye's statement: "But the fascination which *The Golden Bough* and Jung's book on libido symbols have for literary critics is not based on dilettantism, but on the fact that these books are primarily studies in literary criticism, and very important ones." *Fables of Identity* (New York 1963) 17.
4. "Preface to the First Edition," *The Golden Bough*, 3 ed. (New York 1935) I, xii.
5. Ibid.
6. *Fables of Identity* 17.
7. *The Golden Bough*, 3 ed., XI, 307-08.
8. Frazer always denied Comtean inspiration or provenance. Although one of

his teachers at Glasgow, Edward Caird, lectured on Comte (and Hegel) in
the 1870s, Frazer could not bear Caird (see Ackerman, *J. G. Frazer* 15.)

9. "The Branch That Grew Full Straight," in *The Agony and the Triumph* (East
Lansing, MI 1964) 131.

10. "Preface to the Second Edition of *The Golden Bough*," in *ed. cit.*, xix–xx.

11. It must be admitted that his modesty and candor are disarming as he cheerfully reprints his facts with a new theory by which to interpret them.

12. One example of each must suffice. *Euhemerism*: this quotation, coming as
it does in the last volume of the third edition, may be said to represent
Frazer's final view in *The Golden Bough*. Having discussed at length the evidence on all sides about whether or not Balder ever lived, and being finally
persuaded "to incline the balance to the side of Euhemerism," Frazer
writes: "The acceptance of this hypothesis would not necessarily break the
analogy which I have traced between Balder in his sacred grove on the
Sogne fiord in Norway and the priests of Diana in the sacred grove at Nemi;
indeed, it might even be thought rather to strengthen the resemblance
between the two, since there is no doubt at all that the priests of Diana at
Nemi were men who lived real lives and died real deaths" (*The Golden
Bough*, 3 ed., XI, 315). Stanley Edgar Hyman, who also quotes this passage,
comments aptly: "Here the distinction between myth and history, where the
god was once a real man, and the myth as rite, where the god never existed
but is annually personified by men, is hopelessly muddled by the fact that
in both cases men 'lived real lives and died real deaths'" (*The Tangled Bank*
241).

   Intellectualism: "But we still have to ask, how did the conception of such
a composite deity originate? Did it arise simply through observation of the
great annual fluctuations of the seasons and a desire to explain them? Was
it a result of brooding over the mystery of external Nature? Was it the
attempt of a rude philosophy to lift the veil and explore the hidden springs
that set the vast machine in motion? That man at a very early stage of his
long history meditated on these things and evolved certain crude theories
which partially satisfied his craving after knowledge is certain; from such
meditations of Babylonian and Phrygian sages appear to have sprung the
pathetic figures of Adonis and Attis; and from such meditations of Egyptian
sages may have sprung the tragic figure of Osiris" (*The Golden Bough*, 3 ed.,
VI, 158).

   Ritualism: "We shall probably not err in assuming that many myths,
which we now know only as myths, had once their counterpart in magic; in
other words, that they used to be acted as a means of producing in fact the
events which they describe in figurative language. Ceremonies often die
out while myths survive, and thus we are left to infer the dead ceremony
from the living myth" (*The Golden Bough*, 3 ed., IX, 374).

13. "Song is a later invention than the dance, to which it is in its beginnings

secondary and certainly not indispensable." C. M. Bowra, *Primitive Song* (New York 1963) 243.

14. Frazer-Marett correspondence, Trinity College (Cambridge) Add. MS c. 56b; used with permission of the Master and Fellows of Trinity College, Cambridge. Is it possible that Frazer never understood Smith at all, and thus that these letters represent not rejection but incomprehension?

15. *The Tangled Bank* 267.

16. Apollodorus, *The Library*, trans. J. G. Frazer (London 1921) I, xxvii.

17. *The Library* I, xxviii.

18. The titles of these publications tell the story: *Folk-Lore in the Old Testament* (2 vols., 1918); *Myths of the Origin of Fire* (1930); *The Fear of the Dead in Primitive Religion* (3 vols., 1930–36); *Creation and Evolution in Primitive Cosmogonies* (1935); *Aftermath: A Supplement to The Golden Bough* (1936); and *Totemica: A Supplement to Totemism and Exogamy* (1936).

19. *The Golden Bough*, 3 ed., IX, 374–75.

20. Ibid., IX, 384.

Chapter Five

1. In her pamphlet on Russian aspects she lists the languages she has learned, "in a scrappy and discreditable way": three Romance, three Scandinavian, German, three Oriental, and five "dead" languages—plus Russian, of course, which she learned so well in her sixties that she taught it at Cambridge after the war. *Aspects, Aorists and the Classical Tripos* (Cambridge 1919) 6.

2. MacColl is an exception in that he was not a philologist but an art historian (later a curator of the Tate Gallery); at the beginning of her career, however, Harrison was more closely involved with art history than with classical scholarship, so that, mutatis mutandis, his role was the same as that of the scholars to be discussed below.

3. In his obituary of Cornford, Murray emphasizes the crucial influence Harrison had on the younger man's early work. "Francis Macdonald Cornford, 1874–1943," *Proceedings of the British Academy* 29 (1943) 421–32.

4. Jessie G. Stewart, *Jane Ellen Harrison: A Portrait from Letters* (London 1959) 83. The combination of intellectual stimulation, moral support, and generous friendship that Jane Harrison provided is attested in the prefaces of Murray's *Rise of the Greek Epic* (1907) and *Four Stages of Greek Religion* (1912), where he states that his first two chapters are merely recapitulations of *Themis*; and Cornford in his prefaces to *Thucydides Mythistoricus* (1907), *From Religion to Philosophy* (1912), and *The Origin of Attic Comedy* (1914) everywhere acknowledges her extraordinary help and magnanimity. Others of her friends, writing in the *Newnham College Letter* after she died or else in the Jane Harrison Memorial Lectures, gave glowing testimony to her personal qualities. Harrison from her side provides eloquent testimony to

Murray and Cornford for their assistance and friendship in the introductions to *Prolegomena* and *Ancient Art and Ritual* (1913). Cornford's dedication of *Thucydides Mythistoricus* to Harrison reads, in translation: "A dream in return for many beautiful dreams."

5. (London 1925) 88.

6. In a note made in connection with the preparation of her biography (preserved in Newnham College Library), Stewart writes that Harrison was likewise in love with MacColl, with whom she traveled to Greece in 1888. She was told by those who knew Harrison in the 1890s that she went into a deep depression when MacColl married in 1895, despite the fact that she had refused him earlier. For a description of her reaction to Cornford's marriage, and his typically male astonishment when told by his wife what Harrison's real feelings were, see Stewart 112. Sandra J. Peacock, *Jane Ellen Harrison: The Mask and the Self* (New Haven, CT 1988), offers an extended psychoanalytic discussion of Harrison's relations with men.

7. Harrison (MS letter to Murray of 1904) quotes their friend A. W. Verrall's description of her as a person who "simply reeks of 'sentiment.'"

8. Stewart 34.

9. Ibid. In an undated letter quoted by Stewart, Harrison writes, "Nauck's old mottled cheeks are shining with joy because he has got a really sound inscription in him."

10. Stewart 35. A favorite word in Harrison's letters to Murray is "therish," which means anything especially admirable because natural and instinctive.

11. *Classical Review* 24 (1911) 181.

12. W. J. Goode, *Religion Among the Primitives* 255: "Let us remember that standards of criticism in the classics, as well as the quantity of verified data, were both superior to those in anthropology, at the turn of the century."

13. "Scientiae Sacra Fames," in *Alpha and Omega* (London 1915) 107. The paper was originally delivered in 1913.

14. *Alpha and Omega* 3.

15. "Unanimism and Conversion," *Alpha and Omega* 50, 51.

16. MS letter of 1 July 1954, Jessie Stewart papers, Newnham College Library.

17. *Aspects, Aorists and the Classical Tripos* 3.

18. Her last piece of classical work was the review article on "Greek Religion and Mythology" for the *1915 Year's Work in Classical Studies.*

19. Subsequent page references are given in parentheses in the text. The book remained popular enough to reach a fifth edition by 1902.

20. In this connection Harrison tells a delightful story in her memoir [*Reminiscences of a Student's Life* (London 1925) 34]. In her sixties she was appointed Justice of the Peace, and on one case it was reported that the accused had used particularly profane language. The magistrates were interested to know just what had been said, but as it was unbecoming to

utter the offending words, they were written down and passed around the bench. "The unknown to me has always had an irresistible lure, and all my life I have had a curiosity to know what really bad language consisted of. In the stables at home I had heard an occasional 'damn' from the lips of of a groom, but that was not very informing. Now was the chance of my life. The paper reached the old gentleman next to me. I had all but stretched out an eager hand. He bent over me in a fatherly way and said, 'I am sure you will not want to see this.' I was pining to read it, but sixty years of sex-subservience had done their work. I summoned my last blush, cast down my eyes and said, 'O no! No. Thank you so much.' Elate with chivalry he bowed and pocketed the script."

21. MS note in Jessie Stewart papers, Newnham College Library.
22. Stewart 7. This exactly describes the photograph of Harrison, dressed as Alcestis in a student theatrical of 1877, that is reproduced as the frontispiece of Stewart's biography.
23. Stewart 7, 8.
24. MS letter, dated October 1911 in Stewart's hand, Newnham College Library. Pickard-Cambridge's critique, in *Dithyramb, Tragedy and Comedy* (Oxford 1927), is—predictably, from Harrison's words—extremely detailed. It will figure in the discussion of the Ritualists' reception in Chapter Eight.
25. Despite the scandalous behavior of some of those who toiled in the church of art, the 1880s in England seem to offer, mutatis mutandis, an analogy to the mass acceptance of culture that took place in the United States in the 1960s and 1970s. In both decades significant new groups in the population became comfortable enough in the use of their money and position to find it desirable to participate in what had hitherto been an art-culture of a higher class.
26. Stewart 115. She is summarizing an autobiographical essay in Harrison's essay "Unanimism and Conversion" in *Alpha and Omega*.
27. Jane Harrison, "Preface" to translation of Maxime Collignon, *Manual of Mythology* (London 1890) v.
28. *Mythology and Monuments* iii; italics Harrison. Her regret about lack of time derives from the fact that her part of the book was written in three feverish weeks (Stewart 11).
29. *Mythology and Monuments* xlii.
30. Of course she read Smith, and indeed was having her students read him in 1900 (Stewart 14).
31. Jane Harrison, "Preface" to Katherine Raleigh's translation of A. H. Petiscus, *The Gods of Olympos* (New York 1892) vi.
32. Mentioned in neither the bibliography in Stewart nor in Harrison's memoir, it was discovered by chance in the New York Public Library.
33. "Preface" to *The Gods of Olympos* vi, vii.

34. "Notes Archaeological and Mythological on Bacchylides: Odes III, XVII, VII," *Classical Review* 12 (1898) 120–40.

Chapter Six

1. The bitter personal animus between A. J. Evans and A. J. B. Wace offers a good example at a later time of this unfortunate phenomenon.

2. *Proceedings of the British Academy* 12 (1926) 328.

3. Conway (331) says, "In strict logic he was weak, especially from his way of using all kinds of evidence, strong and weak alike, in support of a theory of whose truth he was convinced. . . ."

4. Cook, *The Rise and Progress of Classical Archaeology* (Cambridge 1931) 57.

5. The most acrimonious controversy involving Harrison was provoked not by Ridgeway but by one of his friends and fellow conservatives, M. R. James, the Provost of King's College, in 1916. The *casus belli* is not now important, but James launched a Ridgeway-style all-out attack, accusing her of doing "the worst service that anyone responsible for the direction of young students can do them," and charging her with "falsifying evidence." Ridgeway then wrote to James, saying, "Never was such an audacious, shameless avowal of charlatanism, debauching young minds wholesale, and that too in a generation whose loose thinking has been doing immense harm to national life and international politics." The quotations, along with a fuller account of the controversy, are to be found in Stewart 88. The battle was conducted in the correspondence columns of the *Classical Review* for 1916.

6. *Fifty-five Years at Oxford* (London 1945) 66.

7. An early example of the new, more liberal attitude is Sir Richard Jebb, Murray's predecessor at Glasgow.

8. Jane Harrison, *Reminiscences* 82–83.

9. Stewart 12.

10. Eduard Fraenkel, in the introduction to his edition of *Aeschylus, Agamemnon* (Oxford 1950) 57. Verrall's daring and his brilliant textual conjectures earned him the witty nickname of "splendid emendax." See also the "Memoir" of Verrall by M. A. Byfield in A. W. Verrall, *Collected Literary Essays Classical and Modern* (Cambridge 1913) ix–cii.

11. *Prolegomena to the Study of Greek Religion* (Cambridge 1903) xiv.

12. In his introduction to a translation of Munk's *The Student's Manual of Greek Tragedy* (London 1891).

13. Stewart 56–57.

14. This letter appears in Stewart 57, in slightly different form.

15. See L. R. Farnell, *An Oxonian Looks Back* (London 1934).

16. *The Evolution of Religion* (London 1905) 19–20; subsequent citations will be given in the text in parentheses.

17. Stewart xi.

18. For an account of the celebrated controversy between Nietzsche and

Wilamowitz that arose from the latter's scathing review of *The Birth of Tragedy*, see J. H. Groth, "Wilamowitz-Moellendorf [*sic*] on Nietzsche's *The Birth of Tragedy*," *Journal of the History of Ideas* 11 (1950) 179–90.

19. Friedrich Nietzsche, *The Birth of Tragedy from the Spirit of Music*, trans. Francis Golffing (New York 1956) 7; subsequent references will be given within parentheses in the text.

20. Philip Wheelwright, *The Burning Fountain* (Bloomington, IN 1954) 219.

21. R. R. Marett, *A Jerseyman at Oxford* (London 1941) 163.

22. Émile Durkheim, *The Elementary Forms of the Religious Life*, trans. Joseph W. Swain (London 1915) 422.

23. Harrison cites Durkheim's long essay, "De la définition des phenomènes religieux," from *L'Année Sociologique* 2 (1898-9), 1ff; "Réprésentations individuelles et réprésentations collectives," in *Revue de Metaphysique et Morale* 6 (1898) 273ff; and "Sociologie religieuse et théorie de la connaissance," *ibid*. 17 (1909) 733ff, which became the introduction to *Les formes élémentaires*. Citations from *Themis* 486 n. 3. She does not say when she read them, however, but it cannot have been before 1907.

24. Marett writes (152) that in 1904–05, when he was dissatisfied with rationalism and had heard that some French scholars were publishing interesting and possibly congenial new ideas, he could not find a copy of *L'Année Sociologique* in Oxford—this after the journal had been in existence for six years. No information exists on this point for Cambridge.

25. Cook also had published relatively little by 1898 but was absorbed in gathering material on Zeus; he presented some of the results of his prodigious erudition and researches in what began as an extended review of the second edition of *The Golden Bough* and soon grew to monograph size in 1903–05. This was the core of *Zeus*, the first volume of which would appear a decade later. For more on Cook and Frazer, see Ackerman, *J. G. Frazer* 197–200.

26. F. M. Cornford, then a fourth-year student, attended the lectures on religion and mythology and soon thereafter made her acquaintance.

27. *Journal of Hellenic Studies* 16 (1896) 77–119.

28. Stewart 31. "Pandora" in the letter refers to her essay, "Pandora's Box," *Journal of Hellenic Studies* 20 (1900) 99–114.

29. Stewart 84. It is unclear whether Harrison was writing to Murray or to Stewart herself.

30. *A History of Ancient Greek Literature* (London 1897) 272. Bibliographical citation given by Stewart on copy of letter in Newnham College Library.

31. "Preface," *A History of Ancient Greek Literature* xi.

32. Gilbert Murray, "The Author of *The Golden Bough*," *Listener* 51 (7 January 1954) 13-4.

33. In view of the fact that Frazer was an unknown classical don writing on a subject for which no real audience yet existed, the first edition of *The Golden*

Bough was well and widely reviewed. It is worth mentioning that in 1890 his book was noticed along with three others, including *The Religion of the Semites,* by Joseph Jacobs in *Folk-Lore.* (Not surprisingly, Jacobs found Smith's book the most substantial of the lot.) By comparison, the second edition in 1900 was reviewed in that journal alone by no fewer than eight critics. Frazer's reputation grew most dramatically in the 1890s, at least partly because of his splendid translation and commentary on Pausanias. For more on the reception of the first edition of *The Golden Bough,* see Ackerman, *J. G. Frazer* 98, 323 nn. 4, 5.

34. *Prolegomena to the Study of Greek Religion* (Cambridge 1903) viii; subsequent references will be given in parentheses in the text.

35. She regretted this guess and retracted it in *Themis.*

36. Stewart 25.

37. *The Religion of Ancient Greece* (London 1905) 63.

38. (Cambridge 1950).

39. Guthrie, "Memoir," *The Unwritten Philosophy* viii.

40. Quoted by Guthrie, *loc. cit.*

41. Stewart 85.

42. *Bacchae* and *Hippolytus* (1904); *Electra* (1905); *Iphigenia in Tauris* (1910); *Medea* (1912); *Rhesus* (1913); *Alcestis* and *Suppliant Women* (1915).

43. (Oxford 1909).

44. Edited by R. R. Marett (Oxford 1908).

45. "A Modern Carnival in Thrace and the Cult of Dionysus," *Journal of Hellenic Studies* 26 (1906) 191–206.

46. Notably "Théorie générale de la magie," *L'Année Sociologique* 7 (1903) 107–66; "Essai sur le sacrifice," *L'Année Sociologique* 2 (1898) 130–77; and "La réprésentation du temps dans la religion et la magie," in *Melanges d'Histoire des Religions* (Paris 1909).

47. Stewart 96.

48. *"In Europe from around 1750 onward a shift of emphasis is evident in philosophical and scientific thought from static toward process concepts which is still in progress today. . . .* The transformation from 1750 onward found its best known expression in the development of evolutionary ideas, but it coincided with the progressive recognition of unconscious mental processes." Lancelot Law Whyte, *The Unconscious Before Freud* (Garden City, NY 1962) 44; italics Whyte's.

49. *Reminiscences* 81. Despite these words, one should recall note 47, above, in which Stewart noted that during the writing of *Themis* Harrison's appetite for philosophy had not (yet) become jaded. This disparity is one indication among several that the memoir represents an idealized version of what happened and is not reliable in matters of detail.

50. Immediately and characteristically she began to proselytize for Bergson. An

MS letter to Murray that can be dated by Stewart no more closely than 1908 says: "Have you read Bergson's *L'évolution créatrice?* If not, it is likely that I may be a nuisance when I come [to see you]." And in May 1908 she writes again: "Yes there is going to be a boom in Bergson and I already begin to loathe him [for that reason]—but all the same he's splendid."

51. *Themis* xii. It is unclear what she had in mind when she attributes to herself this momentary lapse into rationalism. If she did drift into believing that primitive religion was a "tissue of errors leading to mistaken conduct," she never said so in any of her books or letters. In the last sentence, "representations" seems to be used in its French sense to mean "ideas."

Chapter Seven

1. That *Ancient Art and Ritual*, a work of 1913, is treated after two works of 1914 is unimportant; all these books and essays were being written more or less simultaneously and in collaboration,and in large measure the accidents of publication schedules determined the order of their appearance.

2. Stewart 169–70.

3. *Euripides and His Age* (London 1913), 115.

4. *Euripides and His Age* 183–84.

5. The end of the hymn is as follows, in Murray's translation: "To us leap for full jars, and leap for fleecy flocks, and leap for fields of fruit, and for hives to bring increase; leap for our Cities, and leap for our sea-borne ships, and leap for our young citizens and for goodly Themis." *Themis* (Cambridge 1912) 8.

6. In fact that is how Harrison wrote all her books. She writes to Murray in October 1910 that the main lines of the book were clear in her mind and "I hope and trust to get it written out quickly now. I am in the stage that, bad or good, I have to get rid of it before I can think in any other form. I believe that this never happens to you. You always command your material. Mine commands me." Stewart 97.

   Cornford in a reminiscence wrote: "For a long time she would brood over the 'plot,' as she called it. Once the plot lay clear before her, she would write very rapidly, drawing with ease upon the treasure of materials stored in her memory. When she was writing *Themis* she astonished me by producing, week by week, a new chapter almost in its final shape. The mood of inspiration would last as long as the words were pouring out upon the paper. Then she would be glad to throw the thing aside, quarter the ground to pick up some fresh scent." (*Newnham College Letter*, 1929, 74.)

7. All page numbers in *Themis* taken from the photographic reprint of the second edition, of 1927, by Meridian Books (Cleveland, OH 1962); this quotation from xi. Subsequent references given in text in parentheses.

8. Freud's main anthropological authorities in that book are Smith and espe-

cially Frazer; they gave him the "evidence" he sought concerning the evolution of culture that corresponded to the development of the individual
he had worked out. Sociology recapitulates psychology. Not really interested in social process, Freud never cared to revise the book although it was
brought to his attention more than once that Smith and Frazer were no
longer held in esteem by anthropologists. See Edwin Wallace, *Freud and
Anthropology: A History and Reappraisal* (New York 1983).

9. Verrall was translating *Bacchae* 75.

10. As late as 1907, in the preface to the third edition of *A History of Ancient
Greek Literature*, Murray accepted Ridgeway's view that "one most important
element in the origin of tragedy was the ritual performed in so many parts
of Greece at the grave of an ancestor or dead hero." These performances,
says Murray, were later transferred to Dionysus. "Almost every tragedy, as a
matter of fact, can be resolved into a lament over the grave of some canon-
ised hero or heroine mixed with a re-enacting of his death." But he doesn't
as yet know how a full historical case for the origins of tragedy can be made
and awaits Ridgeway's book (xxv). I believe that it was the discovery by
Harrison of Bergson and Durkheim in 1908 that converted him instantly
and totally to the eniautos-daimon hypothesis. Indeed it is impossible to be
sure about who came to this idea first, for Harrison (*Themis* 334 n. 1) says
that she dates her inquiry into the ritual origins of dramatic forms from a
lecture delivered by Murray in the spring of 1910. This date seems much
too late, however; one would expect 1907–08.

11. William Ridgeway, *The Origin of Tragedy* (Cambridge 1910) 28; translation
Ridgeway's.

12. See Chapter Eight for a discussion of Roger Tiddy's book *The Mummers'
Play*.

13. All references to Murray's "Excursus on the Ritual Forms Preserved in
Greek Tragedy" (in *Themis*) will be given in the text in parentheses.

14. "The world of mythical imagery is usually represented by the conception
of heaven or Paradise in religion, and it is apocalyptic, in the sense of that
word already explained, a world of total metaphor, in which everything is
potentially identical with everything else, as though it were all inside a single infinite body." Frye, *Anatomy of Criticism* 136. "To the literary critic, ritual is the *content* of dramatic action, not the source or origin of it. *The
Golden Bough* is, from the point of view of literary criticism, an essay on the
ritual content of naive drama: that is, it reconstructs an archetypal ritual
from which the structural and genetic principles of drama may be logically,
not chronologically, derived. It does not matter two pins to the literary
critic whether such a ritual had any historical existence or not. It is very
probable that Frazer's hypothetical ritual would have many and striking
analogies to actual rituals, and collecting such analogies is part of his
argument. But an analogy is not necessarily a source, an influence, a cause,

or an embryonic form, much less an identity. The literary relation of ritual to drama, like that of any other aspect of human action to drama, is a relation of content to form only, not one of source to derivation." *Anatomy of Criticism* 109.

15. (Garden City, NY 1953) 22; orig. pub. 1949.

16. (New York 1965) 20; orig. pub. 1950.

17. Gilbert Murray, "Introduction" to *Oedipus the King* (London 1911) x.

18. For a trenchant analysis of this tendency in postwar criticism to bootleg religion into art via myth, see Philip Rahv, "The Myth and the Powerhouse," *Partisan Review* 20 (1953) 635–48.

19. F. M. Cornford, *The Origin of Attic Comedy* (London 1914) 2. I quote throughout from the second (identical) impression (Cambridge 1934). Page numbers of all subsequent quotations are indicated within parentheses in the text. The reprint edited by T. H. Gaster (Garden City, NY 1961) is to be avoided because in it Gaster has "rearranged" the text wholesale, transposing many sections so that the reader gets the argument as Gaster would have written it, not as Cornford wrote it.

20. At least by all readers of the *Anatomy of Criticism*, as well as, of course, by those classical scholars acquainted with the rather esoteric *Tractatus Coislinianus*. The latter was edited by G. Kaibel, *CGF* I.1.50–53.

21. Many years later Murray followed up Cornford's argument on this point in "Ritual Elements in the New Comedy," *Classical Quarterly* 37 (1943) 46–54.

22. For the passage, somewhat altered, see *Five Stages of Greek Religion* (Garden City, NY 1955) 31.

23. T. H. Gaster, "Editor's Foreword" to his edition of *The Origin of Attic Comedy* (Garden City, NY 1961) xxiii.

24. The lecture was printed first in the *Proceedings of the British Academy* for 1914, then issued separately as a pamphlet (Oxford 1914), and finally, in a slightly revised form, was the eighth Norton lecture Murray gave at Harvard in 1925; these lectures were published as *The Classical Tradition in Poetry* (Cambridge, MA 1927). Page references within parentheses in the text are to this latter edition.

25. Hermann Usener, "Heilige Handlung," *Archiv für Religionswissenschaft* 7 (1904) 281–339.

26. Stewart 87, quoting Cornford's obituary notice in the *Newnham College Letter* for 1929.

27. "Psychology and the Drama," orig. in *Transactions of the Eighth Annual Conference on New Ideals in Education* (1922) rpt. in *The New Adelphi*, n.s., 1 (September 1927) 2–11; (October 1927) 138–44.

28. See Bettina L. Knapp, *A Jungian Approach to Literature* (New York 1984); Morris H. Philipson, *Outline of Jungian Aesthetics* (Ann Arbor, MI 1963).

29. Cornford is quoted as saying that he never understood *Themis* until he read *Ancient Art and Ritual*. MS letter, Harrison to Murray, 1913.

30. Stewart 135. "Ker" (spirit) was one of her regular signatures.
31. *Ancient Art and Ritual* (London 1913) 9-10. I quote from the New York edition of the same year; subsequent citations give the page number in parentheses in the text.

Chapter Eight

1. *Journal of Hellenic Studies* 11 (1890) 218-20.
2. First edition 1907, second edition 1911, third edition 1924, fourth edition 1934.
3. As acknowledged by Murray in the preface to the first edition.
4. In his eulogy, "Jane Ellen Harrison 1850-1928: An Address Delivered at Newnham College, October 27, 1928" (Cambridge 1928) 10; usefully reprinted in the edition of *Themis* and *Epilegomena* published by University Books (New Hyde Park, NY 1962).
5. Stewart 54.
6. J. A. K. Thomson, *The Greek Tradition* (London 1915) 128-31.
7. *Classical Review* 27 (1913) 197-98.
8. *English Literature and the Classics*, ed. G. S. Gordon (Oxford 1912), rev. by Shorey in *Classical Philology* 9 (1914) 202-05; passage cited from 204.
9. *Classical Review* 27 (1913) 132-34.
10. Ibid. 134.
11. Harrison, "Year-Gods and Olympians," *Spectator* 108 (13 April 1912) 589-90.
12. *Principium Sapientiae: The Origins of Greek Philosophical Thought*, ed. W. K. C. Guthrie (Cambridge 1952); "A Ritual Basis for Hesiod's *Theogony*," in *The Unwritten Philosophy and Other Essays*, ed. W. K. C. Guthrie (Cambridge 1950).
13. Stewart 160.
14. Stewart 102.
15. In that regard it is a happy accident, although to Harrison a source of continuing sadness, that Murray resided in Oxford and she in Cambridge because it forced them to communicate by letter. Had they all lived in Cambridge, there would probably have been too few letters for a biography to be possible.
16. *Prolegomena* 441.
17. MS letter in Murray papers in Bodleian Library, Oxford. I suspect that Cook's reservations (rather than the pressure of his work) caused him not to contribute to *Themis* along with Murray and Cornford.
18. MS letter, Jessie Stewart papers, Newnham College Library.
19. But Murray was to change his mind on this too—see below.
20. Murray, "Introduction" to Aristotle, *Poetics* (Oxford 1920) 13; subsequent references in parentheses in the text.
21. Arthur Pickard-Cambridge, [rev. of *Themis*, 2 ed.], *Classical Review* 41 (1927) 146; Gilbert Murray, [rev. of *Dithyramb, Tragedy and Comedy*], ibid. 221-3.

Page references to Murray's review appear in parentheses in the text.

22. A modern example: enjoining classicists to engage in dialogue with social scientists as well as humanists, the ancient historian M. I. Finley wrote, "We all know the standard retort: look at the mess Jane Harrison and even Cornford for a time got into, playing about with Frazer. Let's have no more of that. Indeed not, but then Frazer is neither the alpha nor the omega of sociology." "Unfreezing the Classics," *Times Literary Supplement* 65 (7 April 1966) 289-90.

23. *Classical Quarterly* 37 (1943) 46-54; subsequent page references in the text in parentheses.

24. *Journal of Hellenic Studies* 71 (1951) 120-28; subsequent page references in the text in parentheses.

25. *The Mummers' Play* (Oxford 1923): "The contents of the present book formed the basis of a course of lectures delivered in the Spring of 1914 to students of the School of English Literature at Oxford" (3); subsequent page references in the text in parentheses.

26. See Alan Dundes, "Who Are the Folk?" in *Interpreting Folklore* (Bloomington, IN 1980) 1-19.

27. C. L. Barber, in *Shakespeare's Festive Comedy* (Princeton, NJ 1959), has explored this line more fully.

28. For more of the texts and background, see Robert Ackerman, "Some Letters of the Cambridge Ritualists," *Greek, Roman and Byzantine Studies* 12 (1971) 131-32.

29. Letter of 30 July 1921; Stewart 183.

30. (London 1920); I quote from the Anchor rpt. (Garden City, NY 1957); subsequent page references in the text in parentheses.

31. It should be noted, however, that although she draws many examples from Frazer, she understands fertility as a spiritual rather than a material attribute. See Robert A. Segal, *Joseph Campbell on Myth: An Introduction* (New York 1987) 70-71.

32. For this account of Jessie Weston's early life I am indebted to Stanley Edgar Hyman's informative "Jessie Weston and the Forest of Broceliande," *Centennial Review* 9 (1965) 509-21.

33. She was a member of the Order of the Golden Dawn. Remarks dropped here and there in *From Ritual to Romance* give teasing hints of her affiliations and allegiances: thus, "Without entering into indiscreet details I may say that students of the Mysteries are well aware of the continued survivals of this ritual under circumstances which correspond exactly with the indications of two of our Grail romances" (171 n. 15).

34. Some curious parallels exist between the careers of Jessie Weston and Jane Harrison. Exact contemporaries (1850-1928), both began their intellectual work from the aesthetic side and only gradually came to anthropology and comparative religion, both were strongly influenced by *The Golden*

Bough, both employed as primary evidence in their respective major works a text from a mystery cult that was criticized as being so late as to be useless. The main difference between them was that Jane Harrison never strayed far from the academic world, and thus from intellectual rigor, whereas Jessie Weston never went to university but instead got her start in the inbred world of amateur folklore studies. From there it was perhaps too easy a step to occultism.

35. The use of the book made by its most famous reader, T. S. Eliot, needs no discussion here.

36. Hyman, "Jessie Weston," 521. Jane Harrison in an MS letter of 20 June 1920 to Murray: "Have you read *From Ritual to Romance* by Miss Weston—she finds the Eniautos D. at the back of the Holy Grail—very satisfactory."

37. Gerald F. Else, *The Origin and Early Form of Greek Tragedy* (Cambridge, MA 1965) 4.

38. Gilbert Murray, "Introductory Address" to *Jane Harrison, Rationalism and Religious Reaction* (London 1919) 7; see also Harrison's words on 13.

39. Else 4.

40. Although I take issue with Else's argument here, I do not mean to imply by that a more sweeping rejection of his important book.

41. Northrop Frye, *Anatomy of Criticism* (Princeton, NJ 1957) 109.

42. T. H. Gaster (ed.), *The New Golden Bough* (New York 1959) 392.

43. A harder-to-classify scholar, because (like Robert Graves) nonacademic, is Jack Lindsay, who concludes the foreword to *The Clashing Rocks* (London 1965) thus: "[I] feel, humbly enough, that my book belongs to the line of English works in cultural anthropology that was largely founded by Jane Harrison and extended by thinkers like Cornford, Cook, and others. This great school is rather out of fashion today in England; and I am therefore all the happier in making a gesture of piety towards it."

44. Although his sympathy for ritualism was clearly implied in "Some Thoughts on the Pre-history of Greek Drama," *Institute of Classical Studies, University of London Bulletin,* no. 5 (1958), 43–8.

45. A. Pickard-Cambridge, *Dithyramb, Tragedy and Comedy,* 2 ed., T. B. L. Webster, ed. (London 1962) 128.

46. Ibid. 76.

47. This attribution of anthropological sophistication to the mass of classical scholars may be either premature or overly generous. Note, for instance, that E. R. Dodds at the outset of his brilliant Sather Lectures published as *The Greeks and the Irrational* (Berkeley 1950) felt obliged to explain such rudimentary distinctions as that between shame cultures and guilt cultures to his largely classical audience. That things had not changed much in the next generation may be inferred from the similar lack of familiarity on the part of his audience with anthropology assumed by G. S. Kirk in his 1969

Sather Lectures, *Myth: Its Meaning and Function in Ancient and Other Cultures* (Berkeley, CA 1970).

48. I would have included a notice of Joseph Fontenrose's important study of Delphic myth and its origins, *Python* (Berkeley and Los Angeles, CA 1959), but his polemic monograph *The Ritual Theory of Myth* (Berkeley and Los Angeles, CA 1966) indicates that his views changed substantially thereafter.

49. See V. Propp, *Morphology of the Folktale*, trans. L. Scott and ed. S. Pirkova-Jakobson, *Indiana University Research Center in Anthropology, Folklore and Linguistics*, no. 10 (Bloomington, IN 1958); C. Lévi-Strauss, "The Structural Study of Myth," in *Structural Anthropology*, trans. C. Jacobson and B. G. Schoepf (New York 1963). A useful distinction between the implications of formalism and structuralism was drawn by Alan Dundes in his introduction to the second edition of Propp's book (Austin, TX 1968).

50. See Thompson's contribution to *Myth: A Symposium*, already cited, and his *The Folk Tale* (New York 1946); see also William Bascom, "The Myth-Ritual Theory," *Journal of American Folklore* 59 (1957) 103–14.

51. See H. H. Rowley, *The Old Testament and Modern Study* (Oxford 1969) 291 ff.

52. T. H. Gaster, *Thespis*, rev. ed. (New York 1961) 19.

53. Although one does occasionally encounter clear and straightforward statements of indebtedness such as the following by Susanne K. Langer: "The scholar to whom we are most indebted for a truly coherent picture of religious origins is Jane Harrison, whose *Prolegomena to the Study of Greek Religion* sets forth with all detail the evolution of Olympian and Christian divinities. . . ." *Philosophy in a New Key*, Mentor Books ed. (New York 1949) 136.

54. *Anatomy of Criticism* 140.

Appendix

1. Note the Frazerian touch in the appendices that make up the second half of the second volume, especially Appendix I, "The Indian Village Feast."

2. To Frazer's statement in the preface to the second edition of *The Golden Bough* that, in the event of his "light bridges" of hypothesis breaking down, his book might yet claim "utility and interest" as a "repertory of facts" (I, xix–xx), cf. Chambers, characteristically less metaphorical than Frazer, in the preface to *The Mediaeval Stage*. "I wanted to collect, once for all, as many facts . . . as possible. These may, perhaps, have a value independent of any conclusions which I founded upon them" (I, vii).

3. See the excellent first chapter in O. B. Hardison, *Christian Rite and Christian Drama* (Baltimore, MD 1963), which discusses Chambers' theoretical orientation more fully and sets him in the current of historically minded scholarship then so strongly flowing.

Bibliography

I: Unpublished Sources

The Jessie Stewart Papers (I): more than eight hundred letters of Jane Ellen Harrison to Gilbert Murray. Lent by Murray to Stewart for use in preparing her biography and deposited by the latter in Newnham College Library, Cambridge. The papers consist of the original letters, plus typed copies of the letters made for Stewart, plus miscellaneous working papers of, and letters from, various persons to Stewart. Quotations from unpublished letters have been made from the typed copies, accuracy being assured by checking these against the originals. Some of these letters have been published, in whole or in part, by Stewart in *Jane Ellen Harrison: A Portrait from Letters* (London 1959), and by Sandra J. Peacock in *Jane Ellen Harrison: The Mask and the Self* (New Haven, CT 1988).

The Jessie Stewart Papers (II): miscellaneous drafts, letters, and papers written to and by Stewart in the process of writing her biography of Jane Harrison, now in possession of her daughter, Jean Pace of Cambridge.

The Gilbert Murray Papers, Bodleian Library, Oxford.

The Cornford Papers (I): a series of letters from F. M. Cornford to Gilbert Murray, and (II) a series of letters from Jane Harrison to Frances Darwin; in the British Library.

J. G. Frazer—R. R. Marett Correspondence, Trinity College (Cambridge), Add. MS. c.56b.

II: Published Sources

Ackerman, Robert. "Some Letters of the Cambridge Ritualists," *Greek, Roman and Byzantine Studies* 12 (1971) 113-36.

———. "Jane Ellen Harrison: The Early Work," *Greek, Roman and Byzantine Studies* 13 (1972) 209-31.

———. "Frazer on Myth and Ritual," *Journal of the History of Ideas* 34 (1973) 115-34.

———. "The Fortunes of Cambridge: Myth and Ritual in Anglo-American Criticism," *Social Science Information* (Paris) 15/6 (1976) 919-28.

———. *J. G. Frazer: His Life and Work.* Cambridge 1987.

Aeschylus. *Agamemnon*, ed. Eduard Fraenkel. Oxford 1960.

Altizer, Thomas J. J. "The Religious Meaning of Myth and Symbol" in *Truth, Myth, and Symbol*, ed. T. J. J. Altizer et al. Englewood Cliffs, NJ 1962.

Annan, Noel. "The Intellectual Aristocracy," in J. H. Plumb (ed.), *Studies in Social History: A Tribute to G. M. Trevelyan* (London 1955) 241-87.

Apollodorus. *The Library*, trans. J. G. Frazer. 2 vols. London 1921.

Aristotle. *On the Art of Poetry*, trans. I. Bywater; intro. G. Murray. Oxford 1920.

Arlen, Shelley. *The Cambridge Ritualists: An Annotated Bibliography*. Metuchen, NJ and London 1990.

Barber, C. L. *Shakespeare's Festive Comedy*. Princeton, NJ 1959.

Bayle, Pierre. *Historical and Critical Dictionary: Selections*, trans. R. H. Popkin. Indianapolis, IN 1965.

Besterman, Theodore. *A Bibliography of Sir James George Frazer OM*. London 1934.

Black, John Sutherland, and George Chrystal. *The Life of William Robertson Smith*. London 1912.

Block, Haskell M. "Cultural Anthropology and Contemporary Literary Criticism," *Journal of Aesthetics and Art Criticism* 11 (1952) 46-54.

Bobbitt, Mary R. *With Dearest Love to All*. Chicago, IL 1960.

Bowra, C. M. *Primitive Song*. New York 1963.

Buckley, Jerome H. *The Triumph of Time*. Cambridge, MA 1966.

Burkert, Walter. "Greek Tragedy and Sacrificial Ritual," *Greek, Roman and Byzantine Studies* 6 (1966) 87-121.

Burrow, John W. *Evolution and Society*. London 1966.

Calder, William M., III (ed.). *The Cambridge Ritualists: A Reconsideration*. Urbana, IL, 1990.

Chambers, E. K. *The Mediaeval Stage*. 2 vols. Oxford 1903.

Chase, Richard. *Quest for Myth*. Baton Rouge, LA 1949.

Collignon, Maxime. *Manual of Mythology in Relation to Greek Art*, trans. and enlarged by Jane Harrison. London 1899.

Conway, R. S. "Sir William Ridgeway, 1853-1926," *Proceedings of the British Academy* 12 (1926) 327-36.

Cook, A. B. "Zeus, Jupiter and the Oak," *Classical Review* 17 (1903) 174-86, 268-78, 403-21; 18 (1904) 75-89, 325-8, 360-75.

——. "The European Sky God," *Folk-Lore* 15 (1904) 264-315, 369-426; 16 (1905) 260-332.

——. *Zeus*. 5 vols. in 3. Cambridge 1914-40.

——. *The Rise and Progress of Classical Archaeology*. Cambridge 1931.

Cornford, F. M. *Thucydides Mythistoricus*. London 1907.

——. *From Religion to Philosophy*. London 1912.

——. *The Origin of Attic Comedy*. London 1914; rpt. (Garden City, NY 1961), ed. T. H. Gaster.

——. "Psychology and the Drama," *The New Adelphi*, n.s., 1 (September, 1927) 2-11; (October, 1927) 136-44.

——. [Memoir of Jane Harrison]. *Newnham College Letter* (1929).

——. *The Unwritten Philosophy and Other Essays*, ed. W. K. C. Guthrie. Cambridge 1950.

——. *Principium Sapientiae*, ed. W. K. C. Guthrie. Cambridge 1952.

Dawkins, R. M. "A Modern Carnival in Thrace and the Cult of Dionysos," *Journal of Hellenic Studies* 26 (1906) 191–206.

Dieterich, Albrecht. "Die Enstehung der Tragödie," *Archiv für Religionswissenschaft* 11 (1908) 163–99.

Donalson, J. W. "Philology," *Encyclopaedia Britannica*, 8 ed. (Edinburgh 1853–60) 17: 522–39.

Dorson, Richard M. "The Eclipse of Solar Mythology," in *Myth: A Symposium*, ed. T. A. Sebeok. Bloomington, IN 1958.

——. *The British Folklorists: A History*. Chicago, IL 1969.

Doty, William G. *Mythography: The Study of Myths and Rituals*. Tuscaloosa, AL 1986.

Douglas, Wallace W. "The Meaning of 'Myth' in Modern Criticism," *Modern Philology* 50 (1953) 232–42.

Downie, R. Angus. *James George Frazer*. London 1940.

——. *Frazer and The Golden Bough*. London 1975.

Dundes, Alan. "Who Are the Folk?", in *Interpreting Folklore*. Bloomington, IN 1980.

Durkheim, Emile. *The Elementary Forms of the Religious Life*, trans. Joseph W. Swain. London 1915.

Else, Gerald F. *The Origin and Early Form of Greek Tragedy*. Cambridge, MA 1965.

Evans-Pritchard, E. E. *Theories of Primitive Religion*. Oxford 1965.

——. *A History of Anthropological Thought*, ed. André Singer. London 1981.

Farnell, L. R. *The Evolution of Religion*. London 1905.

——. *The Cults of the Greek States*, vol. 5. Oxford 1909.

——. *An Oxonian Looks Back*. London 1934.

Feldman, Burton, and Robert Richardson. *The Rise of Modern Mythology, 1680–1860*. Bloomington, IN 1972.

Fergusson, Francis. *The Idea of a Theater*. Princeton, NJ 1949.

Finley, M. I. "Unfreezing the Classics," *Times Literary Supplement* 65 (7 April 1966) 289–90.

Fontenrose, Joseph. "The Ritual Theory of Myth." *Folklore Studies* 18. Berkeley and Los Angeles, CA 1966.

Frazer, J. G. *The Golden Bough*. London, 2 vols., 1890; 3 vols., 1900; 12 vols., 1911–15.

——. "William Robertson Smith," in *The Gorgon's Head and Other Literary Studies*. London 1927.

——. and Theodor H. Gaster. *The New Golden Bough*. New York 1959.

Frye, Northrop. *Anatomy of Criticism*. Princeton, NJ 1957.

——. *Fables of Identity*. New York 1963.

Gardner, Ernest. "[Review of] *Primitive Athens*," *Classical Review* 21 (1907) 115.

Goldenweiser, A. A. *Totemism: An Analytic Study*. New York 1910.

Goode, William J. *Religion Among the Primitives*. Glencoe, IL 1951.

Grundy, G. B. *Fifty-five Years at Oxford*. London 1945.

Guthrie, W. K. C. *The Greeks and Their Gods.* London 1950.

Haigh, A. E. *The Attic Theatre.* Oxford 1889.

———. *The Tragic Drama of the Greeks.* Oxford 1896.

Hardison, O. B. *Christian Rite and Christian Drama in the Middle Ages.* Baltimore, MD 1965.

Harris, Marvin. *The Rise of Anthropological Theory.* New York 1968.

Harrison, Jane Ellen. *Myths of the Odyssey in Art and Literature.* London 1882.

———. *Introductory Studies in Greek Art.* London 1885.

———. "[Review of] Rohde's *Psyche*," *Classical Review* 4 (1890) 376–77.

———. "Notes Archaeological and Mythological on Bacchylides: Odes III, XVII, VII," *Classical Review* 12 (1898) 120–40.

———. "The Dawn of Greece," *Quarterly Review* 194 (1901) 218–43.

———. *Prolegomena to the Study of Greek Religion.* Cambridge 1903; 2 ed., 1908.

———. *The Religion of Ancient Greece.* London 1905.

———. *Primitive Athens as Described by Thucydides.* Cambridge 1906.

———. "The Influence of Darwinism on the Study of Religion," in *Darwin and Modern Science*, ed. A. C. Seward. Cambridge 1909.

———. "Year-Gods and Olympians," *Spectator* 108 (13 April 1912) 589–90.

———. *Themis.* Cambridge 1912. 2 ed., 1927.

———. *Ancient Art and Religion.* London 1913.

———. *Alpha and Omega.* London 1915.

———. *Russia and the Russian Verb.* Cambridge 1915.

———. *Aspects, Aorists and the Classical Tripos.* Cambridge 1919.

———. *Rationalism and Religious Reaction.* London 1919.

———. *Epilegomena to the Study of Greek Religion.* Cambridge 1921.

———. *Mythology.* Boston, MA 1924.

———. *Reminiscences of a Student's Life.* London 1925.

———. and Margaret Verrall. *Mythology and Monuments of Ancient Athens.* London 1890.

———. and D. S. MacColl. *Greek Vase Paintings.* London 1894.

Hodgart, M. J. C. "In the Shade of *The Golden Bough*," *Twentieth Century* 157 (1955) 111–19.

Hodgen, Margaret. *The Doctrine of Survivals.* London 1936.

Hutchinson, W. M. L. "[Review of] *Themis*," *Classical Review* 28 (1913) 132–34.

Hyman, Stanley Edgar. "The Ritual View of Myth and the Mythic," in *Myth: A Symposium*, ed. T. A. Sebeok. Bloomington, IN 1958.

———. *The Tangled Bank.* New York 1962.

———. "Jessie Weston and the Forest of Broceliande," *Centennial Review* 9 (1965) 509–21.

Jacobs, Melville, and John Greenaway, eds. *The Anthropologist Looks at Myth.* Austin, TX 1966.

Jarvie, I. C. *The Revolution in Anthropology.* London 1964.

———. "Academic Fashions and Grandfather Killing—In Defense of Frazer," *Encounter* 26 (April 1966) 53-55.

Jones, Robert Alun. "Robertson Smith and James Frazer on Religion: Two Traditions in British Social Anthropology," in *Functionalism Historicized: Essays on British Social Anthropology*, ed. George W. Stocking, Jr. Madison, WI 1984.

Keith, A. B. "[Review of] Farnell's *The Cults of the Greek States*, vol. 5," *Classical Quarterly* 4 (1910) 282-85.

———. "The Origin of Tragedy and the Akhyana," *Journal of the Royal Asiatic Society* (1912) 411-38.

Kirk, G. S. *Myth: Its Meaning and Function in Ancient and Other Cultures.* Cambridge 1970.

Kissane, James. "Victorian Mythology," *Victorian Studies* 6 (1962) 5-28.

Kluckhohn, Clyde. "Myth and Ritual: A General Theory," *Harvard Theological Review* 35 (1942) 45-79.

Knapp, Bettina L. *A Jungian Approach to Literature.* New York 1984.

Lang, Andrew. "Mythology," *Encyclopaedia Britannica*, 9 ed. (Edinburgh 1884) 17: 135-58.

———. *Myth, Ritual and Religion.* 2 vols. London 1887.

———. *Custom and Myth.* London 1893.

———. *Modern Mythology.* London 1898.

———. *Magic and Religion.* London 1901.

Leach, Edmund. "Golden Bough or Gilded Twig?", *Daedalus* 90 (1961) 371-99.

———. "On the 'Founding Fathers': Frazer and Malinowski," *Encounter* 25 (1965), 24-36.

Leaf, Walter, *Homer and History.* London 1915.

Lindsay, Jack. *The Clashing Rocks.* London 1965.

Lowie, Robert H. *The History of Ethnological Theory.* New York 1937.

Malinowski, Bronislaw. "Sir James George Frazer: A Biographical Appreciation," in *A Scientific Theory of Culture and Other Essays.* Chapel Hill, NC 1944.

———. *Magic, Science and Religion.* Glencoe, IL 1948.

Marett, R. R. *Psychology and Folk-lore.* London 1920.

———. *Tylor.* London 1936.

———. *A Jerseyman at Oxford.* London 1941.

———. "Sir James George Frazer, 1854-1941," *Proceedings of the British Academy* 27 (1941) 377-91.

———, ed. *Anthropology and the Classics.* Oxford 1908.

Meyerhoff, Hans, ed. *The Philosophy of History in Our Time.* Garden City, NY 1959.

Müller, Carl [Karl] Otfried. *Introduction to a Scientific Study of Mythology*, trans. J. Leitch. London 1844.

Müller, F. Max. "Comparative Mythology," in *Chips from a German Workshop.* 2 vols. New York 1869.

Muller, Herbert J. *The Spirit of Tragedy.* New York 1956.

Murray, Gilbert. *A History of Ancient Greek Literature*. London 1897.

———. *The Rise of the Greek Epic*. Oxford 1907.

———. *The Interpretation of Ancient Greek Literature*. Oxford 1909.

———. "Greek and English Tragedy: A Contrast," in *English Literature and the Classics*, ed. G. S. Gordon. Oxford 1912.

———. "Excursus on the Ritual Forms Preserved in Greek Tragedy," in *Themis*, by J. E. Harrison. Cambridge 1912.

———. *Four Stages of Greek Religion*. London 1912.

———. *Euripides and His Age*. London 1913.

———. *Hamlet and Orestes*. Oxford 1914.

———. "The *Bacchae* of Euripides," in *Essays and Addresses*. London 1921.

———. *Five Stages of Greek Religion*. Oxford 1925.

———. *The Classical Tradition in Poetry*. Cambridge, MA 1927.

———. "[Review of] *Dithyramb, Tragedy and Comedy*," *Classical Review* 41 (1927) 221-23.

———. *Jane Ellen Harrison: An Address Delivered at Newnham College, October 27, 1928*. Cambridge 1928.

———. "Drama, Greek, Origins," *Encyclopaedia Britannica*, 14 ed. (Chicago 1929) 7: 581-83.

———. *Aeschylus: The Creator of Tragedy*. Oxford 1940.

———. "Ritual Elements in the New Comedy," *Classical Quarterly* 37 (1943) 46-54.

———. "Francis Macdonald Cornford, 1874-1943," *Proceedings of the British Academy* 29 (1943) 421-32.

———. "Dis Geniti," *Journal of Hellenic Studies* 71 (1951) 120-28.

———. "The Author of *The Golden Bough*," *The Listener* 51 (7 January 1954) 13-14.

———. "Memories of Wilamowitz," *Antike und Abendland* 4 (1954) 9-15.

———. *Gilbert Murray, An Unfinished Autobiography*. Jean Smith and Arnold Toynbee, eds. London 1960.

"Mythology," *Encyclopaedia Britannica*, 8 ed. (Edinburgh 1853-60) 15: 759-68.

Newnham College Letter. Cambridge 1929.

Nietzsche, Friedrich. *The Birth of Tragedy*, trans. Francis Golffing. Garden City, NY 1956.

Nisbet, Robert. *Emile Durkheim*. Englewood Cliffs, NJ 1965.

Paris, Pierre. *Manual of Ancient Sculpture*, trans. and enlarged by Jane Harrison. London 1890.

Payne, Harry C. "Modernizing the Ancients: The Reconstruction of Ritual Drama, 1870-1920." *Proceedings of the American Philosophical Society* 122 (1978) 182-92.

Peacock, Sandra J. *Jane Ellen Harrison: The Mask and the Self*. New Haven, CT 1988.

Pedersen, Holger. *The Discovery of Language*, trans. J. W. Spargo. Bloomington, IN 1962.

Petiscus, A. H. *The Gods of Olympos*, trans. K. A. Raleigh; preface by Jane Harrison. New York 1892.

Philipson, Morris H. *Outline of Jungian Aesthetics*. Ann Arbor, MI 1963.

Pickard-Cambridge, Arthur. *Dithyramb, Tragedy and Comedy*. Oxford 1927; 2 ed., rev. by T. B. L. Webster, 1962.

———. "[Review of] *Themis*, 2 ed.," *Classical Review* 41 (1927) 146.

Rahv, Philip. "The Myth and the Powerhouse," *Partisan Review* 20 (1953) 635–48.

Reinach, Salomon. "The Growth of Mythological Study," *Quarterly Review* 215 (1911) 423–41.

Richards, G. C. "[Review of] *Mythology and Monuments of Ancient Athens*," *Journal of Hellenic Studies* 11 (1890) 218–20.

Ridgeway, William. "What People Produced the Objects Called Mycenaean?" *Journal of Hellenic Studies* 16 (1896) 77–119.

———. *The Early Age of Greece*. Cambridge 1901.

———. *The Origin of Tragedy*. Cambridge 1910.

———. *The Drama and Dramatic Dances of Non-European Races*. Cambridge 1915.

Rogerson, John W. *Old Testament Criticism in the Nineteenth Century*. Philadelphia, PA 1985.

Sandys, John. *A History of Classical Scholarship*. 3 vols. Cambridge 1906–08.

Sebeok, Thomas A., ed. *Myth: A Symposium*. Bloomington, IN 1958.

Segal, Robert A. "The Myth-Ritualist Theory of Religion." *Journal for the Scientific Study of Religion* 19 (1980) 173–85.

———. "In Defense of Mythology: The History of Modern Theories of Myth," *Annals of Scholarship* 1 (Winter 1980) 3–49.

———. *Joseph Campbell on Myth: An Introduction*. New York 1987.

Seltman, Charles. "Arthur Bernard Cook, 1868–1952," *Proceedings of the British Academy* 38 (1952) 295–302.

Sheppard, J. T. "Murray's *Four Stages of Greek Religion*," *Classical Review* 27 (1913) 197–98.

Shorey, Paul. "[Review of] *English Literature and the Classics*," *Classical Philology* 9 (1914) 202–05.

Smith, William Robertson. *Lectures on the Religion of the Semites*. 3 ed., S. A. Cook, ed. New York 1927; orig. pub., 1889.

Spens, Janet. *An Essay on Shakespeare's Relation to Tradition*. Oxford 1916.

Steiner, Franz. *Taboo*. New York 1956.

Stewart, Jessie G. *Jane Ellen Harrison: A Portrait from Letters*. London 1959.

Stocking, George W., Jr. "Dr. Durkheim and Mr. Brown: Comparative Sociology at Cambridge in 1910," in *Functionalism Historicized: Essays on British Social Anthropology*, ed. George W. Stocking, Jr. Madison, WI 1984.

———. *Victorian Anthropology*. New York 1987.

Thomson, J. A. K. *The Greek Tradition*. London 1915.

———. "Gilbert Murray, 1866–1957," *Proceedings of the British Academy* 43 (1957) 245–70.

Tiddy, Roger J. E. *The Mummers' Play.* Oxford 1923.

Tylor, E. B. *Anahuac.* London 1861.

———. *Researches into the Early History of Mankind,* ed. Paul Bohannan. Chicago, IL 1964; orig. pub., 1865.

———. *Primitive Culture.* 2 vols. London 1871.

———. *Anthropology.* London 1881.

Usener, Hermann. "Heilige Handlung," *Archiv für Religionswissenschaft* 7 (1904) 281–339.

Van der Meer, H. F. "Euhemerus van Messene" (diss., Amsterdam 1949).

Verrall, A. W. *Euripides the Rationalist.* Cambridge 1895.

———. *Collected Literary Essays Classical and Modern.* Cambridge 1913.

———, ed. "Introduction" to uncredited trans. of Munk's *The Student's Manual of Greek Tragedy.* London 1891.

Vickery, John B. "*The Golden Bough* and Modern Poetry." *Journal of Aesthetics and Art Criticism* 15 (1957) 271–88.

———. "*The Golden Bough*: Impact and Archetype," *Virginia Quarterly Review* 39 (1963) 37–57.

———, ed. *Myth and Literature.* Lincoln, NE 1966.

Von Schroeder, Leopold. *Mysterium und Mimus im Rig-Veda.* Leipzig 1908.

Wallace, Edwin. *Freud and Anthropology: A History and Reappraisal.* New York 1983.

Webster, T. B. L. "Some Thoughts on the Pre-history of Greek Drama," *Institute of Classical Studies, University of London Bulletin,* no. 5 (1958) 43–48.

Weisinger, Herbert. *The Agony and the Triumph.* East Lansing, MI 1964.

Wellek, René. *A History of Modern Criticism: 1750–1950.* Volume 4: *The Later Nineteenth Century.* New Haven, CT 1965.

Weston, Jessie. *From Ritual to Romance.* London 1920.

Wheelwright, Philip. *The Burning Fountain.* Bloomington, IN 1954.

Whyte, Lancelot L. *The Unconscious Before Freud.* New York 1960.

Willey, Basil. *More Nineteenth Century Studies.* London 1956.

Wilson, Duncan. *Gilbert Murray OM, 1866–1957.* Oxford 1987.

Wimsatt, W. K., Jr., and Cleanth Brooks. *Literary Criticism: A Short History.* New York 1957.

Index

Made in the USA
Las Vegas, NV
07 January 2022

40784918R00144